Growing critical: alternatives to developmental psychology

Growing Critical is an introduction to critical psychology, focusing on development. It takes a fresh look at infancy, childhood and adulthood and makes the startling claim that 'development' does not exist.

John R. Morss guides the reader from the early critical movements of the 1970s which gave rise to the 'social construction of development' through the wide range of more recent approaches. He looks in turn at Vygotsky's 'social context of development', at Harré's 'social construction', Marxist critique of developmental psychology, psychoanalytic interpretations of development, and finally post-structuralist approaches following Foucault and Derrida. He surveys the range of alternative positions in the critical psychology of development and evaluates the achievements of Newman and Holzman, Broughton, Tolman, Walkerdine and others.

Marxism, psychoanalysis and post-structuralism – as well as such movements as feminism – challenge our understandings of human development. Morss looks beyond the laboratory, to Marx and Freud, to Foucault and Lacan. What sets *Growing Critical* apart from orthodox psychology is the seriousness with which he has thought through the implications of these challenges.

Contemporary and 'reader-friendly', *Growing Critical* will be of value to both undergraduate and to advanced students, as well as to anyone interested in human development, in psychology, sociology or education.

John R. Morss is Senior Lecturer in Education at the University of Otago.

Critical Psychology
Series editors
John Broughton
Columbia University, New York
David Ingleby
University of Utrecht
Valerie Walkerdine
Goldsmiths' College, London

Since the 1960s there has been widespread disaffection with traditional approaches in psychology, and talk of a 'crisis' has been endemic. At the same time, psychology has encountered influential contemporary movements such as feminism, neo-marxism, post-structuralism and postmodernism. In this climate, various forms of 'critical psychology' have developed vigorously.

Unfortunately, such work – drawing as it does on unfamiliar intellectual traditions – is often difficult to assimilate. The aim of the Critical Psychology series is to make this exciting new body of work readily accessible to students and teachers of psychology, as well as presenting the more psychological aspects of this work to a wider social scientific audience. Specially commissioned works from leading critical writers will demonstrate the relevance of their new approaches to a wide range of current social issues.

Growing Critical

Alternatives to developmental psychology

John R. Morss

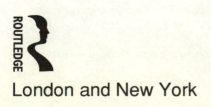

London and New York

First published 1996
by Routledge
11 New Fetter Lane, London EC4P 4EE

Simultaneously published in the USA and Canada
by Routledge
29 West 35th Street, New York, NY 10001

Typeset in Palatino by Michael Mepham, Frome, Somerset
Printed and bound in Great Britain by
TJ Press (Padstow) Ltd, Padstow, Cornwall

British Library Cataloguing in Publication Data
A catalogue record for this book is available from the British
Library

Library of Congress Cataloguing in Publication Data
A catalogue record for this book has been requested

ISBN 0–415–06108–3 (hbk)
ISBN 0–415–06109–1 (pbk)

to Labour in Knowledge is to Build up Jerusalem

William Blake

This book is dedicated to my mother
Win Morss, who grew me

Contents

Preface

Human development is too important to be left to psychology. Whatever the rights and wrongs of the particular claims that developmental psychology might make, it is essential that alternative possibilities are recognized. *Growing Critical* surveys available alternatives to the accounts of human development presented to us by developmental psychology. It is an introduction to the critical psychology of development.

Some of these alternatives are expressed at the fringes of orthodox psychology, some have arisen outside of psychology, and some emerge from the confused territory that is neither inside psychology nor outside of it – psychoanalysis. Critical psychology of development has listened to Freud and Lacan, but it has also listened to Marx and to Foucault. Marxism, psychoanalysis, and post-structuralism – as well as such movements as feminism – challenge our understandings of human development. What sets critical psychology apart from orthodox psychology is the seriousness with which it has thought through the implications of these challenges.

Growing Critical is focused on the claims of critical psychology of development. It does not attempt to offer a comprehensive critique of developmental psychology itself. A clear, up-to-date and lively critique is that of Burman (1994a). *Growing Critical* surveys the intellectual sources of critical psychology, indicates their relevance for the rethinking of 'development', and evaluates the success of critical psychologists in carrying out this project. Thus it evaluates the alternatives that have been proposed in the course of earlier critiques. For if human development is too important to be left to orthodox psychology, it is also too important to be left to critical psychology. It is not enough for critics simply to accuse orthodox psychology of 'positivism' or 'individualism' and to advocate the replacement of such bad 'isms' with good 'isms' (social constructionism, post-structuralism, postmodernism). We must subject the claims of the critics to an examination every bit as rigorous as their examination of the orthodoxy.

In particular, we must ask whether critical work has yet gone far enough in revising developmental psychology. Has critical psychology of development dug deep enough into the substance of the discipline? Has it been too afraid of 'throwing the baby out with the bath-water'? What I will be arguing is that 'the developing baby' does indeed have to be thrown out. It is a changeling. The real bath-tub is occupied not by a naturally-developing baby but by a real baby, whose development has to be made through human activity. Development in babies, children or adults may seem to 'do itself' but this is an illusion, a 'forgetting' (Walkerdine 1993) of the material circumstances in which human change takes place. Development, like history, is someone else's work.

We are all, I suggest, continually making and remaking our own and others' lives. To call the result development is an enormous mistake. It denies mothers (in particular) the credit for their work. Social process is treated as natural process, giving rise to the classic Marxist phenomenon of alienation as the connection between the worker and her work is severed. Development is objectified: it becomes solid and measurable, a field of study and of expertise. Instead of seeing people we see people developing. We read each other and in so doing we deny that we write each other.

The deep problems with developmental forms of explanation are being exposed ever more clearly as successive waves of criticism advance and withdraw. Many of these problems were identified a decade ago in the collectively-written *Changing the Subject* (Henriques *et al*. 1984). Both before and since, critics of developmental psychology have pointed to various limitations in developmental argument. The critique of development has not always been focused clearly nor expressed accessibly. For a combination of reasons, the writings of critical psychologists tend to be complex and demanding. One purpose of *Growing Critical* is to make those writings more accessible and hence more relevant. Reference to technical literature, particularly in the background areas of Marxism, psychoanalysis and so on, has therefore been kept to what I hope is an adequate but minimal level.

Individual books, and the contributions of individual writers, are not dealt with in isolation but in terms of some general trends in the critical literature – appeals to Marxism, appeals to psychoanalysis, and so on. Since particular books and writers make contributions that cross these boundaries, some repetition is inevitable as the attempt is made to construct a larger picture out of various fragments.

If it works, *Growing Critical* will stimulate discussion about the claims and counter-claims of the critical psychology of development. It will do this by increasing the exposure of those claims, and by suggesting some lines of weakness and of strength. If it works, it will worry at critical debate as well as troubling the dreams of developmental psychology. It will be a small, cheeky boy running in and out of the conference hall. The forgetting of development may be a remembering of childhood.

John R. Morss
Dunedin
Aotearoa/New Zealand
December 1994

Acknowledgements

Many people have given me generous help and encouragement in connection with this project. I have not always succeeded in making the most of their advice. First and foremost, John Broughton has devoted enormous time and care to the consideration of draft versions. David Ingleby and Valerie Walkerdine have provided support and tolerance as well as editorial advice. Ben Bradley, Erica Burman, Ian Parker, Rex Stainton Rogers and Wendy Stainton Rogers have commented on drafts and much more. Much of this book was written during a year's study leave at the Centre for Family Research, University of Cambridge. I acknowledge the financial assistance of the University of Otago and I would like to thank Pat Bateson, Jill Brown, Gerard Duveen, Dave Good, Colin Fraser, Ginny Morrow, Shirley Prendergast, Sally Roberts and especially Martin Richards. Many other colleagues have given me encouragement and assistance in sorting out and trying out my ideas – my thanks to Raymond Barglow, Lise Bird, Henriette Bloch, Isabelle Brent, Ian Burkitt, Michael Cole, Alan Costall, Joe Diorio, Margaret Donaldson, Barbara Esgalhado, Dave Fryer, Russell Gray, Lois Holzman, Paul Light, Tim Linzey, Shona Neehoff, Mark Olssen, Ann Phoenix, Alan Prout, Jens Qvortrup, John Shotter, Hank Stam, Colwyn Trevarthen, Jaan Valsiner, Graham Webb and Margaret Wetherell.

Chapter 1

Introduction

What is human development? The answer to that question, one might think, is to be found in the science that specializes in it: developmental psychology. Developmental psychology has told us what development is: it has told us what babies are like, what children are like, and (more recently) it has told us what adults are like. It is to be found in text-books, academic courses, advice to parents, training for teachers, and all sorts of places. If we were to decide to be sceptical about developmental psychology, we would have to start asking some difficult questions. We would have to rethink its claims, even those which seem the most self-evident. We would need to start worrying about development, and to start looking for alternatives to developmental psychology.

I shall argue in this book that the problem with the orthodox, psychological approaches to development is quite simple – they are too developmental. This strange claim should make sense after you have read the book. The book as a whole has a simple aim: to stimulate a self-consciousness about the word 'development'. We should, I think, worry about that word and its effects. We should be on our guard against the implications of the developmental attitude to people's lives and hopes. It treats others as behind or below ourselves, but destined to follow the same path. The search for *anti-developmental* alternatives must therefore be seen as an emancipatory project. This seems odd, because freedom has often been defined as freedom to develop. But when we unpack the notion of development we find that there are problems and that 'freedom to develop' is a freedom with strings attached. We must take care to read the small print before we sign the contract. Developmentalism may be antithetical to human freedom.

One way of starting the investigation is to look at some of the different ways in which people have written about their own or others' lives. Mark Freeman's *Rewriting the Self* (1993) focuses on specific life-stories of very different kinds, starting with the autobiographical *Confessions* of St Augustine. What, he asks, do we learn about development from such narratives? Freeman points out the retrospective nature of life-stories, particularly autobiographical ones. Sense is made of a life by looking back on it:

From the present moment of writing, in other words, one often gazes back upon the past and charts that 'upward' trajectory whereby one has managed, despite the trials and travails that have come one's way, to prevail, to come into being.

(Freeman 1993: 9)

Autobiography would seem to consist of the narration of one's development. Narration, Freeman argues, involves the imposition of some kind of pattern on a sequence of events. In the case of autobiography, these events are themselves imperfectly and selectively remembered. The making of sense requires not only selection but also interpretation, and perhaps distortion. 'The process of narrating the past', Freeman comments 'has a markedly fictive dimension' (ibid.).

Might this 'fictive dimension' apply to the notion of 'development' as well? This would depend on the relationship between developmental psychology and the forms of writing in which Freeman is interested. It may seem that the boundaries between developmental psychology and the novel are fairly clear-cut, but those between developmental psychology and autobiography or biography are much less distinct. True, developmental psychology tends to describe general features of children (most frequently) rather than features of specific individuals as in biography. But is this 'safety in numbers' really an adequate position? Is there really no contact to be made between the general and the particular? Freeman thinks that such contact must be acknowledged. The claims of developmental psychology, he implies, are claims about the kinds of people who write autobiographies or who are the subjects of biographies, as well as about those whose lives are not thus recognized. 'The conclusion', he suggests, 'may once again appear to be inescapable. . . . If narratives are ultimately to be regarded as fictions, and if the selves who write them are as well, then the concept of development itself may be too' (ibid.).

The whole point about a narrative approach, in many ways, is its acceptance of the particularity of experience. Every life is different from every other. Freeman's book examines the complex problems that arise when narrative styles are taken seriously in the context of self and development (see also Freeman 1985; Gergen and Gergen 1993). It is thus entirely appropriate that Freeman takes actual examples of narrative life-writing as his base-line. The examples that he has selected enable him to demonstrate the vast and conflicting possibilities of such writing, and to raise challenging questions about developmental theory. Developmental forms of explanation become suspect, wherever they are encountered. Available criticisms of orthodox developmental psychology may therefore be insufficient: 'critical psychology of development' must itself be re-examined.

STRUCTURE OF THE BOOK

The present chapter introduces the critical psychology of development – the work that is the main concern of this book. It also sketches the background to that work. Most of the background consists of traditional research in developmental psychology: confident and well-established experimental programmes, with their associated literature, generally committed to a biological basis for developmental change. Part of the background, also, is the establishment of a progressive tradition of child development research, revising certain aspects of the orthodox account. These revisions have given rise to a set of approaches I label 'social context' approaches. Alongside the traditional and the social context approaches, two further groupings must be identified: the social construction approach, and critical psychology of development in its various forms.

The major theme in the next chapter (Chapter 2) is the work of Vygotsky, and the attempt to assimilate Vygotsky to a relatively orthodox psychology of development. This work can be seen as continuous with the 'progressive' social context approaches mentioned above. The chapter that follows (Chapter 3) focuses on the 'social construction of development' as discussed by Harré, Gergen and Shotter among others, and on some related approaches. There follows a short discussion (Chapter 4) that takes stock of the situation. The appeals to Vygotsky thus far considered, and the social construction work, may all be seen as inadequate. As I attempt to demonstrate, all this work subjects the notion of developmental change to insufficient scrutiny. I suggest that it is the commitment to developmental explanation that is the central inadequacy of the social context and the social construction work, as well as of traditional developmental psychology. What we should be looking for instead is anti-developmental possibilities. Such possibilities are opened up, I suggest, by appeal to the great critical traditions of Marx, Freud, and post-structuralism. This proposal motivates and guides my examination of the critical psychology of development.

The remaining chapters consider the achievements and limitations of the critical psychology of development, in light of the anti-developmental project. Chapter 5 investigates actual and possible appeals to Marxism in critical psychology of development. Appeals to psychoanalysis (Freud and Lacan) are described in Chapter 6. In approaches to development influenced by these traditions, arguments emerge that are, I think, sufficiently distinct to be called anti-developmental. The most distinctly anti-developmental arguments emerge from writings influenced by the post-structuralism of Foucault and others, as discussed in Chapter 7. The textual focus implied by references to 'deconstruction' is also discussed here. Chapter 8 presents some concluding remarks and some more speculative suggestions.

As I suggest above, critical writings in psychology – including as they do critical examination of the psychology of development – do express the promise of alternative formulations. Work is needed, however, to identify these formulations and to separate them out from vestiges of the orthodoxy. That work is, in large part, the task of this book. Critical psychology of development as it now stands makes possible, but does not yet constitute, an alternative to developmental psychology.

FOUR APPROACHES TO DEVELOPMENT

It may be helpful at this point to locate the critical psychology of development in chronological context and in relation to other approaches. Four approaches to development can be distinguished. First is *traditional psychology of development*, emphasizing experimental and observational methods, and aspiring to quantitative precision and predictive validity. Since the 1970s a considerable literature has emerged that expresses doubts about the claims and methods of experimental developmental psychology. These doubts have given rise to three kinds of alternative approach, influencing but not displacing the experimental tradition. The *social context* approach involves the revision of experimental methods to take account of social factors. The *social construction* approach, also first set out in the 1970s, advocates a much more radical rejection of experimental methods. Contributions to both these approaches continued through the 1980s and beyond. The *critical psychology of development* emerged in the 1980s, and distanced itself from the social context and the social construction approaches as well as from the experimental mainstream. The second and third chapters of this book discuss the second (social context) and third (social construction) of these four approaches, but it is the fourth approach that is the main focus of *Growing Critical*. Some more detail on the four approaches will clarify their similarities and differences.

Traditional psychology of development

The most prestigious scientific periodicals in the psychology of development, such as *Child Development*, maintain a particular set of standards. These standards, which operate through the editorial process, are intended to ensure scientific rigour. For historical reasons, the form of science which is prescribed is modelled on the physical sciences. Experimental research, carried out under controlled conditions, represents the preferred form. Where possible, statistical analysis of samples is expected, such that tentative claims concerning large populations can be inferred. Either explicitly or implicitly, a finding concerning a group of 5-year-old children will be treated as at least potentially generalizable to all 5-year-old children. Such general or even universal claims will often be heavily qualified, but the drive to generalize will usually manifest itself. Inferential statistics – represented by tests of 'significance' – presuppose the search for generalizations.

Much research published in the prestigious journals is not experimental in a strict sense, and some may not use inferential statistics, but the general style is relatively uniform. It is assumed that general laws of developmental change are present in the world, to be discovered by appropriate research (Karmiloff-Smith 1992). Systematic experimentation and observation, and appropriate measurement, are taken to represent the means to this end. This approach to science is usually termed 'positivist'. Positivism is an epistemological commitment, a set of assumptions about how valid knowledge is to be acquired. When directed toward issues of development, there tends to be the accompanying presupposition that developmental change is natural. Stage theories of development, such as that of Jean Piaget, represent this presupposition most clearly. Naturalism is however a much more general assumption within traditional psychology of development. Claims concerning children of a particular age, or concerning change in particular areas of development, tend to be accompanied by an appeal to biology, and often to evolution (Morss 1990). The line of argument is a functionalist one: that is, it treats the activity of children (or adults) as a kind of adaptation to a relatively stable environment. Contemporary, mainstream psychology of development might there-fore be said to be positivist, naturalist, and functionalist (a clear overview is provided by Burman 1994a). It sets itself the task of uncovering the universal and natural processes by which human infants are transformed into fully adapted adults.

Social context

Over the last 20 years, many researchers in the mainstream of developmental psychology have expressed doubts about the traditional positivist programme. In particular, the relative oversight of social factors in the tradition has led to attempts to redress the balance. What might be called 'progressive' trends emerged within the mainstream, qualifying but not totally undermining the orthodox programme. These progressive trends have focused on the social context of development (Rogoff 1990).

By and large, the social context approach is an attempt to save developmental psychology by revising its terms. Traditional psychology of development is rewrit-ten in ways that now 'take the social context into account'. The clearest example of this process has been the social revisions to Piaget, whereby children's perfor-mance on cognitive tasks is shown to be influenced by communicative contexts (Light 1986). The growing child, adapting to his or her surroundings, is still at the centre of this picture. Unlike the traditional account, this central figure is provided with a background, but the social 'context' remains just that; social factors remain secondary.

There have been numerous versions of the social context approach. A systems-theory version has been advocated for a number of years by Urie Bronfenbrenner (1979). A version which makes explicit the commitment to biology and adaptation is that of Jerome Bruner (1990). Perhaps the major theoretical figure in the social context literature is Lev Vygotsky, whose work exerts much more influence now than during his lifetime (see Chapter 2). Vygotsky, who died in 1934, left behind a substantial set of theoretical claims and empirical studies that have allowed for a diverse range of interpretations and applications. As we shall see in Chapter 3, appeal is made to Vygotsky's work by writers in the social construction school as well as by the social context movement.

In its social context role, Vygotsky's work takes the form of a demonstration that children's and adults' activity is naturally social. That is to say, it is natural for children and adults to learn from each other and to assist each other's learning (Rogoff 1990). In this version of Vygotsky, the social nature of childhood is based on biological foundations. Learning from others is a form of adaptation, and one that makes possible the transmission of culture from one generation to the next. The importance of Vygotsky's claims should not be underestimated even within this framework. What was novel about Vygotsky was his insistence that 'internal' processes such as thinking are just as much subject to social function as language or activity. However, the social context movement insists, in its turn, that social functions are adaptive functions. It is this appeal to a functionalist biology, whether implicit or explicit, that enables the social context work to coexist with the tradition. It marks off these first two approaches from the social construction and the critical psychology approaches.

Present orthodoxy in the psychology of development might be seen as an amalgam of traditional and social context frameworks. Influential psychologists of development in the 1990s tend to bring together elements of both (Donaldson 1992). In general, the methodological rigour of the tradition is still admired, and experimental findings are incorporated into developmental accounts where considered appropriate. To some extent, the social context claims have been allowed to form a conceptual layer through which orthodox research may be articulated and findings explained. The social context approach has also been seen to provide additional methods of research. Traditional methods, and traditional styles of reporting research, have had little cause to fear the social context movement. It is for this reason that the social context approach may be seen as a progressive wing of the traditional structures. In this book, the social context work is discussed in relation to the work of Vygotsky, chiefly in the following chapter.

Social construction

This approach was first articulated by Harré, Shotter and others in the 1970s (Harré 1986). By social construction was meant the interpersonal processes through which humans create the reality they experience. Through interaction, and particularly through language and other symbol systems, people make sense of themselves and of each other. People's lives and identities, and much of what we call people's development, are negotiated through interpersonal activity. This social construction work appealed to certain claims of Vygotsky and of the philosopher George Herbert Mead, who like Vygotsky had stressed the social origins of thinking and the self. Writers like Harré and Shotter opposed the quantitative experimental methods of developmental psychology. They found the emerging social context work of interest but theoretically inadequate. The revisions to Piaget, for example, they considered superficial. In particular it was the cognitive focus of both the traditional and the social context approaches that the social construction writers rejected. This cognitive focus seemed to be treating humans (whether children or adults) as information-processing machines. This attitude seemed to the social construction writers to ignore all the characteristics that are unique to humans as they interact with each other and with the world. Their orientation was therefore in many ways a humanist one.

This humanism was retained through various revisions and reconsiderations of the social construction approach through the 1980s, during which time various broader intellectual trends were emerging. Most notably, this period saw the emergence of postmodernism and post-structuralism as explanatory frameworks in social science. Feminist theory was also reinvigorated during the 1980s, partly through its discovery of important ideas in Freudian theory. Appeals to Freud and Lacan, and to Foucault, began to displace appeals to Marxism in the wider social sciences and humanities. Some of the social construction writers responded to the notion of postmodernism but all the other movements were largely ignored. It is the response to the other names on this list – in particular Marx, Freud and Foucault – that sets the critical psychology approach apart from social construction.

Critical psychology of development

Critical psychology of development is of increasing significance in international debate. Many of the central concerns of this approach were set out in *Changing the Subject: Psychology, Social Regulation, and Subjectivity* (Henriques *et al*. 1984). The authors sought a new way of theorizing subjectivity that would avoid the deficiencies they saw both in traditional psychology and in the available alternatives. They took a much more detached view of psychology, including the psychology of development, than was to be found in any of the other approaches. They located psychology as a science and as a profession within larger historical and economic contexts. From this perspective, psychology has itself been created by social processes. Psychology's formulations on childhood and developmental change must themselves reflect those larger political circumstances. This remains the case even if it is recognized that psychology plays an active part in maintaining certain kinds of political structure.

Henriques *et al*. argued that the social construction writers (such as Harré and Shotter) made some of the same mistakes as the orthodox psychology they themselves criticized. In particular, so the argument went, a mistaken assumption about individual agency remained unchallenged in the social construction approach. The individual person was treated as a free agent, detached from the social setting, and able to make voluntary decisions about such matters as social interaction. The authors of *Changing the Subject* argued that the relationships between the individual and society were misunderstood within the humanist writings of Harré and Shotter just as much as in the experimental mainstream and its social-context revisions. It was necessary to redefine subjectivity in a more radically social manner. To do so they appealed in part to Marxist formulations, but principally to post-structuralist and to psychoanalytic ones. Their appeal was to Foucault and to Lacan, then (as now) rather exotic figures in the intellectual landscape. Amongst the authors of *Changing the Subject* this quest was continued most vigorously by Walkerdine, in a series of investigations of childhood, gender, and education (Walkerdine 1988, 1991, 1993).

Walkerdine also contributed to *Critical Theories of Psychological Development* (Broughton 1987). This collection contains a variety of critiques of development from Marxist, psychoanalytic, and post-structuralist perspectives. In comparison with *Changing the Subject*, Marxist influence is of somewhat greater significance in the later book. The most general approach is 'ideology critique' – a form of social and cultural analysis derived from twentieth-century descendants of Marxism. The general orientation of this kind of critique is toward the uncovering of the under-lying functions of psychology – in particular, political functions. It is implied that the adoption of a correct analytic method will make it possible to 'see through' the claims and practices of psychology. The different perspectives to which appeal is made are treated as alternatives that, properly selected or in the right combination, will yield the correct method.

The notion of critique as the uncovering of an underlying message is a highly persuasive form of argument. However, the search for single messages or meanings does not sit easily with the post-structuralism adopted by many critical psychologists of development. The 'decoding' of text or of some social practice is more characteristic of structuralist styles of analysis. Structuralist approaches to human activity and experience tend to seek systematic and rather formal frame-works of description. They aspire to comprehensiveness, bringing the most diverse of phenomena into order. Indeed it was the breakdown of this structuralist enterprise that gave rise to post-structuralism, with its acceptance of fragmentation and incoherence. Structuralism sought ways of disciplining difference, whereas post-structuralism seeks to recognize difference for its own sake.

The post-structuralist tendency is therefore a somewhat anarchic one. Even in less extreme forms, it takes seriously the possibility of indeterminacy in analysis. As an influence in the critical psychology of development, it emphasizes the multiplicity of possible interpretations of a given situation. This emphasis is a characteristic of the work of Bradley and of Rex and Wendy Stainton Rogers. Bradley's *Visions of Infancy* (1989) argues that alternative scientific viewpoints on human infancy must all be seen as alternative interpretations, rather than as successive approximations to the 'truth' about babies. Bradley demonstrates the importance of claims about infancy within the various theories of human develop-ment that have risen and fallen over several hundred years, and through his focus on infancy he is able to construct a critique of developmental theory in general.

Like the authors of *Changing the Subject*, Bradley is intensely concerned with the practical implications of conventional theory and methodology in developmen-tal psychology. For example, many developmental explanations for deviance or pathology effectively blame mothers for such outcomes. Bradley argues that psychologists should instead be situating themselves as advocates for babies and for their mothers. A similarly practical agenda informs the work of the Stainton Rogers. *Stories of Childhood: Shifting Agendas of Child Concern* (Stainton Rogers and Stainton Rogers 1992) argues that there are unavoidably story-like elements in any scientific form of developmental psychology. What matters, they suggest, is who is telling the story, and about whom. These issues are given further consider-ation in Curt (1994).

The critical psychology of development is thus a diverse approach in itself, and an approach in which significant chronological changes have occurred. The titles discussed so far give an indication of this diversity. Somewhat less technical in character, Burman's *Deconstructing Developmental Psychology* (1994a) presents a critical overview of contemporary developmental psychology, informed by the various styles of critical psychology. As Burman emphasizes, developmental psychology is not merely an academic discipline but is a part of everyone's life. For example, television and magazine advertising make constant reference to the needs of infants and children as they seek to promote particular products. We might expect such claims to be contaminated by the purposes of the advertising, but similar claims about children's needs are encountered elsewhere – in education for example. Education systems are constructed on the basis of knowledge about children and childhood that may be presented as objective and value free, but critical scrutiny reveals the presence of complex interests and agendas. Burman's book therefore reminds us very forcefully what is wrong with developmental psychology, and why critical psychology of development is important.

It is the aim of *Growing Critical* to evaluate the critical psychology of development. For if there are problems with developmental psychology, and if some of these problems have been recognized for some time, then we must think seriously about any alternative frameworks that have been proposed. We must ask what progress has in fact been made by critical psychology of development, and whether it has been sufficiently radical. Most important, we must be as rigorous in our consideration of these critical writings as those writings urge us to be in our critique of developmental psychology itself. My examination of the writings of critical psychologists of development is carried out in that spirit. In order to make sense of the various versions of critical psychology of development, however, some more detailed consideration must first be given to those approaches that stand between it and the experimental tradition. We start with the notion of social context, and its principal theorist, Lev Vygotsky.

Chapter 2

Naturally social
Vygotsky and the social context of development

What could be more romantic? A Russian genius, coming of age with the 1917 Revolution, is plucked from obscurity to overturn Soviet psychology. Suffering recurrent bouts of tuberculosis, he writes some of his major works in hospital. He gives stirring lectures and founds a dynamic new approach to the study of social life, attracting students and colleagues the closest of whom betray him under political pressure. He lives in one room with his wife and two daughters. Deferring treatment for what turns out to be his final illness, he dies in 1934 before his 38th birthday. With his last breath, perhaps, he echoes the inner speech of Prince Andrei of *War and Peace* – as he watches the spinning, smoking shell before his feet on the battlefield of Borodino – 'I cannot, I do not wish to die. I love life – I love this grass, this earth, this air...'.

Almost everyone agrees that Lev Vygotsky was a genius and a brilliant innovator in developmental psychology. Vygotsky's writings have certainly had a major impact on Western developmental psychology in the last 15 years or so. Growing tired of Piaget, whose work had arrived in the US about 15 years prior to that, developmental psychologists in the late 1970s began to take notice of what Vygotsky had written nearly half a century previously. Vygotsky seemed to provide ready-made answers to the questions that were increasingly being asked about Piaget. The overwhelming majority of post-Vygotskians – both of East and West – describe Vygotsky as refining the notion of developmental change, but not challenging it.

If Vygotsky had not existed, developmental psychologists would have had to invent him – and in a sense they have. For Vygotsky's work is now seen through late twentieth-century eyes, and interpreted from the perspective of contemporary psychology. As we shall see, even the Soviet continuations of his work by those who had direct contact with him involved a variety of shifts of emphasis, not to say distortion.

VYGOTSKY

Born in what was then Russia in 1896, Vygotsky's adult life took place in what was then the Soviet Union (Van der Veer and Valsiner 1991). For reasons related to this socio-historical context, Vygotsky's work had made relatively little impact on the West until the 1960s and required the disaffection with Piaget to make the real breakthrough. In the area of child development theory, the 1980s were in many ways the Vygotsky years. The reaction against Piaget in the English-speaking psychological world was to some extent a critically-minded reaction. Piaget, it seemed, was committed to universal, rational accounts of intellectual development. The Piagetian approach disdained social, cultural, and communicative contexts for cognition. The turn to Vygotsky was not entirely a matter of fashion, or of seeking a replacement for Piaget. It was also motivated by critical reflection on developmental study itself.

A recognition of the importance of social and historical context, as found in Vygotsky, was threatening not just to Piaget but also to the broader assumptions that Piaget reflected. If followed through, a focus on the relative nature of development – on its dependence on context – sets up a major challenge to orthodox developmental theory. The discovery or rediscovery of Vygotsky in the West has therefore been an important element in the establishment of critical perspectives on development.

One complicating factor in the Vygotsky story is the different histories of his work in the USSR and in the West. Although Vygotsky's writings were suppressed in the USSR after his death, students and colleagues continued to work with his ideas through the Stalin era and the post-war period. There are a number of post-Vygotskian traditions in Soviet psychology, some closer than others to Vygotsky's own work. Some have attempted to correct or to revise Vygotsky, or to adapt his work in terms of ongoing Western trends. In turn, Western devotees of Vygotsky have made varying usages of these Soviet post-Vygotsky traditions. The Soviet traditions will be discussed after outlining some basic aspects of Vygotsky's own work.

From outside in

The Soviet Union of the 1920s was a state in turmoil and under siege. The Bolshevik Revolution of 1917 had overthrown the last vestiges of the Czarist regime and replaced it with workers' control of production. But the Revolution was still being contested by armed forces – not only dissident Soviet citizens but also the armies of many foreign nations. The structures of the new Soviet society were all still in a state of flux. The Revolution had not yet congealed into the centralized dictatorship of the Stalin years. There were still real questions about how children should be educated for their future role in the first socialist society, and what role such sciences as psychology should now play. Into these debates, and into Moscow, came Lev Semeonovich Vygotsky, a teacher and art critic from the provinces (Kozulin 1990).

Soviet psychology had inherited various institutions and research programmes from the pre-Revolutionary years. There were several competing methodologies, including versions of the conditioning psychology developed earlier by Pavlov, and versions of behaviourist psychology. Vygotsky was one of a number of young scholars whose views came to be influential in the debate as to likely directions for a Soviet psychology in the 1920s. Later, he sketched out a psychology in which many aspects of development would be treated as the taking-in of a culture. Vygotsky thereby offered a sociohistorical framework for the study of human development, in which the larger cultural values of a society would be taken to define maturity in that society. For Vygotsky, human development involves the 'interiorization' of a culture and hence in large part, what others have called the social construction of mind (Harré 1986). At the same time, he insisted on the significance of biology and evolution in the form of a natural line of development intertwining with the cultural line.

In its opposition to a more traditionally biological theory, and especially in its optimism for human change under changed circumstances, Vygotsky's approach fitted in with the prevailing political style. More specifically, Vygotsky argued that thinking and consciousness can be treated as a kind of problem-solving. If so, thinking would be a covert kind of labour, because labour in general involves the individual interacting with the world in a purposeful way. Moreover, the specific tasks (physical or mental) which a person is called upon to undertake are determined by the cultural setting – in all its economic and historical detail. This interpretation agreed, at least in general terms, with some of the claims of Marx and of Engels. Marx had emphasized the way in which people interact with the environment through work, transforming both nature and themselves in this 'dialectical' process. Engels had derived from Marx a set of philosophical doctrines, massively influential in early Soviet thinking, that attempted to codify this dialectical approach to human beings.

Marx had stressed that human labour takes place within larger structures of social relationship, such as those characteristic of capitalism. Vygotsky tended to treat labour in a somewhat individualistic fashion, as a matter of the individual tackling problems set by the environment. His commitment to the problem-solving orientation probably came more from his reading of European psychology – particularly the Gestalt psychologists – than from his Marxism (Van der Veer and Valsiner 1991). The Gestalt psychologists such as Kohler were studying problem-solving in chimps as well as in human children and adults. In this respect, Vygotsky's work forms part of a long European tradition of 'functionalism', in which human activity of all kinds is considered as a kind of adaptation. The convergence of psychology and political doctrine on a functionalist account of human existence was perhaps a happy one for Vygotsky. Had he been forced to choose between conflicting viewpoints from those two sources, the impression is that he would have attempted to resist political coercion and faced the consequences. Be that as it may, most recent appeals to Vygotsky (especially in the US) have maintained the functionalist emphasis, and are happy to treat this as the major manifestation of Vygotsky's Marxism. Deeper scrutiny of Marxism in Vygotsky is thus, perhaps with relief, avoided.

Mind in society

Many of Vygotsky's writings were published during his lifetime, but shortly after his untimely death in 1934 his books were suppressed. The suppression appears to have been due mainly to shifts in Communist Party doctrine concerning the role of testing in education, one of many professional areas in which Vygotsky was involved. Several colleagues and students kept his ideas in circulation, but Vygotsky remained relatively unknown in the West as well as in the USSR until the 1960s, when the translated collection *Thought and Language* appeared (Vygotsky 1962).

This rediscovery of Vygotsky meant that his ideas were effectively a new contribution to thinking in developmental psychology from the 1960s onwards. However, the critical impact of Vygotsky was somewhat blunted by several factors. First, the 1962 translation of *Thought and Language* had expunged any references to Marxism as being irrelevant to the psychological argument – as is made clear in the later translation (Vygotsky 1986). A higher profile for Marxism might have brought Vygotsky to the attention of some of the more critical commentators. Also, much of the material translated was concerned with concept learning in children and other processes that seemed consistent with the mainstream rather than critical of it. Some developmental thinkers, including Jerome Bruner, James Wertsch and Michael Cole in the US and Margaret Donaldson in the UK, did notice the important differences between Vygotsky's approach and that of Piaget in particular. It was not however until the publication in 1978 of a further translated selection from Vygotsky – *Mind in Society* (co-edited by Michael Cole, Vera John-Steiner and colleagues) – that the importance of Vygotsky became widely acknowledged.

Mind in Society presented an edited translation of a diverse set of Vygotsky's writings. Two related Vygotskian formulations became widely known. First was the principle of 'internalization'. According to Vygotsky:

> Every function in the child's cultural development appears twice: first, on the social level, and later, on the individual level; first, *between* people (*interpsychological*) and then *inside* the child (*intrapsychological*). . . . All the higher functions originate as actual relations between human individuals.
>
> (Vygotsky 1978: 57)

It must be stressed that Vygotsky's claim concerned 'higher' functions (that is, cultural functions). He appears to have considered human infancy to be dominated by 'lower' (that is, 'natural') functions.

The second principle was 'the zone of proximal development'. Vygotsky's accounts of the zone are intended to emphasize the importance of social contexts for intellectual achievement. Vygotsky notes that the achievement of any task always takes place first with assistance or guidance, before the task is solved independently. The difference between collective and individual achievement is one definition of the zone. More precisely, if interpreted in a quantitative way, the zone is the difference between some measure of independent achievement (an IQ test perhaps) and some measure of guided achievement. The notion of the zone of proximal development can thus be treated in a very conventional, quantitative manner – as a measurable feature of a child's performance. The zone can also be treated as an attack on all such measurements. Vygotsky can be read as denying the reality of independent achievement itself – that is to say, arguing that personal achievement is always within a collective context. A human context of guidance, and hence the zone of proximal development, can always be said to be present. Even a child's solitary play can be treated in this way. In imaginative play a child is reaching ahead of herself, guiding herself as it were. What she/he is thinking about, how she/he constructs possible future or alternative selves, is always defined by (and is thus 'within') a specific culture.

As Van der Veer and Valsiner (1991) have pointed out, Vygotsky discussed the zone of proximal development only in the writings of his last two years of life. Arguably, it would have received more attention and refinement had Vygotsky lived longer. His discussions of the zone place emphasis on the dynamic nature of children's achievements – the fact that new competencies are continually emerging. Van der Veer and Valsiner interpret the zone as a formulation designed to grasp something of the immediate ('proximate') future development of a child, by identifying competencies that are currently 'in process'. Achievements possible with help or guidance, or possible by imitation, might thus be treated as near-future independent achievements.

It is unclear however to what extent Vygotsky thought of a child's future achievements as determinate, and to what extent open ended. For the zone of proximal development can be interpreted in a very open-ended way, with a vast number of possible skills being included. There might be little or no prejudgement as to what competencies are to be anticipated as occurring 'next'. At the other extreme, the zone might be interpreted in a closed, rigid way, with a well-defined set of anticipated competencies and even a chronological timetable for their emergence. This latter, more determinate reading would lead to an orthodox developmental account. Western devotees of Vygotsky have usually interpreted the zone of proximal development in terms somewhere between the two extremes (see Newman and Holzman 1993).

Vygotsky's own emphasis is difficult to ascertain, but was probably also between these extreme possibilities. He does seem to have presupposed some predictable changes in children's development, bringing him nearer to the 'closed' pole. His interest in general 'crisis periods' in child development – when significant reorganization is taking place – would corroborate this interpretation (Van der Veer and Valsiner 1991). Such crisis periods were identified by Vygotsky as occurring at birth and at the first, third, seventh, thirteenth and seventeenth years of life. There was thus a rather orthodox developmental side to Vygotsky, comprising a normative and even a prescriptive analysis of childhood. For this reason much of what Vygotsky argued in terms of his two principles seems rather familiar. The first principle – internalization – insists that developments in infancy are somehow 'lower' than those of later childhood. The importance of the achievements of infancy and of early childhood is that they make subsequent achievements possible.

The second principle – the zone of proximal development – suggests a natural hierarchy or sequence of achievements, so that an expert in child development might be able to predict what is 'next' (that is, proximal).

If such normative and prescriptive tendencies are resisted, however, critical possibilities are opened up by the zone of proximal development and by the principle of internalization. A radical interpretation along these lines is provided by Newman and Holzman (1993) whose Marxist reading of Vygotsky as a 'revolutionary scientist' is discussed in Chapter 5. This issue of the alternative readings of Vygotsky is clarified by a consideration of the response to Vygotsky both within and (subsequently) beyond the Russian zone.

SOVIET REVISIONS OF VYGOTSKY

Vygotsky's approach was transmuted by various colleagues and students in the USSR after his death. The most influential, on an international scale, was A.R. Luria. The most significant in terms of Soviet developmental theory was A.N. Leont'ev. Leont'ev's 'activity theory' became the dominant developmental approach in the Soviet Union in recent decades, being seen as the more adequate successor to Vygotsky's theory.

Vygotsky's emphasis on language had already come in for politically-directed criticism in the early 1930s. An emphasis on language, and on cultural meaning carried by language, came to be seen in official Soviet circles as 'idealist' and hence contrary to Marxism. Vygotsky's approach was seen as neglecting the role of practical activity and ignoring the new socialist context of children's development in the USSR. In Vygotsky's accounts, it was verbal interaction between pairs of people – such as that between teacher and pupil, or between parent and child – that carried most explanatory weight. There was no obvious role for social labour or for class conflicts. Vygotsky's theory seemed to rise above such matters, and to address developmental change in an abstract way. Vygotsky's was a general theory of child development, not a theory of socialist child development.

The ideological status of general theory was unpredictable in the USSR of the 1930s. After all, the philosophical writings of Marx and Engels purported to be applicable to all times and places. The general applicability of Engels' philosophy of nature was considered a virtue, not a vice, by Party officials overseeing Soviet academic activity. Within psychology, Pavlov's claims about the importance of physiology and conditional reflexes were not considered less important or less politically correct because they ignored class and society. Instead, they were celebrated as scientific truths even more fundamental, in a sense, than social and economic processes. Brains and the central nervous system were allowed to transcend economics. Luria at least was grateful for this dispensation, for he successfully adapted to changing times by dropping an early enthusiasm for psychoanalysis (suppressed in the USSR in the late 1920s) in favour, eventually, of studies of the localization of brain function. Luria's collaborations with Vygotsky took place in between these two careers.

Whatever was acceptable in brain science, what was wanted in education and psychology was a formulation that recognized and indeed celebrated the special superiority of the socialist system. Vygotsky's treatment of the political structure as largely irrelevant was inappropriate. Without condoning its style or its implications, this aspect of the 'idealist' charge against Vygotsky was not totally unfounded. From a Marxist perspective, Vygotsky's account of a sociocultural setting becoming 'interiorized' is rather a bland one. There seems no place in his system for any kind of conflict within the social world. It might be argued that Vygotsky was writing for a new socialist state from which such conflicts were to have been eradicated. But Vygotsky is usually thought of as having been writing a general psychology, in the European tradition, relevant to but not limited to his own time and place. The extent of European influence on Vygotsky's thinking was cynically exploited and misrepresented in the Stalinist era, when such internationalist tendencies were thought of as counter-revolutionary.

'No illusions': Luria and the Uzbekis

Vygotsky did have one major opportunity to study conflict between alternative cultures within the context of 'development'. Ironically, this opportunity was itself sabotaged by a Western intellectual tradition – ethnocentrism. The circumstance was the study of the 'modernization' of the Uzbekis in Soviet Central Asia. The research was carried out by Luria and colleagues, but under Vygotsky's direction.

The time was 1931. The Uzbekis were Moslems, and operating a peasant, semi-nomadic economy that was considered backward by Moscow. In line with Communist Party doctrine, all agriculture in the Soviet Union was to become collectivized. Anyone deemed to own an inappropriate amount of private property or to own farmland on which others worked was identified as a 'kulak' and was liable to 'liquidation' (Van der Veer and Valsiner 1991). The Uzbek agricultural economy and many aspects of its culture were forcibly transformed to meet the theoretical requirements of the new state. This situation was treated by Vygotsky and, perhaps more enthusiastically, by Luria as a natural experiment, as sociohistorical evolution happening before their very eyes. People at a lower, primitive level were being assisted to develop to a higher level over a few years.

Such an ethnocentric attitude was little different from the colonial attitudes of the imperialist West. Similar attitudes to Vygotsky's and Luria's were expressed at the time by Leont'ev:

> Half-civilized tribes feel a certain repulsion to ordered labour . . . whereas in primitive man the power of uninterrupted, persistent attention was very poorly developed, with us it has attained a very considerable degree. . . . Thus, the transition of the savage from capricious and fitful dissipation of energy to the specific, systematic, and organized labour of man, signifies . . . the transition to a higher form of activity and attention.
>
> (Leont'ev cited in Cole 1988: 141)

It should be emphasized that Leont'ev was not here specifically referring to the Uzbekis as 'savages'. His colleague Luria was using the term 'primitive' in that connection, observing for example that the Uzbekis were 'primitive' and 'underdeveloped under the influence of the Islamic religion' (Van der Veer and Valsiner 1991: 243). But it is noteworthy that the transition to 'organized labour' – that is, to the social life of modern, industrialized society – is treated as a natural evolutionary step. Treating socioeconomic change as natural, evolutionary development was a commonplace of Western social thinking of the nineteenth century, and Leont'ev's words could have come from almost any of the founding figures of developmental psychology (Morss 1990). The endorsement of this position by Leont'ev is a highly significant indication of Soviet developmental thinking. It should also be pointed out that the (geographically) Western Soviets – the Russians and Ukrainians – considered themselves in any case racially superior to the 'ethnic minorities' of the East and South ('minority' here being an evaluative rather than a quantitative judgement).

The actual studies carried out by Luria included evaluations of both 'higher' and 'lower' kinds of mental functioning. 'Lower' thinking, such as 'concrete' reasoning and the susceptibility to certain kinds of visual illusion, was anticipated in all research subjects. 'Higher' (that is, more abstract) thinking was anticipated only in the more Sovietized of the Uzbekis. Comparison was made both directly between Uzbekis who had received more or less of the advantage of formal, Russian-style education and sociocultural transformation, and indirectly, with Russian norms.

Particularly with regard to such 'higher' functions as logical, abstract thinking, the less-educated Uzbekis scored poorly. Indeed, Luria reported considerable evidence of 'concrete' thinking even in the better-educated group (including the president of a collective farm). The less-educated subjects showed no susceptibility (reported Luria) to certain visual illusions which require an understanding of visual perspective. On 'natural' aspects of thinking, and less demanding visual illusions such as the Muller-Lyer arrows figure, they all performed the same. Luria considered these findings to be positive evidence for Vygotsky's formulation of the two lines of development, the natural and the sociocultural. As I suggested above, the opportunity was lost for any kind of consideration of the Uzbeki experience as a clash of cultures (including Islamic versus Communist), because the experience was treated simply as one of primitive culture versus superior, advanced culture. That is to say, difference was treated as development. Of course, the political truth was that the Soviet-Russian culture was indeed superior – through force of arms and organization.

Ironically, Luria's interpretations of his findings were not well received in Moscow. Luria's accounts of the relative superiority of the collectivized Uzbekis – those who, despite illiteracy, had had the benefit of involvement in a socialist form of production – were still not sufficiently positive. Luria described such people as still having traces of concrete thinking and as not yet being fully able to reason on an abstract level. For example, the president of a collective farm referred to above refused to give consideration to the hypothetical situation of a rich peasant owning miserable cattle. According to more politically sophisticated critics in Moscow, this answer showed proper ideological reasoning in the new, collectivized circumstances, since rich peasants no longer existed. Such responses hence demonstrated the success of the collectivization process. Luria was hoist with his own petard.

More bizarre still, Luria's message to Vygotsky (with reference to some of the experimental findings) that the Uzbekis 'had no illusions' was interpreted by Party officials, it is said, as a comment on the Uzbekis' distrust of the objectives of collectivization (Velichkovsky, personal communication, 1993). It is appropriate, perhaps, that Vygotsky's own research programme should present such striking examples of the penetration of culture and politics into the analysis of human development.

Leont'ev's adaptive activities

As well as suffering from the fallout from the Uzbek episode, Vygotsky was also becoming subject to other kinds of political pressure in the early 1930s, as noted above. Vygotsky's emphasis on language and meaning was becoming particularly unfashionable. Official Marxist doctrine insisted that any appeal to conscious experience must be related very closely to practical activity. If it did not, it was likely to be labelled as 'idealist'. Meaningfulness, for Vygotsky, seemed to be granted too much autonomy.

A more particular, but related controversy concerned the distinction between thinking and speech. Vygotsky treated thinking and speech as interrelated from childhood onwards, but distinct and independent in the infant. Thinking (problem-solving) in the baby is as yet uninformed by language, and speech (verbal communication) is emotional rather than cognitive. Such a position came to be seen as unacceptably inconsistent with the claims of Engels concerning the relationships between thinking and speech. According to Engels, whose works first became influential in the USSR during the 1920s, both thinking and speech derive (historically) from the emergence of labour in human society. They are thus linked together in ways that do not depend on the developmental achievements of infancy.

By the early 1930s, the works of Engels had become the foundation documents for an official 'science' of Marxism in the Soviet Union – a science of dialectical materialism that supposedly synthesized an account of nature and an account of economic reality. The Engels contribution was considered to be the definitive Marxist account of natural science and its laws, these laws being identical in form with the laws underlying economic development. The apparently technical inconsistency between Vygotsky and Engels over thought and speech therefore became politically significant. Vygotsky was refusing to accept the intellectual leadership of the Party in its elevation of Engels. Luria and Leont'ev, however, found themselves more able to swim with the tide on these issues.

Leont'ev was already distancing himself from Vygotsky during the last years of the latter's life, and attempted to entice Luria away also (Van der Veer and Valsiner

1991: 291). Leont'ev's own theoretical approach was focused on 'activity', rather than language. Activity was defined as including all practical and sensory engagement with the world. In some respects this move was consistent with Marxism. Certainly, Marx (in the 'Theses on Feuerbach') had insisted that practical activity must take philosophical precedence over contemplation. Vygotsky had treated the 'lower' sensori-motor activities (such as those of infancy) as simply natural ones, not yet overlaid with sociocultural influences. Leont'ev erased, or at least smudged, that boundary of natural-versus-social in Vygotsky. To some extent, in doing so, Leont'ev brought what Vygotsky had treated as natural into the social domain.

In keeping with this change in emphasis, Leont'ev placed much greater emphasis than Vygotsky on the social relations of production, that is, on the capitalist (or communist) context for individual activity:

> [H]uman psychology is concerned with the activity of concrete individuals, which takes place either in a collective – that is, jointly with other people – or in a situation in which the subject deals directly with the surrounding world of objects. . . . However, if we removed human activity from the system of social relationships and social life, it would not exist and would have no structure. With all its varied forms, the human individual's activity is a system in the system of social relations. . . . The specific form in which it exists is determined by the forms and means of material and mental social interaction that are created by the development of production and that cannot be realized in any way other than in the activity of concrete people.
>
> (Leont'ev cited in Wertsch 1985a: 211)

This quotation leads us into issues of Marxist theory that are dealt with more fully in Chapter 5 below. But it should be noted here that Leont'ev's shift from language to activity was double-edged. In redefining the Vygotskian barrier between natural and social, Leont'ev not only brought the natural closer to the social: he also brought the social closer to the natural. He did this by emphasizing continuity between infancy and childhood. Infant 'activity' was treated naturalistically by Leont'ev, as in effect it had been by Vygotsky. But Vygotsky had insisted that from childhood onward development is (almost) entirely a social, historical, and cultural matter. In his elevation of 'activity' as a general process, Leont'ev treated those (language-related) aspects of thinking that Vygotsky had labelled sociohistorical as continuous with early behaviour. By deemphasizing the differences between infancy and childhood, Leont'ev compromised Vygotsky's sociocultural position. Leont'ev's activity theory turned out to be more naturalistic than Vygotsky's theory.

Party functionaries

It would be easy, from a position of safety and of hindsight, to accuse Luria and Leont'ev of political opportunism. Both presented their research and their theoretical claims as consistent with, and informed by, Soviet Marxism (Van der Veer and

Valsiner 1991). Particularly in Leont'ev's case, the appeal to Marxism must be placed alongside some very conventional, 'bourgeois' assumptions concerning developmental change (Kozulin 1990: 121). In his emphasis on practical 'sensuous' activity, as underlying even language and other kinds of 'sign' process, Leont'ev was in important respects duplicating the functionalist psychology of Western Europe. He may well also have been amplifying the functionalism already present in Vygotsky.

Functionalism in psychology, either 'bourgeois' or Soviet, involves an appeal to evolutionary adaptation. The focus on practical activity, as in Leont'ev, seems to allow for continuity across the animal kingdom. This evolutionary treatment of practical activity is in many ways individualistic, and entirely consistent with nineteenth-century evolutionary thinking in the social sciences (such as that of Herbert Spencer). It fits in well with simplistic, linear accounts of human evolution, including Engels' account of the 'origin' of language. Such appeals were popular in the Soviet science of the Stalinist era. Leont'ev used such arguments to a much greater extent than did Vygotsky.

Leont'ev was able to argue that human development involves the interiorization of a set of cultural practices. These practices, or skills, are themselves the result of some kind of evolutionary process occurring in the species. The interiorization might be effected through language but language is no more than a vehicle for the social transmission of culture. The kind of human heritage of skills that Leont'ev treats as objective – as forming the material to be internalized by each growing child – is in many respects simply the result of human social evolution. What appears as an objective social world to the child consists of activities common to all humans. Such activities would include various kinds of tool-use, and indeed language-use itself. These are general adaptive achievements of humankind, to be interiorized by each child as it proceeds toward civilization. Where social conditions are treated as objective and universal in this way, the picture reduces rapidly to the traditional, bourgeois account of adaptation to a stable environment.

Leont'ev's approach to matters of development remains of considerable influence in Russian psychology (Zinchenko 1985). Zinchenko maintains the convergence between Soviet and Western thinking. A focus on adaptation is common to both, and so, paradoxically, is an individualistic orientation. Partly because of Vygotsky, and partly in spite of him, Soviet developmentalism stayed on a track parallel to the developmental psychology of Western Europe.

VYGOTSKY GOES WEST

Cultural lines: Bruner and Cole

Jerome Bruner has told us that he first heard about Vygotsky at a party in 1954 (Bruner 1985: 22). At that time Bruner was mainly concerned with perception and thinking, but he explored the implications of Vygotsky's arguments in a number of ways over the next 30 years, as he became increasingly interested in children's cognitive growth.

In particular, Bruner focused on the 'scaffolding' role played by adults in their interaction with young children – setting up frameworks for language, problem-solving and other activities. This was a direct application of Vygotsky's zone of proximal development. By the early 1980s, Bruner was arguing that language is acquired by children because of the transmission of culture across the generations – another broadly Vygotskian theme. Language, said Bruner, cannot be acquired simply through the automatic workings of an in-built cognitive 'device' (in the way that the linguist Chomsky had claimed). Chomsky's 'language acquisition device' must at least be supplemented by a 'language acquisition support system' involving adults (Bruner 1983). But for Bruner this support system is itself the result of human evolution and hence is grounded in biology. Following Vygotsky and many others, Bruner retained the biological basis for early development. The acquisition of language, of tool-use, of forms of thinking and problem-solving, are all functional and adaptive phenomena.

Michael Cole and his colleagues at the Laboratory of Comparative Human Cognition have explored Vygotskian themes from a basis of cross-cultural psychology. Cole's own interpretation of the zone of proximal development is substantially similar to Bruner's. He adopts it as a formulation for some widespread (perhaps universal) aspects of human culture – ways that adults transmit culture to children. According to Cole, contributing to Wertsch's collection on Vygotsky, the individual engaged in goal-directed activity can be treated as a 'unit of analysis' for both cultural and individual process (Cole 1985). Cole does emphasize that this engagement is 'under conventionalized constraints', a term that includes a whole range of types of social arrangement. But 'the acquisition of culturally appropriate behaviour' (1985: 158) is stated to be an interactive one in which children are guided by adults. As for Bruner, then, the zone of proximal development ('where culture and cognition create each other') is for Cole an index of some universal, adaptive features of human nature. Citing evidence from Taleland in Ghana and elsewhere, Cole explains that the difference between cultures lies in the precise ways in which the zone is manifested – for example, which adults do the teaching and how, and what practices the teaching is about. A similar approach is followed by Rogoff (1990) who expresses the Vygotskian viewpoint in terms of children's 'apprenticeship in thinking'. Humans are naturally interdependent, Rogoff argues, so that it is natural for children to become engaged in processes of 'guided participation' in cultural activities (Rogoff 1990: 210).

Cole and his colleagues at the Laboratory of Comparative Human Cognition state that 'from the sociohistorical viewpoint, a culture maximizes its impact on a child's development by providing regulative contexts that fall within the zone of proximal development' (Laboratory of Comparative Human Cognition 1983: 335). This sounds as if the notion of the zone of proximal development is being used with some precision. But the zone is defined as the interface of culture and the individual, so that anything that happens there is by definition 'within' the zone. For Cole, the zone becomes a loose shorthand for cultural transmission as a general, adaptive process. Critical scrutiny is not given to the notion of development in this context. Everything that happens between culture and the individual is, by implication, a good process, as a result of which good development takes place. Good development means the acquisition of one's culture – anything else is presumably sociopathology.

In their introductory remarks to *Mind in Society*, Cole and Sylvia Scribner discuss Vygotsky's Marxism in some detail. Most concretely, the Marxism is discerned in Vygotsky's focus on the human use of tools, by which humans 'master' external nature (Vygotsky 1978: 7). Tool-use is taken as a form of 'mediation' by which, as for Marx, historical-social change is reflected back in changed consciousness. Cole and colleagues place a quotation from Marx at the start of *Mind in Society*. The quotation is about the planned and purposeful nature of human activity, such as that of the architect (in comparison with the efforts of spiders and bees, which also construct things out of natural components). This quotation presents an individualistic picture of human activity, in which the human wrestles with a universe of objects. This is the tool-story to be found so frequently in anthropological writings.

The tool-story is an adaptation story. It emphasizes general human characteristics, presumably instilled by evolution in some way. Cole's general approach to science is an adaptive-evolutionary one. He has noted, for example, that the long history of attempts to ground cognition in social context should help us to avoid the repetition of theoretical mistakes, in that we should be able to learn from the fate of previous formulations. 'After all' he asks, 'if the previous versions of such ideas were deserving of such merit, why don't *they* represent the dominant paradigm? And if they were found inadequate, why are we wasting our time with them now?' (Cole 1991: 407, emphasis in original). These questions presuppose a Darwinian selection process at work in such scientific debates – survival of the fittest idea, as it were.

The adaptation emphasis is consistent with Cole's insistence on universal constraints in psychological development. Cole and his colleagues note that developmental psychologists 'can point to stages of understanding corresponding to logically connected aspects of the environment' (Laboratory of Comparative Human Cognition 1983: 337). The sequence of achievements in child development are, by analogy, constrained by 'biological structure and environmental contingencies'. For Cole, there are indeed universal features of development. Specifically there is a hierarchy of types of constraint – 'a progression from universal to culture-specific to context-specific' (ibid.: 343). As an application of Vygotsky, Cole's work has consistently framed developmental change within the constraints of universal processes of evolution and adaptation. Children's development is naturally social.

Cognitive lines: Wozniak and Wertsch

Alongside cultural versions of Vygotsky, such as those of Bruner and of Cole, it is possible to distinguish a more cognitive strand. An early contribution to this line of work was made by Wozniak (1975). Wozniak's emphasis has been on structural aspects of explanation, and in this regard, on 'dialectical' aspects of Soviet developmental theory. Here, 'dialectical' refers to such theoretical processes as contradiction and the dynamic interplay between a changing organism and a changing environment. Wozniak himself defines the dialectical method very carefully, in terms of official Soviet scientific methodology. In the course of his exploration Wozniak has noted that aspects of Piaget's theoretical system can also be treated as dialectical (see also Bidell 1988). This convergence reveals some interesting things about the later (post-Vygotsky) Soviet work. In particular, it demonstrates the importance of structure and system to the writing of Leont'ev (see Leont'ev's quoted comments on pp. 18–20 on the human individual's activity as 'a system in the system of social relations').

Wozniak notes the strongly cognitive flavour of this later Soviet work. There is an emphasis on 'active' aspects of mental functioning, just as there was in Western cognitive psychology in the post-war years. There is discussion of the interrelations of control in terms of systems theory. Remarkably perhaps, the convergence of Soviet and Western (cognitive) approaches in the post-war era is most marked in their common neglect of the social context of consciousness. Partly due to the renewed influence of Pavlovian (neurological) explanations in Soviet psychology in the 1950s, 'hard science' accounts became requisite in the USSR at that time. The Soviet Union was, after all, pressing forward to the next achievement in its collective zone of proximal development – the launch of Sputnik in 1957, with all its connotations of technological 'leapfrogging' of the West. Structural convergences between Soviet and Western developmental thinking therefore reveal more about the global situation in techno-politics than about some kind of grand theoretical synthesis. Despite Stalinist efforts – including the suppression of Vygotsky as being too Westernized – Soviet psychology of development remained little more than a variation on European themes.

Wozniak's more recent work has explored ways of conceptualizing the 'social ecology' of children's development. A cognitive emphasis is retained in this analysis, so that Wozniak can conclude that 'the child develops [an] abstract conceptual system that will function as the source of future meaning attribution' (Wozniak 1993: 90). The conceptual system emerges from the interplay of specific cognitive endowments in the newborn and the 'sea of social events' in which children are immersed. Natural processes thus play a key role in Wozniak's analysis, although he emphasizes the complexity of the transactions between the individual and the social and physical environments. As with Vygotsky, it would not be unfair to define Wozniak's position as a claim that children's development is naturally social.

The final contributor to be considered in this summary of the Western uptake of

Vygotsky is James Wertsch. Wertsch has translated and interpreted Vygotsky's writings over a number of years, and has been responsible for collecting together contemporary viewpoints on Vygotsky's work (Wertsch 1985a, 1985b). For Wertsch, Vygotsky's contribution lies in his emphasis on three major themes and on his attempts to synthesize them (Wertsch 1991a). The first theme is the 'genetic method', according to which present states of affairs are to be explained by 'how they came about'. The second theme is Vygotsky's emphasis on social origins of mental functioning. In Vygotsky's words, as cited by Wertsch, 'humans' psychological nature represents the aggregate of internalized social relations that have become functions for the individual and form the individual's structure' (Wertsch 1991a: 89). In his claim that functions in intellectual development appear first as social relations between people, Vygotsky was, Wertsch explains, appealing to a tradition in European psychology as well as to Marxism. The French psychiatrist and psychologist Pierre Janet, for example, had made similar claims concerning the social origins of mind and, from Janet, a version of this claim even emerges in Piaget (Morss 1990: 124).

Neither the first nor the second theme, Wertsch argues, was entirely original to Vygotsky. The third was much more so. This theme is identified by Wertsch as 'mediation'. This claim relates to the importance of tools and signs in human thinking. Like the first and second themes, Marxist support can be found for this point. Human labour can be traced back in an evolutionary sense to tool-use and to animals' manipulation of their environments. However, as Wertsch emphasizes, Vygotsky's emphasis on the role of language in thinking goes well beyond Marx. For Wertsch, this emphasis underpins that which is original in Vygotsky's approach – including his versions of the genetic method and of social origins for thought. Sign systems, including representation of any kind, are taken as having emerged through sociocultural evolution.

Wertsch has carefully indicated what he considers to be limitations in Vygotsky, as well as achievements. In particular he points to Vygotsky's inadequate account of social-institutional settings. Vygotsky, for Wertsch, was too narrowly concerned with a problem-solving approach to labour and with interpersonal communication, in both cases abstracted from larger social structure. Thus Vygotsky's analysis of labour was 'transhistorical' (Wertsch 1985a: 237) in that it ignored the effects of economic structure – contrary to Marx. Again, the focus on interpersonal communication makes it difficult to grasp the historically changing patterns of language-forms made available to speakers. Language-forms, genres, or 'voices', occupy positions of differential privilege. If people come to think in terms of the languages in which they grow up, then the conflicts between alternative languages must be recognized. For Wertsch, Vygotsky's treatment of verbal thinking as incorporating a unified, public language is quite misleading. We must recognize the plurality and heterogeneity of voices at the level of thinking. While maintaining a qualified commitment to Vygotsky, Wertsch has therefore started to explore complementary frameworks, most noticeably the work of Russian literary theorist Mikhail Bakhtin (also see Hermans *et al.* 1992).

A contemporary of Vygotsky, Bakhtin had presented an analysis of texts, particularly literature, in terms of the interplay and interconnection between multiple 'voices'. Voices may be alternative genres or styles, but it is also possible for one voice to speak 'through' another. The complexity of Bakhtin's analysis allows for the homogeneity of Vygotsky's account to be corrected. Wertsch argues that the role of sign systems (that is, of semiotic processes) must be extended. Styles or genres of both written and spoken language will enter the field of inquiry. This will enable interpersonal analysis – that is, the analysis of an immediate social context – to be grounded in a cultural and historical analysis. 'Voices' or styles or genres must be thought of in public terms, Wertsch indicates – as collective products competing for individual consumption. In some respects, this might be seen as an attempt to introduce power relations into Vygotsky's formulations.

Quite explicitly, also, Wertsch intends his appeal to Bakhtin to undermine Vygotsky's developmentalism. Having established the notion of a plurality of voices, both 'inside' and 'outside' people's heads, Wertsch notes that Vygotsky's only recognition of plurality was in the form of a developmental hierarchy (Wertsch 1991b: 99). As with the cross-cultural work – in which cultural difference was interpreted as evolutionary development – for Vygotsky, different systems of thinking were to be ranked on a vertical scale. For Wertsch – who connects his work with the 'cultural psychology' of Cole and of Robert Shweder (1990) – different systems of thinking comprise, instead, a 'tool-kit' of alternatives, none inherently superior to any other.

Elsewhere, however, Wertsch insists that his investigation of socially-constructed thought processes can be no more than a complement to the study of universal processes. 'There are undoubtedly universal as well as socioculturally specific aspects of human mental functioning' (Wertsch 1991b: 7). This position is in agreement with Cole and with Shweder. Further, Wertsch's insistence (following Vygotsky) that human action is always mediated – by tools or by language – would seem to imply that there is an 'unmediated' form of action in animals. Development in human infancy must somehow bridge this gap. 'We' adult humans must therefore see ourselves as having evolved from animals and having developed from babies. Evolution and development are seen as parallel processes, through which higher levels of adaptation emerge. Both processes are described as being sociocultural, but the emphasis on adaptation and on function pulls the explanation in a biological direction. The appeal to universal aspects of functioning has the same effect. The social is naturalized.

Wertsch has also pointed to some non-biological directions in which post-Vygotskian thinking might proceed. He has noted on several occasions that Vygotsky largely failed to consider such classic Marxist themes as the class structure, the process of commodification in capitalist society, and the effects of abstract (wage) labour on individual development. Wertsch has thereby highlighted some of Vygotsky's deficiencies as a Marxist thinker, but his own revisions of Vygotsky have been in a different direction. Nor has Wertsch felt it appropriate to treat Vygotsky's claims as an indication of a thoroughly 'social constructionist' viewpoint. Others, whose knowledge of Vygotsky's work may be less comprehensive than that of Wertsch, have taken this step, as the next chapter describes.

PROGRESS SO FAR

Vygotsky's work is very effective in placing children's development within a social context. However, it is not yet clear, from the versions of Vygotsky so far discussed, whether Vygotsky helps us to proceed beyond that contextualizing. The Marxism in Vygotsky appears to have been an influence towards an emphasis on adaptation and hence an orthodox evolutionary developmentalism. Those who have followed Vygotsky most closely, both in the West and the East, have in the main preserved the functionalism of the original, however much they may have revised other aspects of Vygotsky's work.

It must be emphasized that the Marxist contribution to the critique of development is far from exhausted by the Vygotsky traditions. Nor have we yet done with Vygotsky – since he has inspired work in psychology that differs significantly from that summarized in the present chapter. Chapter 3 describes some readings of Vygotsky as a social constructionist, and Chapter 5 includes a Marxist reading of Vygotsky. The mainstream of late twentieth-century Vygotsky enthusiasts treat him as the discoverer of enculturation as apprenticeship. Children 'develop' through being exposed to the kinds of things that adults value and through the opportunity for 'guided participation' (Rogoff 1990) in valued activities. In this analysis, everything that adults do is related to their culture. Every aspect of the transmission of culture from one generation to the next is now said to involve development. The term development is perhaps being stretched so far as to lose much of its meaning. This stretching process does not however deal with the conceptual problems of developmental explanation. The emphasis on functional adaptation remains. If we are seeking for alternatives to developmental explanation, we are not yet making much progress.

In his published writings, Vygotsky held fast to a distinction between science and literature, while remaining fascinated by their interactions. Yet, in more personal terms, Vygotsky insisted on the significance of 'inner disharmonies, the difficulty of living', as illustrated for example in the writings of Chekhov. 'In particular, all of us, looking at our past, see that we dry up. That is correct. That is true. To develop is to die' (Vygotsky cited in Van der Veer and Valsiner 1991: 16).

Chapter 3

Persons in conversation
The social construction of development

For a number of writers, the term 'social construction' expresses a cohesive point of view on human experience across the lifespan. It places emphasis on the role of interpersonal negotiation in constructing the social world. For Kenneth Gergen, Rom Harré and John Shotter, in particular, face-to-face human engagement must be seen as the most significant arena for the construction of identity and subjectivity. We define ourselves and others, they suggest, in terms that emerge from the conversational activity that so characterizes humans. We tell ourselves, or perhaps story ourselves, into being.

A number of divergent styles of analysis are brought together in the writings of the social construction theorists. The range of these styles is well indicated in the statement of objectives for the Sage series 'Inquiries in Social Construction', edited by Gergen and Shotter. The general objective is described as follows:

> This series is designed to facilitate, across discipline and national boundaries, an emergent dialogue within the social sciences which many believe presages a major shift in the Western intellectual tradition. . . . It is a dialogue which involves profound challenges to many existing ideas about, for example, the person, selfhood, scientific method and the nature of scientific and everyday knowledge.
>
> (Semin and Gergen 1990)

Styles that are mentioned include 'rhetoric and narrative'. For those writers who identify themselves with the social construction approach, argumentation and story-telling are universal elements of people's social life. They are elements that vary however in their details between cultures and with time. The social construction approach is therefore able to appeal to cross-cultural and to historical analyses of human social life, as well as to scrutinize contemporary experience in the West. This range of styles is reflected in this chapter.

The focus on story-telling and its interactive nature connects up with movements in disciplines other than psychology. As George Howard (1991) notes, the move towards story-telling and 'culture tales' in psychology reflects a wider distrust of claims for absolute knowledge in the social sciences. Most generally, this disenchantment with certainty has given rise to notions of 'postmodernism' – a style which has also found its way into social construction writings (Gergen 1992; Shotter 1992). More narrowly, it converges with relativistic views of culture within social anthropology. According to Geertz (1983), for example, ways of knowing the world are intrinsic to cultures. All of human knowledge is 'local knowledge' – relative, at least in some respects, to the culture in which it makes sense. Western modes of thinking – through which 'alien' cultures have traditionally been analysed – are only superior by reasons of history and accident.

As assimilated by psychologists interested in development, an element of universality is retained. Story-telling and other narrative processes may be treated as generically human. Instead of treating developmental change as natural in itself, it may be argued that it is natural for people to tell developmental stories. This view of the interaction between culture and narrative – as discussed by Bruner for example – forms an important background for the more focused considerations of 'the social construction of development' by Harré and Shotter.

Making sense of a life – one's own or someone else's, of whatever age – can be said to involve the construction of stories (Freeman 1993; McAdams 1993). More broadly still:

> Stories are habitations. We live in and through stories. They conjure worlds. We do not know the world other than as story world. Stories inform life. They hold us together and keep us apart. We inhabit the great stories of our culture. We live through stories. We are *lived* by the stories of our race and place. It is this enveloping and constituting function of stories that is especially important to sense more fully. We are, each of us, locations where the stories of our place and time become partially tellable.
>
> (Mair 1988: 27, emphasis in original)

Developmental psychology should perhaps be seen as a set of stories 'of our place and time'. The multiplicity of these stories can be overwhelming. Not only is there Vygotsky's story, as against Piaget's, but there is also Wertsch's version of Vygotsky's story alongside Wozniak's version, and so on. We are captured by whichever authority we are in conversation with, and begin to see the world as they do.

Developmental stories are indeed diverse, but common themes and structures can perhaps be discerned. The developmental claim might itself be seen as one of the 'great stories of our culture'. Developmentalism, if it can be satisfactorily defined, might turn out to be one of the grand narratives by which modern, industrialized societies regulate themselves. After all, much of the state's intervention into its citizens' lives is rationalized in terms of the developmental needs of particular age-groups. At the same time, much of the entrepreneurial effort of the private sector is directed at the redefinition of those needs in terms of the products and services that it wishes to sell. That children have certain characteristics, that adults have others, and that it is natural to grow from one to the other, are messages that we receive from all forms of mass communication (Burman 1994a).

Some of the stories that 'inform life' are thus rather small in scale, some very large. Some seem more negotiable than others, but they are all interpersonal. All are in some ways carried by people, and constantly recreated through people's interactions with each other. The stories that people tell to, and about, each other are constructed through social processes. This is the line of argument that is taken up by the social construction writers.

In the last chapter, we saw how psychologists have responded to Vygotsky's claims about human development. There is a recognition of the social context, including the cultural setting, and hence of the diversity of human experience. But Vygotsky and his followers have placed little emphasis on conflict between different value systems and their effects on development. As Mair (1988) would put it, they have discussed how stories 'hold us together' but have neglected to deal with how they 'keep us apart' (1988: 127). One of the more innovative of the contemporary Vygotskians, James Wertsch, has moved in that direction with his attempt to incorporate the ideas of literary theorist Bakhtin on the multiplicity of 'voices' within a text. Literary theorists, along with feminists, social historians and many others, are included in the participants of the 'emergent dialogue' as described by Gergen and Shotter's statement of objectives.

In this chapter, the major focus of attention is the relatively cohesive work on 'the social construction of development' by Rom Harré, John Shotter, Kenneth Gergen and others. First, however, some comments are made on the more cultur-ally-based approaches to the human making of human development. This work forms a bridge between the post-Vygotsky and the social construction traditions, and also merges with the narrative approach, especially in the case of Bruner.

TELLING TALES: CULTURE AND NARRATIVE

Bruner: the 'push to narrate'

Jerome Bruner has responded to recent movements in the social sciences while retaining a broadly orthodox perspective on development. In the last ten years or so, narrative approaches have gained a prominent place in Bruner's writings but he has been at pains to demonstrate the consistency of this literary form of analysis with a more biological emphasis on adaptation.

For Bruner, children grow up in a certain culture, and interiorize it, so that its forms of knowledge become theirs. This analysis focuses on ways in which different cultures *are* different, perhaps radically different, from each other, and hence casts doubt on any claim for universal patterns. Bruner did not however want to relinquish his grasp on universal aspects of development. How is it, he asked, that despite this diversity of human cultures, all cultures manage to transmit themselves to the next generation?

The answer, for Bruner, lay in treating some aspects of Vygotsky's account as universal (and presumably biological), as well as looking elsewhere for universal processes. The latter task brought Bruner to the issue of narrative. Bruner came to believe that there are two kinds of thinking made available to humans as a consequence of evolution: a logical, analytical kind, and a sequential, sense-making kind. Logical forms of thinking – such as Western science – had been treated by Vygotsky, as well as by Piaget and many others, as the pinnacle of cognitive development in the individual. Story-telling, for Bruner, is just as important, both as a cultural process and for what it tells us about the human mind.

Bruner thus treats narrative as something like a cultural universal. He argues that all humans must be treated as having some kind of predisposition or readiness to think in narrative terms – that is, in terms of coherent sequences of events. There is a 'push to narrate' (Bruner 1990: 138). Such a predisposition underlies the various forms of intuitive or 'folk' psychology that different cultures generate, and thus, according to Bruner, narrative has general cultural functions. Most significantly, narrative forms of interpretation serve a peace-keeping function, to 'promote negotiation and avoid confrontational disruption and strife' (ibid.: 67). Bruner treats the narrative style of thinking as a functional device which assists the smooth running of a society. The peace-keeping function is common to all cultures – all, that is, that have survived. For 'this method of negotiating and renegotiating meanings by the mediation of narrative interpretation is, it seems to me, one of the crowning achievements of human development in the ontogenetic, cultural, and phylogenetic senses of that expression' (ibid.). Bruner neatly articulates the evolutionist, universalist tendency inherent in his version of the role of narrative. Narrative competence emerges as the goal of individual growth – also (to be somewhat facetious) it will save the world.

Bruner's use of Vygotsky is functionalist. It focuses on the adaptive, survival value of the processes Vygotsky described. Even when emphasizing that people's lives are lived through story-telling, Bruner insists that children are 'predisposed naturally and by circumstances' towards certain employments of narrative; 'we equip them with models and procedural tool kits for perfecting those skills. Without those skills we could never endure the conflicts and contradictions that social life generates. We would become unfit for the life of culture' (Bruner 1990: 97).

Bruner's use of story-telling and narrative, which he finds compatible with Vygotsky's overall framework, is designed to explain how human society works so smoothly. Developmental change seems to be thought of as a functional component of this larger system. More generally, Bruner's 'cultural psychology' steers a middle course between extremes that he has termed a 'trivial' universalism and a 'rubbery relativism' (1990: 20). Bruner's universalism is anything but trivial. It supplies a foundation for his arguments. He may not however have given enough thought to the issue of whether relativism can be other than 'rubbery'.

Shweder and the 'cultural psychology' of human development

Orthodox versions of 'cross-cultural psychology' have often fallen prey to ethnocentrism (see Burman 1994a: 160). More recent approaches, such as the 'cultural psychology' of Richard Shweder – an approach influenced even more by anthropology than is that of Bruner – are making a serious effort to grasp cultural diversity. In Shweder's words:

> Cultural psychology is the study of the ways subject and object, self and other, psyche and culture, person and context, figure and ground, practitioner and practice live together, require each other, and dynamically, dialectically and jointly make each other up.
>
> (Shweder 1990: 1)

For example, Shweder refers to the work of Higgins and Parsons (1983) in which 'stages' of development are reinterpreted as 'subcultures'. Older children in the US tend to be more skilled than younger children at transmitting abstract information, but it is not necessary to attribute this to some underlying developmental change – for children of different ages live in different subcultural worlds. The home subculture emphasizes social relationships at the expense of the transmission of information; the reverse is the case in the school subculture. The ways children think, and changes in the ways they think, should be thought of as cultural, not natural phenomena:

> [T]he child's emerging ideas are, to a great extent, transmitted to him. . . . There are a lot of messages implicit in social discourse: messages about what to presuppose, what to value, what to feel, how to classify; messages about what it is to be a person, how to relate to a group . . . and so on. The 'language games' of American parent – child discourse redundantly transmit the thematic content of American culture. . . . 'You're old enough now to ...', 'Let's make a deal', 'What if everybody did that?'.
>
> (Shweder 1984: 56 – 7)

Human life is thus a complex cultural construction. Cultures, and subcultures, are immensely varied. But cultural psychology insists on some general, underlying processes that allow culture to happen. Human beings, it is claimed, are 'highly motivated to seize meanings and resources out of a sociocultural environment that has been arranged to provide them with meanings and resources to seize and use' (Shweder 1990: 1). Shweder's definition of human nature is a functionalist one, placing emphasis on the way different components work together to yield the proper outcome. Shweder's approach thus converges with that of Bruner and with the Vygotskian accounts described in the previous chapter. The functional attitude tends to treat human activity as harmoniously (perhaps 'ecologically') attuned to the natural and social environment, and implies that this state of harmony is the consequence of evolutionary processes. In so doing, it defines developmental change as a reflection or a working-out of this happy interaction. 'How' development happens, in terms of detail and of cultural diversity, is seen as problematic in an empirical sense. But *that* it happens, and what it is in broad terms, is regarded as unproblematic.

Unlike the Vygotskians, however, Shweder has given some thought to the problematic aspects of 'developmentalism' (the term is his) as a theoretical commitment in the analysis of the human mind (Shweder 1984). He sees developmentalism as an approach to mind that treats differences as a matter of progression on a scale. Piaget's theory is one version of this approach. Shweder emphasizes that developmentalism is a theoretical position, a set of claims or presuppositions, and hence intrinsically open to challenge. Alternatives to developmentalism are, at one extreme, 'relativism' (in which differences are considered irreducible) and, at the other extreme, 'universalism' (in which differences are considered illusory).

Shweder insists that his framework of alternatives for theory in cultural psychology – universal, developmental, relative – is itself fairly robust. Unlike Bruner, Shweder does not want to chart a middle course between universalism and relativism, but to find the correct place for each of those interpretations. He insists that each type of theory must have some sphere of validity. Some aspect or aspects of human life or experience must indeed belong in each slot. Some things people do *are* properly described in terms of universals, some in terms of relatives, and some in terms of developmental formulations. It is the boundaries between the categories that present the theoretical problems (how do we decide what belongs where?) rather than the categories themselves.

Shweder is unwilling to relinquish his categorical system of types of theory. In doing so he limits the possible critique of 'developmentalism'. What is open to debate, he allows, are the boundaries of applicability of developmentalism rather than the concept itself. To attempt to eliminate any of the alternatives in his system, Shweder warns, is imperialistic. 'What we must resist is the temptation to imprison all mental events in the same cell' (Shweder 1984: 60). He thus warns us against overextending the category of relativism, for example (bringing us back to Bruner's rubber imagery). Shweder insists that developmental explanation, likewise, should be tightly disciplined and not allowed to exceed its range of validity. But its place in the system is guaranteed.

Shweder's approach to human development is substantially akin to that of Cole, discussed in the previous chapter (although without the debt to Vygotsky), and perhaps shares its limitations. Cultural psychology observes developmentalism at work, and scrutinizes it to some extent, but ultimately defends it. Some aspects of human thinking, it says, are indeed properly thought of as lying along some inherent and invariant scale. The fact that this might seem to be a version of the universal approach goes unremarked.

Probably neither Shweder nor Cole would object to the proposal that human development is to be thought of as 'socially constructed'. Nor, it is quite likely, would Bruner. However, none would wish that term to be taken in too open-ended a manner. In that respect they would probably not wish to be identified with those writers most emphatic on the significance of that term: Rom Harré, John Shotter, and Kenneth Gergen.

THE SOCIAL CONSTRUCTION OF DEVELOPMENT: HARRÉ AND FRIENDS

Rom Harré: the wilderness years

Rom Harré has consistently urged that psychologists should take seriously the social processes through which their objects of study are constituted. Following the philosophical traditions of G. H. Mead and Wittgenstein, he insists that human mental life is socially produced through such processes as interaction, language and the sharing of values (Harré 1983, 1986).

Experimental forms of social psychology – Harré's early target – ignore the role played by people's expectations and obligations in such settings. Similarly, stage-based accounts of childhood make the pretence that a sequence of stages unfolds through some natural process. Instead, Harré argues, stages are at best a description of a particular way in which some person is obliged to behave. There are always alternatives. Harré takes any hierarchical account of children's (or adults') growth and turns it on its side: a set of stages becomes a set of alternatives. This procedure is a challenging one. Harré has told and re-told this story many times over the last 20 years. The main reason he has had to repeat it so often has been that psychologists have been reluctant to listen.

The term 'social construction of development' was introduced in the 1970s by a number of critical voices within (and outside of) psychology. The concerns emerged first in the context of social psychology, and were subsequently applied to developmental psychology. These critics went beyond the progressive 'social context' writers who simply added communicative context to the orthodox formulas. In such books as *The Explanation of Social Behaviour* (Harré and Secord 1972) an experimental mainstream in social psychology was examined and found wanting. Methods being applied to human social experience were derived directly from the laboratory study of such processes as learning and perception. The critics argued that human social experience is different in kind from phenomena that can be studied with the methodology of natural science.

The attitude of these critics of social psychology was broadly humanistic and liberal. Traditional psychology, they argued, was treating people as if they were merely passive objects of naturalistic causal forces. The model of 'man' (even these critics tended to say 'man') was a mechanistic or behaviouristic one. This model seemed to fit into an ongoing tradition of natural science – a tradition based on the search for universal laws. The uncovering of such laws would allow for the prediction of an individual's behaviour. This mechanistic assumption was simply a mistake, said the critics. People are not merely passive; they are moral agents who must be allowed, or even required, to take responsibility for their actions and choices. Psychological research, said Rom Harré, must learn to treat humans 'as if they are humans' – that is, in ways that fully recognize people's capacities.

After dealing with social psychology, critical attention was turned to developmental psychology. One of the first collections to include these new criticisms of developmental psychology was *The Integration of a Child into a Social World*, edited by Martin Richards in 1974. Contributors included Shotter and Harré. Harré's focus had thus far been on methodology in social psychology. Shotter had already, in journal articles of the very early 1970s, employed quite novel forms of interpretation in child development, especially in the context of play.

Harré's chapter in Richards (1974) was concerned with the notion of autonomous social worlds in childhood – with culture-like systems of meaning located at different times. For example, children's interaction in the playground may be seen in terms of a special culture or subculture. The world or worlds of the child, Harré argued, have to be described not as if biologically determined but more as forms of culture. Moreover, they cannot be seen simply as early steps or stages on the way towards maturity. The notion of maturity has to be redefined as well. Adulthood, Harré argued, is controlled by social conventions and 'moral orders', not by the completion of a natural process. The social activity of children is also subject to moral orders, once language has been acquired. Piaget, as Harré observed, treated early forms of experience as 'stages toward adult mastery' (1974: 245), with particular emphasis on logical – mathematical forms of reasoning. The social construction viewpoint that Harré was outlining was a direct challenge to Piaget's notion of cognitive development, and to any half-hearted revisions of it. Harré gave more direct consideration to the Piagetian mainstream as the 1970s proceeded. The ways in which the mainstream had revised Piaget were inadequate, for too much status was still being given to stage-like analyses. The mechanistic approach to developmental process was itself misconceived, so that an amalgamation of this approach with any version of Piaget would necessarily fail. Orthodox developmental psychology, it appeared, was incapable of facing Piaget head-on.

During the 1970s a social construction movement gathered momentum, particularly in Britain. Its theoretical appeals were directed towards Vygotsky and G. H. Mead, as well as to Goffman's analyses of the rule-boundness of human activity. It should be noted that the term 'social construction' itself had been in the literature since 1967, when Berger and Luckmann's *The Social Construction of Reality* was published. This book was an accessible account of the social phenomenology of knowledge, derived from a collection of sociological traditions. It focused on the ways in which social reality is constructed by the activity of adult humans in their interaction. Little of the detailed argument of the book was adopted by those interested in the social construction of development. In fact, the occasional comments on individual development in the book are of an orthodox character – for example, early infancy is treated as a time in which the baby is in a biological sense still a part of the mother (Berger and Luckmann 1967: 66). Development is merely socialization – a biological being comes to be human and capable of a social life. The title was enough, as far as psychologists were concerned, since it legitimized the term 'social construction'.

Rom Harré: *Personal Being*

Harré's *Personal Being* (1983) sums up his approach to human development as worked out in the 1970s and sets it in a more systematic framework. Harré insists that 'the primary human reality is persons in conversation' (Harré 1983: 58). 'Conversation' is taken to refer to any communicative system of meanings in which people participate – not just spoken language, but also gestures, or the selection of clothes or activities. This primary reality gives rise to a set of secondary structures, to a 'practical order' of work and to an 'expressive order' of honour, respect, and other displays. Human minds are also secondary structures, and depend on the articulation of theories or accounts derived from the public arena. Humans exist as participants in conversation before they conceive of themselves (or others) as minds with subjective properties – and in principle they may never take this step. This is Harré's version of the Vygotskian notion of the social origins of mind.

Among other claims, *Personal Being* includes some pictorial formulations of the processes by which individuals come to interiorize their culture (Harré 1983: 258). (Figure 3.1.) Harré sets out a two-dimensional scheme constructed from a public–private axis (vertical, with public above) and an individual–collective axis (horizontal, with individual on the left). The public–private dimension is a

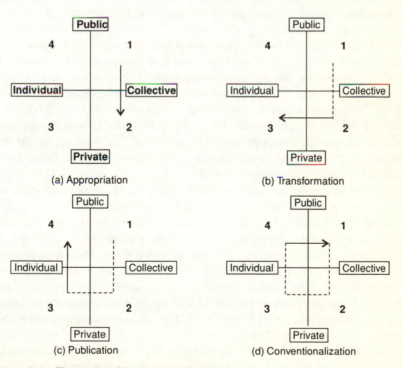

Figure 3.1 The cycle of human development
Source

dimension of display (display to others versus display to oneself). The individual–collective dimension is a dimension of 'realization' or 'grounding'.

Harré insists that the two dimensions are distinct and that they cannot be reduced to one dimension of personal versus social. That which concerns individuals may not necessarily be private – identifying someone as 'smart' is a public matter, but refers to an individual. That which is privately displayed may reflect collective systems of representation. For another example, language is related to both axes but in different ways. Language allows a continuum of representation from public to private, and it also allows a continuum of action from individual to collective (from 'I command' to 'this is what we do'). The whole array is itself 'within' language, that is, within the conversational world.

The two-dimensional scheme, with its four cells, is meant to clarify the social nature of psychological processes. Development will largely be defined by movement from one cell to another. Most generally, and most fundamentally, development in the individual is represented by the movement from the public-collective cell (cell no. 1) 'down' to the private–collective cell (cell no. 2). This is Harré's version of Vygotsky's 'appropriation' of cultural forms of interaction. For Harré, this process goes on all the time in human action, but achieves particular significance in infancy and childhood where it dominates mental life.

As explained in the final chapter of *Personal Being*, further transitions around the four sectors are also of importance to development. Further transitions beyond appropriation are of particular significance to adults, whose mental life is increasingly made up of complex cycles of movement around the four cells. In the adult, Harré represents the process of appropriation as a transition from 'persons' to 'selves'. The transition 'across' from private–collective to private–individual is 'transformation' (Figure 3.1b). This involves 'the creation of distinctive personal being by the transformation of one's social inheritance' (1983: 257). The next transition is 'up' to the public–individual cell (cell no. 4), in which some individualized character is publicly presented or 'published'. As Harré emphasizes, the individualized character thus broadcast was itself of course derived, before transformation, from the public–collective world.

Finally, the transition 'across' from public–individual to public–collective is a process of 'conventionalization' in which a formerly individualized procedure is taken up by the social collective. The whole series of transitions around the quadrant is a 'cycle of development'. At least for the adult and older child, the two-dimensional diagram represents a landscape in which many different events and transitions are taking place simultaneously. The transitions are all to be understood in terms of the one overall framework of four cells, and it is important for Harré that the transitions take place in the same clockwise direction around the landscape (broadly speaking, from social to personal). The outcome of the processes thus represented is what we call 'development'.

Some qualifications to Harré's formulation must be noted. Developmental change is not entirely defined by the cyclic processes pictured in the diagram. Some larger assumptions about development frame Harré's diagrammatic formulation.

The issue of quantitative advance in development is of major significance here. Important as the cyclic aspects are for Harré, they are incomplete in themselves for they must be complemented by more quantitative processes. This quantitative claim of Harré's is most clearly indicated in the discussion of moral thinking (Harré 1983: 227). The rigid (Piagetian) stage theory of Kohlberg for the development of moral judgement is seen by Harré as unacceptably prescriptive. Kohlberg had described a fixed sequence of quasi-Piagetian stages in moral judgement – younger children, for example, being self-centred and older children seeking the approval of others (Kohlberg *et al.* 1983). Harré, instead, discerns flexible strategies. Citing observational evidence, he argues that all of Kohlberg's moral 'levels' can be found simultaneously in children of school age. They are in fact situationally governed, and represent aspects of interactional style rather than some inherent developmental sequence.

Harré's critique of developmental stages is quite incisive here. However, his own alternative 'admittedly speculative' account of the acquisition of moral orders reintroduces a developmental proposition. He suggests that 'there is a cognitive capacity that does change. This is the ability to deal with more complex tasks and to handle greater masses of material' (ibid.: 225). This suggestion seems to presuppose that complexity and amount (of information) are absolutes, standing outside of cultural negotiation. In itself, the proposal that children are naturally less able to deal with complexity than adults – and that infants are even less able to do so than children – is a classic developmental claim.

It is difficult to define complexity in ways that do not depend on some cultural framework. The difficulty level of a task is not an intrinsic property of that task. As contexts change, so do levels of difficulty (as the Vygotskian tradition has emphasized). Treating difficulty level as an inherent property of a task is associated closely with the construction of graded sequences of materials (for example, reading materials) with which to educate children in a particular skill area. Progress through this sequence is routinely treated as a naturalistic development. Piaget would have agreed that the conservation task (usually solved by 7-year-olds) is a more difficult task than the object-permanence task (sometimes solved by 7-month-olds). Indeed he considered these tasks to be related in a logical – mathematical sense, and their ontogenetic sequence to be logically guaranteed. Piaget would have considered it impossible for the conservation task to be solved earlier than the permanence task. Similar assumptions are commonplace in post-Piagetian accounts of cognitive development, especially those influenced by 'information processing' accounts of cognition.

Harré's apparent commitment to the naturalistic notion of a developmental increase in capacity is therefore an unfortunate one. However, he does insist that capacity must always be treated together with issues of rights to display such capacity (ibid.: 226). Potentially at least, this qualification undermines the developmental claim, and places the issue of capacity back in a sociocultural context where, I would argue, it belongs. Harré's general conclusions on the developmentalism of

Piaget are strongly expressed. Piaget's work is 'a normative scheme presented in the rhetoric of science':

> A social-educational scheme whose products will fulfil the person-specifications of the Gallic, francophone social universe will present a developmental schedule which *must* culminate in the cognitive style appropriate to the normative classifications of that universe. If the culture is aimed, so to speak, at producing people who reason abstractly and formally, then its practices will necessarily appear as a sequence of stages by which one of the many possible modes of human thinking comes to overtake and supersede the others. Piaget's work is a brilliant exposé of a cultural tautology. But so too, in a more pedestrian way, is the work in which *that* judgement appears, namely this one!
>
> (Harré 1983: 252, emphasis in original)

Having criticized Piaget for a complex kind of ethnocentrism, then, Harré concedes that his own theoretical framework must surely derive, likewise, from his own culture. This is an important admission, since it corrects an impression that the theoretical framework (of the cycle of appropriation, transformation, publication and conventionalization) is somehow above culture. This impression is of a rather formal and structural analysis of mental life, too closely wedded to notions of regularity and rule-following. Structural analysis tends to detach the scientific observer from the scene, preserving the special status of that observer's knowledge.

It must be emphasized in conclusion that the approach set out in *Personal Being* and elsewhere is the most rigorously worked out of all the social constructionisms of development. Harré has brought together persuasive evidence and convincing theory on the negotiability of children's thinking and experience. It is Harré's misfortune, perhaps, to have been working out these formulations over a sufficient length of time, and in sufficient detail, for others to detect limitations in his approach.

Shotter and Gergen

Although pride of place must be given to Harré in a discussion of the social constructionists, John Shotter and Kenneth Gergen have been arguing for closely related points of view for a similar period of time. In comparison with Harré, Shotter (1993b, 1993c) has represented a more tentative and anti-systematic position. Shotter's eclecticism should be viewed as a reflection of his long-standing interest in interpretive approaches to scholarship. He is unwilling to settle on any one style of interpretation, being acutely aware of the arbitrary nature of doing so. Gergen (1985, 1991) might perhaps be placed between Harré and Shotter – open to new ideas, but extremely concerned to be responsible in their application. It is Shotter and Gergen, rather than Harré, who have recently embraced the notion of post-modernism, and Shotter who has come closest to the associated techniques of deconstruction. This section gives a sketch of the long-standing claims of Shotter and Gergen. A review of their current positions, as they respond to the notion of postmodernism, is discussed on pp. 42–5.

Shotter (1974), like Harré, made a contribution to Richards' *The Integration of a Child into a Social World*. He emphasized the personal and hence moral nature of psychology at large – characteristics which he treated as antithetical to causal, mechanistic kinds of explanation. The activities of persons, said Shotter, should be thought of in terms of 'powers' rather than causal mechanisms. Shotter explored the implications of the moral nature of the person for an understanding of very early, including infant, development. How, he asked, do human babies come to acquire personal powers? It cannot be a natural (biological) process since powers are intrinsically social. It must happen, Shotter argued, through babies being treated as human by adults. Babies become human by being treated as such.

Shotter's analysis involved an assumption about the role of interpretation in human interaction. 'Interpretation', in this context, is being used in a non-technical way. It relates to alternative possibilities for making sense or for constructing a representation of something. It does not refer to a search for a single truth, or for an underlying message in some text. Throughout the chapter in *The Integration of a Child into a Social World*, Shotter emphasized the general role of interpretation in the study of human development – the interpretation of children's actions by adults, by each other, and by themselves. Once able to use language, children were described by Shotter as living in a world of shared representations in which they play a part in constructing their own development. As far as infancy is concerned, the construction is however largely the responsibility of adults. Shotter thought of this account as broadly consistent with the arguments of Vygotsky.

Shotter's writings of the 1980s included more detailed explorations of Vygotsky, but paid less attention to the specific contexts of infant and child development compared to his earlier writings. His concerns were now with broad metatheoretical issues in psychology (Parker and Shotter 1990). His approach has remained a humanist one, in which a place is carefully retained for human agency and subjectivity, so that 'moral' perspectives remain of central interest (Shotter 1992). At the same time, rather more technical approaches to interpretation are explored so that literary forms of analysis become increasingly significant. In an examination of Harré's notion of 'persons in conversation' as the primary human reality, for example, Shotter (1993a) appeals to literary theorist Bakhtin. Bakhtin, as Shotter describes, outlined an approach to language and to the structure of meaning (semiotics) that emphasized interpersonal negotiation. Hence 'it is in the creative work of semiotically linking ourselves, meaningfully, both to each other and to our surroundings, that we . . . socially construct our identities' (1993a: 468).

Personal identity, as socially constructed, is now the major point of contact between Shotter's interests and developmental psychology. A concern with identity and the self in the modern (or postmodern) world is also central to the writings of Kenneth Gergen. Gergen has made several position statements on the social constructionist approach, both in general and in the context of human development. In *The Social Construction of the Person* Gergen outlines some major tenets of a

social constructionist orientation. Each, in a different way, emphasizes the negotiated, social-collective nature of human knowledge. Thus, 'the terms in
which the world is understood are social artifacts, products of historically situated
interchanges among people. . . . Forms of negotiated understanding are of crucial significance in social life' (Gergen and Davis 1985: 4–7). The Gergen and
Davis collection as a whole emphasizes humanistic interpretations of human life
and its development over time. Shotter's own chapter in this book is typically
wide-ranging.

The Social Construction of the Person discusses empirical as well as theoretical
issues in development. Despite considerable scepticism about experimental research, the social construction approach is not entirely hostile to more qualitative
kinds of empirical inquiry. Partly as a result of the earlier writings of Shotter,
Gergen and Harré, some empirically-minded psychologists of development (particularly in Europe) began framing their research in terms of social construction
(see for example Semin and Gergen 1990). In some ways this reflected the greater
continuity and higher profile of larger critical traditions on the continent of Europe
than in the UK and US. Psychologists in Germany, for example, would have been
much more aware of Marxism and the sociology of knowledge, and their possible
implications for research, than those in the English-speaking world. Awareness of
psychoanalysis as a kind of critique of the mainstream would also be much greater
in Europe, whereas few of the Anglo-American social constructionists have given
much attention to either Freud or Marx.

This situation has resulted in more complex interactions between empirical
research and theoretical criticism in the European setting than in the UK or the US,
where the critical voices have tended to remain distinct. This difference is illustrated
by the case of adult and life-span development as an area of empirical research. In
the UK and the US the study of adulthood tends to be narrowly empirical, with its
theoretical frameworks derived by the extension of childhood theory (see Dannefer
1984, 1989). Research is often framed in terms of a stage theory of adult development, thus risking the 'ontogenetic fallacy' (Dannefer 1984: 101). On the continent
of Europe, where life-span study has a long history, investigations of adulthood are
more commonly undertaken in a manner that recognizes the role of social construction (Kohli and Meyer 1986). The nature of adulthood in contemporary Europe is
described in societal terms, including the notions of modernization and stratifica-
tion. One consequence of this is that historical changes are taken more seriously in
the context of developmental theory. As noted above, Gergen has emphasized that
the terms in which the world is understood 'are social artifacts, products of
historically situated interchanges among people' (Gergen *et al.* 1990: 108). Closely
related to the claims of the social constructionists, then, are arguments for the
historically relative status of childhood and of developmental change.

HISTORY AS RELATIVISM

Kenneth Gergen's approach to human development is in many respects an historical approach. In this sense the social construction approach converges with more directly historical considerations of the nature of development. In particular, the idea that human development is culturally and historically defined has been urged over the last decade by Yale psychologist William Kessen, whose work is described by Gergen as the 'most radical' contribution to the area and who has made use of the term 'the social construction of development' (Kessen 1979: 819).

Kessen's paper 'The American child and other cultural inventions' (1979) was a key early statement. As Kessen noted in that paper, it had been recognized for some time that conceptions of childhood changed over long periods – as from the middle ages to modern times. The writings of French historian Philippe Ariès were the major contribution to this debate. Ariès had claimed that Western European society in the middle ages lacked any kind of 'concept of childhood' – that is, children were treated simply as small, underprivileged adults. The treatment of children as special, as needing protection and so on, was for Ariès an 'invention' of modern times. Whether or not the Ariès analysis was strictly correct (Pollock 1983), it made the point that adult treatment of children has changed with history.

Kessen emphasized that history does not stop. If adult treatment and perception of children in the middle ages or in the nineteenth century was in any way historically dependent, then it must also be historically dependent today. It is inconsistent to treat child labour in the nineteenth century, for example, as an example of historical dependence, while at the same time neglecting the role of present-day circumstances in defining childhood. If child labour happened as a consequence of economic conditions, then it follows that present-day treatment of children must also be recognized as in some ways relative to circumstances. Kessen was arguing that modern-day perceptions of childhood were not the be-all and end-all of a science of human development:

> Not only are American *children* shaped and marked by the larger cultural forces of political maneuverings, practical economics, and implicit commitments . . . [but also] *child psychology* is itself a peculiar cultural invention that moves with the tidal sweeps of the larger culture in ways that we understand at best dimly and often ignore.
>
> (Kessen 1979: 815, emphasis in original)

This was a threatening proposal. The scientific study of child development, Kessen was proposing, is itself an accident of history. What we study, how we study, and how we formulate our conclusions, are all in a sense relative to our historical and economic circumstances. In referring to 'the social construction of development' (ibid.: 819), Kessen placed such an attitude in a much larger framework. 'Social' construction – as between people – must be considered a component of 'cultural' construction. In particular, Kessen linked these notions by a discussion of the importance of individualism, showing that a focus on the individual is central to Western psychology of development:

> The child – like the Pilgrim, the cowboy, and the detective on television – is

invariably seen as a free-standing isolable being who moves through development as a self-contained and complete individual.

(1979: 819)

This individualist ideology, Kessen argued, must be seen as directing research
programmes and also as determining the objectives for intervention. Such unexamined commitments are still part of our science: 'we are both creators and performers
in the cultural invention of the child' (ibid.: 820).

Such historical awareness both reinforced and also extended the notion of the
social construction of development. At the same time Kessen's work represents an
analysis of the history of ideas as exemplified in the science of child development.
In more recent writings, Kessen has examined the role of such broad intellectual
commitments as the notions of progress and evolution in their relation to developmental psychology (Kessen 1990). He has examined the early years of what we
now refer to as developmental psychology, particularly in the US context, and
analysed the influence of the evolutionary claims of Darwin and Spencer (I explored
related issues in *The Biologising of Childhood* (Morss 1990)). Kessen's argument
about the role of individualism has also been carried forward by Sampson (1990)
and by Shotter (1990). These analyses are profoundly critical of the aims and
presuppositions of contemporary developmental psychology. Indeed they extend
the notion of social construction far beyond its usual interpersonal framework. The
persons who are in conversation must it seems be located within a larger social
structure, and large social changes will have effects on the way the conversation is
carried out. One of the most general social transformations to be diagnosed in recent
decades is the emergence of 'postmodernity'.

THE POSTMODERN TURN: 'TELLING IT AS IT MAY BECOME'

By the 1980s, and somewhat in contrast to previous circumstances, the social
constructionism of Harré, Shotter, and Gergen had become well established as a
line of argument. From a style of confrontation with the orthodoxy and the radical
advocacy of a new approach, the mood shifted towards the explication and
application of a methodological programme.

At the same time, a new generation of critically-minded psychologists was
emerging. As graduate students in the 1970s, these critical psychologists had been
exposed to the writings and teachings of Harré, Shotter, and Gergen. They were
sympathetic towards the social construction arguments and were taking account of
them in their own ongoing critical work (Broughton 1987; Henriques *et al.* 1984).
They felt themselves able to subject those arguments to critique. This cohort, who
were publishing their own books in the 1980s, were able to treat Harré, Shotter,
and Gergen as a kind of Old Guard – almost as an establishment against which to
define their own arguments.

Moreover, the wider social mood was different. The 1980s were years of
radically conservative governments in the UK and the US, years of stark divisions

between privileged and non-privileged. Liberal responses – characteristic of left-wing thinking in the 1970s – no longer seemed adequate. To the more politicized critical psychologists of the 1980s – Broughton, Urwin, Walkerdine – the liberalism and humanism that they saw in the social construction movement seemed to condemn it. Therefore the recent statements of that 'Old Guard' came to be seen in the context of two kinds of antagonism. Not only were the old battles against mainstream orthodoxy still being fought, albeit in a more gentlemanly manner, but new battles were taking place against avowedly more radical, and younger, women and men. The ground was shifting. Gender issues for example, had been invisible in the earlier debates, but this negligence was no longer acceptable.

The critique of the social construction position was expressed most forcefully at the beginning of the collection *Changing the Subject* (Henriques *et al.* 1984). As part of the introductory section to that book, Urwin, Walkerdine and their colleagues summarized what they saw as the humanism, individualism, and liberalism of that position. The aim of that difficult but important book was, among other things, to articulate a more effective form of critical approach to psychology. The social construction movement in psychology, having originated in the 1970s, was thus being challenged in the next decade as being insufficient. Larger changes in the social sciences were also taking place to which the social constructionists were responding on their own behalf. In particular, the notion of postmodernity was becoming widely diffused in academic discussion. Recent writings of Shotter and Gergen, in particular, combine interests going back several decades with an enthusiastic reception of new movements in the wider intellectual world. The 'postmodernist' formulations of Shotter's and Gergen's ideas are both innovative and consistent.

Shotter and Gergen have discussed the implications for psychology of the 'postmodern turn' identified by scholars in the humanities (Gergen 1992; Shotter 1992). Postmodernism defines itself in terms of some particular notions of 'modernism' in science and society. Modernism – in the sense repudiated by postmodernism – involves optimistic commitments to progress, including technological, educational and scientific progress. Shotter's version of postmodernism is consistent with his general framework. For Shotter, psychology of orthodox varieties has been modernist. It has sought for universal, abstract theories of human activity – the kinds of theory that allow for detached contemplation of the experience of others.

In contrast to this, a postmodern attitude would for Shotter involve practical, socially involved and responsible consideration of human lives. Shotter's postmodernism is thus a distinctly humanist one. Accounts would be negotiated and re-interpreted in a context of the intentionality of communicating individuals, although intentionality would be defined in social terms. There would be a focus on local and personal perspectives, and a recognition of plurality and fragmentation. Accounts and narratives would replace theories. Postmodernism, for Shotter, is a corroboration of the style he has been advocating all along.

Kenneth Gergen has also written on the possibilities of a 'postmodern psychology'. Like Shotter, Gergen finds the postmodern attitude consistent with his own position. He contrasts the 'modernist' project represented by traditional psychology – with its search for universal truths about human nature by means of prescriptive methodologies – with the demands of postmodernism:

> The challenge for the postmodern psychologist is to 'tell it as it may become'. Needed are scholars willing to be audacious, to break the barriers of common sense by offering new forms of theory, of interpretation, of intelligibility.
>
> (Gergen 1992: 29)

For Gergen, a valid psychology would accept a plurality of stories, whereas modernist psychology has been dominated by the 'grand narrative' of scientific progress. The assumption of progress in the science of psychology – the assumption that progress has been made and will continue to be made – is little more than a literary device. Progress is a way of framing a story about psychology. Indeed, for Gergen, story-telling is an unavoidable aspect of what we might prefer to call 'science'. But those who tell a story are obliged, according to Gergen, never to forget the constructed and negotiated character of that story. Individual responsibility is increased, rather than decreased, in the world of a postmodern psychology of social construction.

Such matters arise just as much in the supposed privacy of one's own self as in the more patently public domain. As Gergen describes in *The Saturated Self* (Gergen 1991), the self of our times is constructed out of culturally available materials. It will always be a struggle to maintain any kind of coherence in the self. The inhabitant of the industrialized North of our globe, and increasingly the inhabitant of the South, is exposed to massive international communications and information whether or not he or she participates actively in such processes. We are also exposed to increasingly diverse alternative lifestyles – to stories that we can see making sense for other people, and that we can less and less easily dismiss as deviance. Nor can we seek the comfort of ignorance concerning different possibilities, for no culture is truly foreign any more: the whole social world of humankind is opened up to us. Nothing that is human is beyond our ken. Gergen's postmodern self is saturated with possibilities, as the number and variety of persons with whom it is in conversation expands, seemingly without limit.

Harré, Gergen and Shotter have conversed with each other and with many others in seeking to untangle the processes of the social construction of human experience. They share many commitments and values, and they agree on many points of criticism of orthodox psychology – including the psychology of development. Differences between them should not be neglected however. Harré has tended to adhere to a realist approach, emphasizing the solidity of the processes he has described. Gergen has been more willing to accept the inevitability of some kind of relativism in a social construction approach. There can be no objective, absolute foundations for knowledge, but 'because of the inherent dependency of knowledge systems on communities of shared intelligibility, scientific activity will always be governed in large measure by normative rules' (Gergen 1985: 273). Thus, 'there is stability of understanding without the stultification of foundationalism'.

Shotter, especially in his recent work, casts doubt even on the 'stability of understanding' that Gergen has wished to maintain. Gergen himself, as we have seen, now calls for a breaking of 'the barriers of common sense'. For Shotter, most emphatically, life is flux. Shotter (1993b: 191) is beginning to distance himself from the humanism that he has always adhered to. He is now suspicious of the focus on consensus and on communal intelligibility that has been so characteristic of the social construction writings, including his own. His 'rhetorical – responsive' version of social construction (Shotter 1993c) focuses on ways of being, rather than ways of knowing. Other and earlier versions of social construction he now sees as falling into the trap identified by Marx – treating reality as an object of contemplation rather than as sensuous human activity (Shotter 1993b: 220). In exploring his more open-ended version of social construction, Shotter endorses the criticisms made of its more established versions by a younger generation of scholars.

PROGRESS SO FAR

The work of the social construction writers has constituted a consistent and coherent critique of orthodox psychology, including developmental psychology. It has insisted on the social construction of our selves and of our lives. But somehow the movement has failed to live up to the promise of its early years. The term 'social construction' has begun to sound a little tired, and its repetition threatens to turn it into dogma. There is a kind of stubborn humanism and an optimism that is sometimes a little cloying. There is a tendency to self-centredness that sometimes prevents a scrutiny of the positioning of that self within larger structures of society.

Meanwhile, the social construction position has been out-flanked by the faster-moving forces of critical psychology – somewhat younger, and riding more manoeuvrable steeds. The battle has moved on. Even the postmodernism of Shotter and Gergen is a social construction version of postmodernism. The social construction position still insists that human development is a matter of negotiation. It seems to suggest that anything is possible in human development – so long as we just have faith in our conversational resources. We're born free. Together, we can be what we want to be. . . .

The style of the social construction writers is reminiscent of philosophical literature – in particular, the existentialist novels of Sartre. The world-weary humanism of the existentialist movement was still influential in the social sciences at the time when Harré, Shotter and Gergen were in the early stages of their careers. There is in social construction a focus on the intellectual individual facing the rigours of a social world, which in some ways 'he' hates but which he cannot do without. Making sense, Sartre indicates, is itself a social process. Here is Sartre's Roquentin, of the novel *Nausea*, as reported by Mark Freeman (1993: 82–3): 'When you live alone . . . you no longer know what it is to tell something: the plausible disappears at the same time as the friends.' Roquentin continues: 'Suddenly you see people pop up and who speak and who go away, you plunge into stories without beginning or end.'

Sartre himself, in due course, turned to Marxism for a way of making sense of consciousness and identity. It is to Marxism, also, that a number of critical psychologists have turned in seeking to improve on the formulations of social construction. The turn to Marx – like the turns to Freud and to Foucault – represents a major reorientation of debate about psychology and about development. It involves reaching back through several centuries of Western thinking. It is therefore an appropriate time to take stock of the situation and of the story so far.

Chapter 4

The problem of development

Before following the line of argument into Marxism and the critical psychology of development, some reorientation is required, for the notion of development has not yet been tackled head-on.

The previous two chapters have surveyed some versions of the social context approach to development (focusing on appeals to Vygotsky) and some versions of the social construction approach. Both contemporary and somewhat earlier formulations have been reviewed. The appeals to Vygotsky described in Chapter 2 insist that 'the social is natural'. Developmental change may be treated as social in important ways, but remains directed by functional adaptation. Development itself is taken for granted somewhat, and not subject to critical examination.

Vygotsky's ideas also play a major role in the social construction arguments of Harré and colleagues (discussed in Chapter 3). There is little appeal to biological forms of adaptation here, and yet a naturalistic argument is still to be found. For the social construction writers, people's experience of their own and of others' lives can take place only through social interaction. Developmental change is refracted through interpersonal negotiation. Such social processes are treated as generically human ones. The image, perhaps, is of small communities in which much interaction is face-to-face and on equal terms. Such direct interaction is taken to guarantee equality and authenticity of communication.

The social construction approach has not been considered adequate by the critical psychologists of development, for reasons that I think are cogent ones. In moving on from those social construction writers, and even in talking about 'progress', I am not suggesting with any degree of confidence that I am moving 'up'. It seems to me however that the social construction writers do not see development itself as enough of a problem. Perhaps it is simply that Harré, Shotter and Gergen all have interests in psychology that are much broader than the areas covered by 'development'. In any event these writers, and those they have influenced, will remain present in this book as further approaches are discussed.

DEVELOPMENTALISM AND ANTI-DEVELOPMENTALISM

In moving the discussion on to the various critical psychologies of development, the notion of developmental change becomes subject to increasing scrutiny. It becomes urgent to examine whether development makes sense as a form of explanation. If there are alternatives to developmental forms of explanation, then we may have found alternatives to developmental psychology. Critical psychology of development, much more than the social context or even the social construction approach, makes possible the articulation of such alternatives.

Alternatives to developmental explanation approached within critical psychology I call 'anti-developmental' positions. The single common feature of anti-developmental formulations, in suggesting alternatives to developmentalism, is the claim that there must be such alternatives (Dannefer 1989; Stainton Rogers and Stainton Rogers 1992; Walkerdine 1993). An anti-developmental account is one that establishes a critical distance from developmental explanation. It is not enough to be *non*-developmental. That would be to miss the point, and to fail to take developmental argument seriously. Indeed, developmental arguments have a way of seeping back into such supposedly non-developmental formulations as those based on learning theory (Morss 1990).

One way of establishing this critical distance is to treat developmental explanation as discourse. Discourses are coherent systems of meanings that are historically located and that reproduce power relations (Parker 1992). Attention would be focused on developmental statements, that is, on particular claims appealing to developmental explanation. Developmental statements can be made about individuals (John is suffering a mid-life crisis because he is 40 years old) or about populations (40-year-olds are prone to mid-life crisis). In discourse analysis, both statements would be looked upon as having been produced: produced in particular circumstances, for particular reasons, and perhaps in the interests of particular persons or groups. A professional organization might have services to offer John and people like him; John himself might prefer to think of his problems in developmental terms – if this helps him to feel less at fault for those problems.

A developmental statement cannot be seen in any circumstances as a neutral 'reading-off'. Developmental change must always be treated as 'produced', so any naturalistic account of development has to be rejected. As a phrase, 'the social production of development' captures a number of important aspects of the critique of developmental explanation. The phrase offers a neat contrast to 'the social construction of development'. Too much weight should not perhaps be placed on this exact form of words, however, because the replacement of the term 'construction' with the term 'production' would be of little value unless the terms could be precisely distinguished. It should also be observed that the term 'production' has been identified rather narrowly with Marxist forms of analysis of social life. Marxist perspectives are not the only relevant ones.

Critical psychology might be said to offer alternative readings of 'the social production of development'. As will become clearer in the remainder of this book, I do not believe that critical psychology yet offers us ready-made anti-developmental formulations. The work of separating out the developmental arguments from the alternatives largely remains to be done. This objective provides the framework for the chapters that follow. Several attempts have been made in my earlier chapters to indicate the major characteristics of developmental argument. Before commencing the search for anti-developmental formulations, is it possible to define developmentalism with any precision?

Broadly speaking, developmentalism involves the assumption of regulated natural change (Walkerdine 1993). This may take the extreme form of a series of stages through which the individual is said to progress. More generally, it involves statements concerning directional change during the human lifetime: for example, the proposal that adults are more rational or complex in their thinking than children. More generally still, and converging more closely with everyday discourse, developmentalism takes the form of 'Children are like X'. Children, it may be said, can only think or act in certain ways. Infants, perhaps, may be said to think and act in certain other ways, adolescents in others, adults in yet others. If these different statements are reasonably consistent with each other then a coherent stage theory may be detected. But it is the assumption of natural regularity that underpins the stage theory, not the reverse.

There is an explanatory drive involved here. Natural regulation is appealed to as a kind of explanation in the developmental argument: that's how things are. It would be setting up a straw man to suggest that contemporary developmental psychology offers such explanations in a crude sense. Only rarely would developmental psychologists claim that a child of a particular chronological age does something simply 'because' she or he is that specific age. Some examples might perhaps be found in the psychological literature on infancy, such as the notion of 'stranger anxiety' being timetabled at nine months of age (Bradley 1989: 110). Developmental statements are usually expressed at a more general level, in the 'ball park' terms of infancy, early childhood, and so forth. Such guardedness might be seen as a recognition that the explanatory appeal to an age-group is inherently problematic. On the other hand, the imprecision might be a device for protecting the developmental statement from scrutiny. That is to say, the statement may be offered as a generality or perhaps as a norm which may not quite fit any specific case. It thus survives any such mis-match, should it occur.

Psychologists, indeed, have rhetorical devices at their disposal for discounting single cases should they appear to disconfirm some general statement (by calling them 'anecdotes' for example). At the same time, developmental psychologists frequently wish to link up their technical research with everyday developmental discourse. In spoken presentations of research particularly, reference is often made to the researcher's own children or family members, or to characters in some television show. When there seems to be a match between the general claim and the specific case, the 'anecdote' becomes an 'example'.

The point here is that the knowledge being produced by the research of the developmental psychologist exists in a close relationship with everyday knowledge about children. Most notably, the expert knowledge relies on the lay knowledge. The arguments of the developmental researcher are never based entirely on specific empirical 'findings', but on some combination of such findings and more general claims and assumptions. Some aspect of lay knowledge may indeed be challenged by a researcher's conclusions, but this will almost always involve appealing to some other aspect of lay knowledge. Everyday knowledge about babies, children, adolescents, and adults may well be less consistent than the accepted scientific account of the day. There will be diversities and conflicts in this everyday knowledge reflecting class, culture, and demographic distinctions. Consistency can, however, be attained by appropriate selection. This process of judicious selection from lay accounts may be an important aspect of the way psychological science works.

The inherent contestedness of everyday knowledge about development points us towards the anti-developmental position. Within everyday knowledge there is likely to be a range of alternative explanations for any particular action. Suppose a particular child has said or done a particular thing (for example, been abusive to another child). One available explanation is likely to be a version of the developmental explanation: 'That is what children (of that age) do'. But there will probably be alternative explanations to hand ('She just saw someone else do it', for example). Developmental explanation, as employed in developmental psychology, however, tends to be employed as if there were no alternative. It may be said to be hegemonic.

If this is an accurate analysis then the functions of the developmental statement must be examined. What is the point of making a general, developmental statement about children, adolescents, or adults – especially in the context of discussion of a particular case? It is possible, at least, that the appeal to development as an explanation causes other potential accounts to remain unconsidered:

> The very idea of development is not natural and universal, but extremely specific and, in its specificity, occludes other marginalized stories, subsumed as they are within the bigger story. The big story is a European patriarchal story, a story from the centre which describes the periphery in terms of the abnormal, difference as deficiency.
>
> (Walkerdine 1993: 455)

It might be suggested that certain forms of explanation would be more challenging than others to the professional status of the person (such as a psychologist) expressing the judgement. Some hypothetical examples might be drawn from legal situations involving young children's testimony. An expert opinion might be presented that a particular child's testimony is not to be trusted *because* 'young children do not understand the difference between reality and fiction'. This general claim might be used to support a particular agenda, such as the case for the defence of an adult accused of molestation, or a general scepticism towards child abuse statistics.

The 'anti-child' aspect of this example should not be over-emphasized. It is the form, rather than the content, of the developmental statement that is of concern here. Other, 'pro-child' kinds of developmental statement are available in the same situation. It might be said, for example, that a particular young child's testimony is totally reliable *because* 'children under a certain age are not yet able to lie'. Such a statement might itself meet various professional agendas, such as a case for the prosecution or a crusade for government action on abuse. What I am suggesting is that developmental explanation is always made for a purpose. Those purposes, and their moral contexts, are as varied as human social life allows.

Developmentalism therefore consists of the production of, and reliance on, explanatory statements concerning general natural regulation of changes in the human life-span. The anti-developmental approach involves the critical scrutiny of developmentalism, and the search for systematic alternatives to developmental explanation. If it is correct to describe developmentalism as hegemonic, then it must be seen as violently suppressing alternative ways of thinking and of being. Hegemony is threatened only by resistance.

DEVELOPMENTALISM AND THE SOCIAL SCIENCES

An attempt has been made above to define developmentalism analytically. It is also possible to define developmentalism historically. Critical psychology of development looks to Marxism and psychoanalysis, as well as to feminism and various social science traditions, in order to re-think developmental change. In doing so it recognizes that the problem of development has a long history in Western thinking. The discussion that follows should be seen as a brief overview of some of the historical dimensions to developmental explanation.

Developmentalism can be thought of as a set of assumptions that emerged in the eighteenth and nineteenth centuries, and found expression throughout the intellectual products of that period. The work of Darwin – at least as understood by psychology and other social sciences – is one such expression (Mörss 1990). An examination of critical psychology in terms of its scrutiny of developmentalism therefore requires some background in the intellectual history of the West. A focus on Hegel and Marx raises the relevant issues, including the notion of evolution in the natural and social sciences of the nineteenth century. What follows is intended as no more than an introductory sketch of some of these issues. It sets the scene, most particularly, for the discussion of Marxist critical psychology in Chapter 5.

Development from Hegel to Marx

Marxism can be treated as a vantage-point from which to view the intellectual currents of the nineteenth century. Marxism can be seen as having grown out of the confluence of a number of intellectual traditions and social movements. First, it owed a great deal to the rationalist analysis of political economy made by Adam Smith and his followers. Smith stressed the role of individuals' self-interested decision-making in giving rise to large social institutions such as the market. This individualist approach – literally, 'minding one's own business' – would subsequently be called 'bourgeois' economics. It can be seen as reflecting the rationalism of the Enlightenment of the eighteenth century. Second, Marx was attempting to make sense of contemporary events in the world of labour as Europe became industrialized. Third, Marx was responding to the Romantic movements of the early nineteenth century – that had portrayed the world as in some sense the expression of human consciousness. The most sophisticated version of this Romantic argument – a developmental version – had been presented by the philosopher Hegel. Thus Marx himself was at the same time an analytic rationalist of human nature, a politically committed journalist and an inspired romantic of human developmental potential.

Marx was of the generation after Hegel, one of the 'young Hegelians' who sought to correct and revise Hegel in the decades after Hegel's death in 1831 – just as Hegel's generation had revised Kant. Conventionally, it was Hegel's method of analysis – his 'dialectic' – that is said to have most influenced Marx. Marx himself claimed to have inverted Hegel's dialectic, turning an idealist philosophy into a materialist one. But it could be argued that it was Hegel's developmentalism that Marx inherited. Developmentalism took many forms in Hegel. First, general upward progress was discerned in human society through ascending forms of structure and institution. Second, this progress was linked, at least in conceptual terms, with a notion of evolutionary change in the natural world. Finally, progress and evolution were combined with development in the individual such that the growth of self-consciousness paralleled the larger processes.

While they were synthesized in a unique manner, these developmental claims of Hegel themselves reflected ongoing intellectual traditions. The first claim, that of general progress in human society, was a presupposition of the rationalist arguments of the Enlightenment. The second, linking human obligations with the natural world and its evolutionary processes, was urged by the idealist 'nature-philosophers' who were trying to correct Kant. Kant had insisted on the disjunction of human and natural processes, but Hegel, with the nature-philosophers, insisted on their intimate connection. Finally, the interrelation of a developing, self-realizing self or ego and a world known to that self was at the heart of another German revision of Kant – that of Fichte.

All these developmental presuppositions of Hegel's time were retained in Marxism to a greater or lesser extent. The first, a historicist progressivism, provided a framework for Marx's own analysis of social change. The second, a naturalistic progressivism, played little part in Marx but was strongly reasserted by Engels later on. The two together were then to constitute a scientific Marxism for the twentieth century, with history and the natural world both obeying the same set of laws. The third developmental claim, that of a self-realizing self, was a Romantic or humanist attachment of Marx, manifested in his concept of alienation. Alienation is in a sense the loss of identity. For individuals to move out of a state of alienation – and this would be one consequence of a Communist revolution – would be for them to develop.

Marx's notion of alienation is also related to Hegel's account of recognition. Recognition of oneself by others is central to Hegel's accounts of the development of self-consciousness. Individuality is, for Hegel, created and maintained by social processes. In a sense this makes Hegel the first social constructionist, but for Hegel these social processes are more like warfare than like a conversation. Hegel's metaphor for this situation is the parable of the master and slave, who constitute each other in their drive for recognition. Their needs, which are mutually dependent, drive them through certain kinds of change in their relationship and hence in their identity. Hegel's notion of continual (perhaps unending) struggle is basic to what he meant by 'dialectic', and Marx wanted to keep hold of this insight. It is the struggle that creates the individuals as subjects, rather than the other way around. The dialectical approach therefore treats social relations as more fundamental than the subjectivity of individuals. In Hegel this appeared to be an idealist position. Indeed, Hegel's position owed something to idealist traditions in Western philosophy running back to Plato. But Marx was able to argue that the relational position could be cleansed of idealism. Social relations could be given primacy within a materialist framework. This pointed Marx towards an objective account of human nature in which definite social structures and processes would be correlated with specific forms of consciousness and subjectivity.

Hegel's dialectic was intensely developmental, and so was that of Marx. The conflicts of the dialectical process in Hegel seemed to give rise to some kind of forward movement, either in the individual or in history. Sometimes, Hegel suggested, later moments could be identified as consummations of earlier conflicts, transcending them while preserving them in the subsequent structure. Such overcomings were themselves subject to further conflict and further spirallings of the dialectical process. The notion of a three-step sequence of 'thesis, antithesis, synthesis' was never more than a crude reduction of Hegel, but it was a reduction that fitted Marx's objectives. The dialectic, for Marx, was a progressive process, to be observed in particular in historical change. Struggles between major historical forces (social classes) take place, and history is the result. The creation of individuals, and of their subjectivities, thus takes place within a social world, which, through conflict, is itself developing.

Hegel's writings are complex and subtle, and he frequently undercuts his own arguments in an ironic fashion (Morss 1993). But to Marx's generation, the developmentalism apparent in Hegel was widely accepted. That developmental change indeed characterizes the humanly knowable world went largely unquestioned. The middle part of the nineteenth century was replete with conflicting readings of Hegel, alongside that of Marx. More were to emerge at the end of the century, and yet more during the twentieth. Most of these readings of Hegel were developmental either at the level of the individual, or of society, or both.

Meanwhile, biological accounts of developmental change were emerging. As noted above, Hegel's arguments derived in part from a philosophical approach to nature connected with the Romantic movement. According to 'nature-philosophy', the world of nature is in some sense developing as a whole. The emergence of 'higher' kinds of animal, especially humankind, was seen as an expression of this great process. Broadly speaking, this is what was meant by 'evolution' before Darwin. Indeed it is what was meant by evolution long after Darwin (Morss 1990). Most significantly, Darwin's claims were seen in the latter part of the nineteenth century as giving support to developmental accounts of the natural world. Treating evolution as a form of development – that is, treating a sequence of animal types as ascending a scale – is not, with hindsight, particularly Darwinian. Indeed Darwin outlined alternatives to that conventional viewpoint. But the Darwin assimilated by the early psychologists of individual development was one who endorsed a linear hierarchy of animal types, and indeed of human types.

Whatever alternatives we may now discern, it is a developmental Hegel and a developmental Darwin that we must acknowledge in terms of historical consequence. This is certainly the case in the context of social science. One of the nineteenth century's most influential social scientists, Herbert Spencer, put together an explanatory model of human psychology and the natural world based explicitly on what he called 'the development hypothesis' (see Morss 1991). Spencer's evolutionism might be seen as a crude synthesis of Hegel and Darwin, but it enjoyed considerable popularity among psychologists a century ago (Kessen 1990). Bringing together, as it seemed to do, the philosophical and the scientific discoveries of the nineteenth century, Spencer's account exemplifies the developmentalism from which more recent social science has had to emerge.

Spencer's account of social evolution soon came to be seen as inadequate by social scientists of the present century. But such extreme and global versions of developmentalism were easier to shrug off than more subtle forms. As the history of Marxism shows – and more particularly as the history of Marxist psychology shows – developmentalism proved obstinate.

Chapter 5

Marxism and the critique of development

Far from being exhausted, Marxism is still very young, almost in its infancy; it has scarcely begun to develop.

(Sartre 1963: 30)

To introduce a Marxist perspective, we might sketch a Marxist response to the social construction position described in Chapter 3. If the social construction position can be summarized as 'Together we can be what we want to be', then the Marxist response might be 'Let's stop fooling ourselves!'

The social constructionists make out that people are free to negotiate social reality between themselves. They pretend that people interact with each other on equal terms. But (the Marxist continues) people are unequal, and every aspect of people's interactions is affected by their inequalities. Most fundamentally there are economic differences – differences resulting from the unequal distribution of wealth. Pretending that people are equal goes along with pretending that they can control their own lives. The social constructionists make out that people are voluntary, rational agents, choosing freely from among a range of alternatives. But equality and freedom are both delusions under capitalism, and capitalism is now world-wide – including what used to be the Soviet Union. If people could control their own lives, how many would choose the lives they have?

Shotter, Harré and Gergen give different accounts of how social construction takes place. All three agree however in focusing on rather small-scale, even intimate forms of social life. The interest is primarily on pairs of individuals interacting ('conversing') one on one. The image is of a debate between two equal partners, or perhaps a dance. Apart from the problematic assumption of equality in these models (are there not power relationships even within a pair of individuals?), there are other deficiencies. Any reference to larger processes in social life – such as class struggle, the exploitation of minorities, the role of the state and so on – are kept out of the picture. The Marxist critic would point out that just as Piaget ignored the realities of social communication in his account of cognition, rendering his descriptions practically worthless, so Gergen and company ignore the realities of economic structure.

With its focus on freely-acting rational individuals – choosing whether or not, as well as how, to interact with others – the social construction approach presupposes a liberal analysis of society. It takes it for granted that people are primarily distinct individuals, with some rational self-awareness of their needs. Such individuals are seen as entering into contractual relationships with other free individuals, in order to satisfy their needs. To strike such contracts, individuals agree to curtail some freedoms. The system of parliamentary representation, with occasional elections on a one-person-one-vote basis, is an example of this kind of social contract. This picture of human society is the picture of a free market, a picture that has formed the basis for the development of Western capitalism over the past three centuries.

The illusion of freedom and equality is an essential part of the capitalist system. If people were to become fully aware of the power structures underlying the capitalist economy then they might be less willing to keep on playing their part in it. The raising of consciousness of these economic realities might be necessary (even if not sufficient) for any political change to take place. The myths of freedom, equality, and choice fostered by capitalist societies are perfectly mirrored by social constructionist accounts of human development. As Elizabeth Grosz has noted, 'a kind of theoretical and political self-making . . . marks the worst of liberal humanism', laying it open to 'charges of self-indulgence and the aura of an advertising slogan ("Become whatever you want to be")' (1994: 174).

The image of human society that is presupposed by the social construction approach is thus itself a political one. If the social construction writers appear to assume that they are dealing with natural, universal aspects of human reality, then they are deceiving themselves as well as us. In effect, then, the social construction accounts are 'mystifying'; they are concealing political oppression, even though unintentionally. What they take to be general features of human social life – the kinds of interaction which, among other things, allow 'human development' to be constructed – are actually historical facts, true only for certain places and times. To ignore larger social realities is to collaborate in the oppressive character of the modern industrial, democratic, capitalist state. Or so the Marxist critic would say.

The object of this chapter is to review the role of developmental argument in Marxist forms of psychology. To what extent has Marxism, either directly or indirectly, provided alternatives to developmental explanation? Rhetoric aside, has it made any advance on the social constructionist position? Broadly speaking, claims made from within Marxism are dealt with first, and claims from Marxist psychologies of various kinds next. The survey of relevant issues within Marxism starts with Marx, and includes the Critical Theory of the Frankfurt School as well as the Western Marxism of Louis Althusser and Lucien Sève. The discussion of Marxist psychologies of development that follows focuses on contemporary accounts.

DEVELOPMENT AND MARXISM

A general Marxist viewpoint would seem to be opposed to the social construction approach. Its opposition focuses on the individualism and the humanism that it perceives in the emphasis on interpersonal negotiation. Such features seem to the Marxist to ignore social and political realities. Instead of placing explanatory weight on individual choice, it is implied that attention should be directed to the ways in which people's lives are constrained. The kind of freedom that social construction seems to take for granted seems to the Marxist to be illusory, for people's consciousness is in some sense the reflection of their social and political status.

In *Capital*, Marx seems to endorse a rigid determinism by which human activity in all its manifestations is prescribed by economic circumstances – by the nature of the production and distribution of wealth. Economic modes of production determine modes of consciousness. This picture can be formulated in terms of an economic 'base', and a 'superstructure' that contains everything else: culture, technology, the arts, consciousness, and science. This picture is sometimes called 'economism'. From this perspective, human development is simply the production of persons appropriate to the economic needs of a society.

What we or psychologists call development must for the Marxist surely be socially produced. If people's thinking is, like consciousness in general, the reflection of their social and political status, then changes in that thinking must be thought of in the same way. If there is some regularity in the way adults (of a certain class) think, and if this kind of thinking seems different from the thinking of those people's children, then one might expect the explanation of the change to be sought in social circumstances. If the way the adults think seems desirable from the point of view of the owners of wealth, then it would be misleading to describe it as 'mature'. 'Maturity' implies natural change, from a lower to a higher level. Instead, the different kinds of thinking observed, and the fact that individuals tend to move from one state to the other, would be interpreted as consequences of the social and political situation.

This would only be the first approximation to a Marxist analysis, and one might expect psychologists influenced by Marxism to have fleshed out the skeleton. The situation is less straightforward however. Marxist psychologists have been reluctant to treat the thinking of children as socially determined in the same sense as that of adults. To a surprising degree, childhood has been treated as a kind of 'pre-history' by Marxists: as a biological phase prior to the individual's entry into the social world. Marxist analysis of consciousness has sometimes been thought to apply only to the inhabitants of the factory – not to their children, and sometimes not to their wives.

Added to this 'blind spot' towards childhood is the undeniable developmentalism to be found in Marxism itself. Given the historical context of the emergence of Marxism (as summarized in the previous chapter) the presence of developmental assumptions in Marxism should not be surprising. What has to be done, therefore, is for Marxist accounts that touch on 'developmental' change to be very carefully scrutinized. This must start with Marx's own writings.

Developmentalism in Marx

For Marx, communism is the developmental end-point of human history and it is the point when all people will become fully developed as individuals. True human development will only take place when communism is established.

In books such as *Capital*, Marx is concerned with establishing the human consequences of modern industrial society – in particular its place in history. Given an accurate analysis of the present circumstances, together with an adequate theory of historical change, it should be possible to anticipate future developments in economic structure and class relationships. The analysis would also generate an account of the consciousness of those who live under capitalism, and of the anticipated consciousness of the citizens of a post-capitalist economy. Marx was making the case for a new way of analysing social reality, that is, a new way of conceptualizing human social life. The social relations in which he was most interested were those of capitalism, in which large numbers of people work for wages and hence participate in a money-based economy. Profits are extracted from people's labour, so that people's labour is no longer their own. Workers become detached or alienated from their own actions. Only under communism would this situation be remedied, claimed Marx.

According to Marx's analysis, the motor of historical change is the conflict between social classes. The forming of class interests, and their coming to consciousness and expression, are at the same time manifestations and causes of history. But Marx was no Darwin, content to establish general mechanisms without prejudging the direction of change. Quite definitely, for Marx, class conflict and economic processes in general give rise sooner or later to radical improvement in the conditions of human existence. Forms of society get better, although some earlier stages may linger on in certain locations. People's development as people also gets better. Instead of stagnating (to mix the metaphors somewhat) people will blossom.

This evolutionary, developmental account can easily be found in Marx's own writings. In the Preface to *A Contribution to the Critique of Political Economy*, for example, Marx puts it this way:

> At a certain stage of their development, the material productive forces of society come in conflict with the existing relations of production. . . . Then begins an epoch of social revolution. . . . No social order ever perishes before all the productive forces for which there is room in it have developed; and new, higher relations of production never appear before the material conditions of their existence have matured in the womb of the old society itself. . . . In broad outlines Asiatic, ancient, feudal and modern bourgeois modes of production can be designated as progressive epochs in the economic formation of society. The bourgeois relations of production are the last antagonistic form of the social process of production.
>
> (Marx 1969: 84–5)

A range of world-views can be identified within Marx's writings, without extending to the writings of other Marxists. One version might be called humanist. The development of non-privileged individuals is systematically distorted under capitalism, but the true form of development would be revealed under communism. Thus, in a sense, privileged individuals in a class society do in fact develop in something like a 'true' or 'natural' way. Hence, it could be argued, Marx treats actual human development in the leisured class (under capitalism) as approximating true development, except insofar as it prevents the true development of others. Under communism it would be open to all to lead the life of choice and eclectic activity previously available only to the few.

More persuasively perhaps, the truly-developing individual might be identified not with the capitalist but with the person who struggles militantly against capitalism. Thus the life of the militant is taken by the contemporary Western Marxist Lucien Sève (1978) as in some ways a prototype of proper development. Either way – treating either the leisured member of the ruling class, or the militant, as a prototype of true development – there is a distinctly naturalistic cast to the interpretation. If what happens to the typical worker under capitalism is thought of as repression of development, then there must be some form of natural, organic development or 'flowering' that would otherwise take place. This is a naturalistic appeal. Even if some workers become militant, and throw off their developmental shackles, the 'repression hypothesis' will still apply to the mass of their comrades. What we have here is an individualist picture consistent with the Romanticism of the early nineteenth century. The *man* who is true to himself is able to reject the coercive forces of the social world. In doing so, he changes that world and creates new possibilities for human consciousness.

For Marx, the usual condition of the worker under capitalism is one of 'alienation'. Alienation is to some extent a Romantic notion in that it involves separation from one's true self. Alienation stands in the way of self-realization. The notion of organic, natural development that this book is concerned to challenge is in many ways an intellectual heritage of that Romanticism, and Marxism is not free of it.

The humanist Marx – the Marx who seems concerned with the individual subject and his or her development, alienation and so on – is the Marx predominantly of the early writings. This humanist Marx has been championed by some later Marxist traditions, repudiated by others (Geras 1983). Some later Marxists, such as Sève, have sought for continuations of these early interests of Marx in the 'mature' works such as *Capital*. For Sève, the early Marx was humanist in a speculative sense and the later Marx was humanist in a rigorously scientific sense. Other communist writers, most notably Louis Althusser, have insisted that Marx's early writings were simply an apprenticeship. They argue that Marx was progressively disentangling himself from humanist concerns and formulations, as he worked towards a fully-fledged and anti-humanist science of life under capitalism.

This debate serves to introduce some of the diverse post-Marxist traditions of the present century. In Russia, Marxist theory contributed to the Bolshevik revolution by which the Soviet Union was established. Among other crucial revisions of

Marx, Lenin identified the theoretical role of the Bolshevik party as representative of the interests of the proletariat. The Bolsheviks came to be perceived, quite literally, as the most developed members of their class. With their maturity of political awareness and judgement, and with their maturity of organization and self-discipline in the service of their class (and thereby of history), members of the Party would lead their more backward brothers and sisters into the new society. With hindsight, it seems almost inevitable that such an attitude would degenerate into repression even without a Stalin to accelerate the process.

THE FRANKFURT SCHOOL: FOR AND AGAINST DEVELOPMENT

Of the many twentieth-century Marxist formulations on modern social life and consciousness, those articulated by the Frankfurt School of 'Critical Theory' have had perhaps the greatest impact on psychologists' critique of development. This has certainly been the case in the US. In the context of critical work on development, Critical Theory is best represented by Theodor Adorno and (later) Jürgen Habermas. The work of Adorno is explored in its developmental implications by Buck-Morss in her contribution to Broughton's (1987) collection. The 'ideology critique' of developmental psychology practised by Broughton himself is closer to Habermas than to Adorno. These contemporary appeals to Critical Theory are evaluated at the end of this chapter.

Within Western Europe, Marxists of the twentieth century had to recognize the achievement of the Bolsheviks in establishing the USSR, and to consider its theoretical implications. Marx himself had, it appeared, been too developmental. He had looked for the first successful workers' revolutions in the most 'advanced' industrial economies of Western Europe, not in the peasant empire on Europe's margins. In the 1920s, mainstream Marxism in Western Europe was subordinated to the dictates of the Communist Party as internationally organized. Partly in response to this, a group of independent-minded Marxist thinkers became established in Frankfurt as the Institute for Social Research. The 'Frankfurt School' comprised, by the 1930s, such writers as Horkheimer, Adorno, and Marcuse (Jay 1973). In establishing Critical Theory the Frankfurt School maintained a critical distance from both Soviet and Western versions of Marxism, while sharing many of the attitudes of Marx, Engels and their successors to the capitalist society in which they lived.

In their analysis of that society, the Frankfurt School also took careful note of the position outlined by the non-Marxist sociologist Max Weber in the early years of the century. Weber had presented an account of the gradual impact of bureaucracy and rational organization on modern life that was as sophisticated as that of Marx, but which held out no hope of revolutionary salvation. Weber had analysed the connections between the capitalist economy and personal subjectivity and motivation. Rationalization, for Weber, is a trend by which people's actions and consciousness become increasingly defined according to instrumental functions. Thinking in terms of means and ends comes to replace thinking in terms of values.

By the 1930s, when taken up by the Frankfurt School, rationalization could be seen as a process of the scientizing of daily life, in parallel to the scientizing of work (through mass-production and so on). With their minds open to non-Marxist ideas such as Weber's, the members of the Frankfurt School therefore re-examined Marxism with respect to such twentieth-century 'developments' in capitalism as mass-production and mass-consumption.

The Frankfurt School was unconvinced by the official Soviet analysis of Western capitalism. The official line was expressed in the 'materialist' terms of base and superstructure. According to this framework, the consciousness of the capitalist citizen was governed by ideology. For Marx, ideology was the incorrect and misleading belief-structure of a pre-communist society. It functioned to prevent the oppressed classes from rising to a level of consciousness at which they would see their situation for what it was. Much of popular culture under capitalism can be seen as ideology in this rather simple sense. Popular culture includes messages about how people should live, how they should treat their children and so on, as well as what they should buy. However, the contemptuous treatment of popular culture as simply a form of oppression soon runs out of steam. Few cultural processes can be shown to represent deliberate manipulation by a ruling class. Many flow from structural properties of large industrial societies somewhat irrespective of political persuasion. Nor does it seem satisfactory to treat cultural processes as mere 'superstructure' – simply expressing the economic realities of the time. For the Frankfurt School, a focus on culture involved taking it seriously as a level of reality, and the Frankfurt version of 'ideology critique' emerged as a subtle and many-sided analysis of modern life.

In the pre-war years the School (including Adorno) was re-located from Frankfurt to New York. After the war it contributed to a more widespread and fairly optimistic scrutiny of Marxism. Adorno remained in the US until his death in 1969. The School returned to Frankfurt, and in recent years has been dominated by the thinking of Jürgen Habermas, who has paid as much attention to Weber's analysis of modern life as he has to that of Marx.

Adorno and Habermas share many concerns. Both despise the capitalist economy for its oppression of people, and both believe this oppression to be insidious as well as explicit. Both believe that the forms of consciousness available to the subjects of late capitalism are themselves distorted and distorting. Their agreement is essentially an agreement with the emancipatory aims of Marx. But the differences between Adorno and Habermas are in many ways greater than their similarities, particularly with respect to issues of development. In this respect, as I explain further below, it is Adorno's line of argument that offers more to the anti-developmental debate. In chronological order, Adorno and Habermas – the most representative figures of Critical Theory – have been respectively against, and for, development.

Adorno: against development

Adorno's position is sometimes referred to as 'negative dialectics'. By negative dialectics Adorno meant a whole range of critical standpoints and reactions to the 'positive dialectics' of official Soviet Marxism and of its version of Hegelian philosophy (Buck-Morss 1977; Rose 1978). One aspect of the official (Soviet) Marxism that Adorno called into question was the commitment to inevitable progress in human affairs.

According to official Marxism, progress is inbuilt by virtue of the dialectical nature of reality. Contradictory elements (such as different classes) struggle against each other, and higher levels inevitably emerge from this conflict. This positive aspect of the official version of twentieth-century Marxism appeals to an increasing convergence, over historical time, between nature and human consciousness. Forms of consciousness exert ever more complete mastery over nature, as technology advances. Hence nature becomes known ever more completely. This more complete knowledge of nature feeds back into consciousness, making it ever more perfect. With the advent of communism, it is assumed, reason and reality will coincide. The truth about the natural and social worlds becomes fully accessible to the communist citizen.

Adorno treated this assumption of progressive convergence as a developmental or evolutionary claim. As Habermas was later to observe, Adorno 'distrusted the concept of a developmental logic' (Habermas 1979: 72). Adorno traced the notion of progressive convergence back through Marx and Engels to the influence of Hegel. One version of it, for Adorno, was the developmental approach to history in Soviet Marxism. As Adorno was well aware, Soviet science also endorsed this vision of progress, in the form of biological evolution. The evolution of 'higher' animals from 'lower' animals, and humans from animals, was treated in terms of a steady ascent. The image was of the climbing of a ladder. This (pre-Darwinian) picture of evolution, which had dominated Western social science in the nineteenth century, is a developmental picture. There is an inexorable ascent, a 'march of progress'. In its Soviet form it was presented as the materialist account of human history.

Adorno's negative dialectics rejected these claims wholesale. He perceived that the assumption of convergence between reason and reality was an assumption about functional adaptation – just as characteristic of Herbert Spencer's sociology as of Soviet Marxism. That is to say, twentieth-century Marxism, in its official version, merely rephrased the nineteenth-century bourgeois view of the progressive evolution of human society. Adorno steadfastly opposed this 'philosophy of reconciliation'. His was a philosophy of inevitable and endless struggle between thinking and the world. Concrete things will never meekly fall under a system of concepts, argued Adorno. Conceptual systems will always do violence to reality. They aim at completeness, at closure: they try to explain everything, to eat everything. In Adorno's striking phrase, 'the system is the belly turned mind' (Buck-Morss 1987: 259). Nor should it be thought that there is some other, easy way to grasp reality. Reality cannot be known outside of that violent and unending struggle with some conceptual structure.

Adorno's is a philosophy of difference, of non-identity. It presents major challenges to Western thinking on development, in psychology and elsewhere. Thought and things are, for Adorno, defined by a radical non-identity one with the other. Thought is not developing – in the individual, the species, or the society – towards a closer connection with reality. It cannot be casually assumed, Adorno implies, that adult thinking is in any sense more valid or truthful than that of children. Nor can the identity of a thing with itself be presumed, so that the notion of continuity is undermined. A person today, and a person with the same name yesterday, are only 'the same' person by the mediation of some conceptual framework. Adorno's questioning opens up a whole series of issues concerning change that the developmental approach usually evades.

Adorno himself explored the implications of his ideas for the understanding of history, and its relations with nature, rather than in the area of psychology. He examined the notion of 'second nature': that which is treated as natural and non-negotiable but which is itself the product of history. This analysis connects with the Marxist account of 'commodity fetishism', by which phenomena constituted through social relations come to be treated as real. By implication, development can be looked upon as commodification. That is to say, changes in people's lives that are entirely social and contingent might come to be looked upon as natural and necessary. Adorno's arguments undermine the developmental position, and keep on undermining it. I will return to Adorno towards the end of this chapter, in the context of Buck-Morss' appeals to his negative dialectics within critical psychology of development.

Habermas: for development

Despite his Frankfurt School location, Habermas shares rather little of the critical style of Adorno. Habermas is an eclectic thinker, much concerned in recent years with communication in modern society and its democratic potential (Habermas 1979). He presents his claims and analyses within an evolutionist framework. In this context he is extremely sympathetic towards the arguments of Piaget and Kohlberg in orthodox psychology of development. With little distortion, Habermas can be represented as Frankfurt's developmentalist, whereas Adorno was its anti-developmentalist.

Habermas seeks an explanation of the smooth functioning of modern industrial society. As Pusey notes, Habermas 'has made very substantial concessions to the functionalist paradigm' (Pusey 1987: 207). He retains a faith in the rational progress of humanity and in the emancipation that will accompany that rationality. He thus endorses what has been called the 'project of modernity' – a vision of human betterment and enlightenment first established in the eighteenth century. This is, at the same time, a developmental and an evolutionary vision.

Habermas' extensive writings present several versions of the social and intellectual history of the West. Some are more stage-like than others, but the general commitment to an evolutionary form of analysis is clear. The direction of evolution involves the convergence of reason and reality; there is something close to an inner logic to the succession of social forms:

> Adorno failed to recognize the communicative rationality of the life-world that had to develop out of the rationalization of worldviews before there could be any development of formally organized domains of action at all. It is only this communicative rationality, reflected in the self-understanding of modernity, that gives an inner logic . . . to resistance against the colonization of the lifeworld.
>
> (Habermas 1987: 333)

The full significance of this claim, and of such processes as 'the colonization of the lifeworld', can only be established with reference to Habermas' own text. However, a general commitment to developmental argument is reasonably clear. This attitude stands in marked contrast with the writings of Adorno, as Habermas is well aware. To complete the quotation given earlier, Habermas comments that:

> Adorno, despite his Hegelianism, distrusted the concept of a developmental logic because he held the openness and the initiative of the historical process (of the species as well as the individual) to be incompatible with the closed nature of an evolutionary pattern.
>
> (Habermas 1979: 72)

Habermas, in contrast to Adorno, wished to defend a version of developmentalism in human history. Developmental patterns are to be reconstructed through conceptual analysis. Habermas argued that 'social evolution can be discerned in those structures that are replaced by more comprehensive structures in accord with a pattern that is to be rationally reconstructed' (ibid.: 140). Here developmental psychology plays an explicit role in Habermas' general theory:

> The stimulus that encouraged me to bring normative structures into a developmental-logical problematic came from the *genetic structuralism* of Jean Piaget as well, thus from a conception that has overcome the traditional structuralist front against evolution.
>
> (1979: 124)

As will be discussed in the following section, 'structuralism' entered Marxist thought most dramatically with Althusser. For Habermas, it was evolutionary or genetic versions of structuralism that were to be sought out. Such accounts, best typified by Piaget and Kohlberg, set out a normative sequence of stages through which thinking must pass. For Piaget, immature thought is 'egocentric' and hence unable to take account of alternative viewpoints. For Kohlberg, following Piaget closely, moral reasoning proceeds through a series of levels each more abstract than the last. Immature moral reasoning, as in the child, is egocentric and concrete. It is not yet even aware of the norms of its immediate social setting, that is to say it is 'pre-conventional'. The child, for Kohlberg as for Piaget, lives in a world of immediate rewards and punishments, of personal needs and adult authority. 'Conventional' reasoning dominates adolescence, and indeed adulthood in many cases, and involves reference on matters of moral judgement to some code, practice, or law. Finally, according to Kohlberg, 'post-conventional' moral reasoning frees the individual from the constraints of social expectation, but subjects him or her to the demands of some universal system of ethics.

Habermas has been happy to endorse Kohlberg's account in quite explicit terms, as an example of the correspondence between social evolution and individual development:

> The rationalization of law [through human history] mirrors the same succession of pre-conventional, conventional and post-conventional fundamental concepts that developmental psychology had demonstrated for ontogenesis.
>
> (Habermas cited in Jay 1984: 505)

As Jay notes, Habermas' analysis here is both developmental and evolutionary.

Habermas has also contributed to the psychological exploration of 'the development of the self' (Döbert *et al.* 1987). This is consistent with Habermas' emphasis on the theoretical significance of a contemporary 'sharpening of the adolescence problematic' (Habermas 1987: 388). The jointly-written chapter on the self discusses adolescence in explicitly developmental terms. Stress is placed on the convergence between Piaget's theory of cognitive development, Mead's theory of interactive development, and Freud's theory of psychosexual development (Döbert *et al.* 1987: 279). These various developmental schemes are treated as so many objective facts, valid (but partial) descriptions of what regular changes take place. The attempt is made to synthesize the claims of developmental psychology (including psychoanalysis) with the developmental sociology of Habermas. What emerges is a stage theory of the socialization of moral consciousness. The intention is to anchor the account within Habermas' theory of communicative action, such that 'the developmental levels of moral consciousness must be derived as a special case from the developmental levels of interactive ability' (ibid.: 297).

The collaborative work on the development of adolescent identity is a good example of Habermas' overall objectives. He is not merely appealing to the psychology of development for corroboration of his claims. Rather, he is assimilating the developmental programmes of Piaget and Kohlberg to his own evolutionist project (Habermas 1987: 389, 399). In so doing he demonstrates the implications and the significance of what I am calling developmentalism. In terms of social theory, as Habermas demonstrates, the treatment of the thinking of children as developmental is one with the treatment of history as developmental. If developmentalism is a mistake, it is a big mistake.

WESTERN MARXISM: ALTHUSSER AND SÈVE

Two recent Western Marxists have had important things to say about development. Louis Althusser and Lucien Sève – French communist philosophers of the 1960s and 1970s – both thought it necessary, as we shall see, to find a way of describing human subjectivity that is compatible with Marxism. Both found it essential to deal with questions of how children grow up to become the kind of adult human described by Marxist theory. Althusser and Sève were agreed on the theoretical importance of the relationship between childhood and adulthood. As is the case with Adorno and Habermas, their specific claims differed markedly from each other. Unlike the Frankfurt School thinkers however, it is not possible to cast one as developmentalist and the other as anti-developmentalist. Of the two, Althusser has been of considerably greater influence on critical psychology (Henriques *et al.* 1984). Indeed, Althusser's approach has been the most influential form of Marxism in the social science of recent times.

Althusser and Sève were both writing in the context of the Communist Party of France, which in the 1960s was trying to respond to changes in Soviet Marxism. The hard-line economism which had dominated the Stalin years was being re-thought to some extent. It no longer seemed adequate to explain culture and subjectivity as the reflection of an economic 'base', as *Capital* seemed to insist. Marxist theory in the West had to face up to the kinds of issues that the Frankfurt School had been addressing since before the war. How are we to conceptualize human subjectivity without losing a Marxist grasp on reality? Within French communism, some theorists were turning towards a humanist kind of Marxism, an approach closer to the earlier Marx than to the Marx of *Capital*. For Althusser, this reaction to the inadequacies of economism was in precisely the wrong direction. Humanism, for Althusser, involved an appeal to some human essence outside of history. He insisted that Marx had rejected this approach and claimed that Marx in 1845 'broke radically with every theory that based history and politics on an essence of man' (Althusser 1969: 227). The later Marx was, for Althusser, the scientific Marx – analysing history and consciousness in an objective manner. Althusser set his face absolutely against humanism of any kind. Marxism was to be scientific or it was nothing. Humanist Marxism was however the position that Sève was later to defend.

Althusser: structure without genesis

Althusser is of interest because of his attention to childhood and the family within a stringently Marxist analysis. As part of his theoretical programme, he wished to demonstrate how people come to acquire subjective selves that incorporate and sustain capitalist social relations. This takes place, Althusser argued, through the 'hailing' of the subject by ideological systems. Subjectivity is created by the individual being 'recognized' by some larger institution such as family, school or church. People, Althusser argues, can only know themselves through the mediation of such ideological institutions, and some of the most important of these institutions focus their attention on children. Subjectivity reflects the process by which 'raw' individuals are incorporated into the diverse functioning of capitalist existence.

Althusser's Marxism emphasized the integrated totality of social structure, including its economic, cultural and intellectual components. There was no neat distinction to be made between 'base' and 'superstructure'. He did not accept that the realities of human life could be explained simply as the reflection of economic factors and of the production of wealth. Althusser did maintain that in principle – 'in the last instance' – it is in economic forces and relations that any final explanation will be located. Such final explanation may never be reached: 'The lonely hour of the "last instance" never comes' (Althusser 1969: 113). Althusser insisted that the anti-humanism of the economicist approach be retained – he denied to human subjects the kind of autonomy and free will that were claimed by humanist accounts of human nature. He insisted that it is the social world that makes individuals.

Althusser argued that a satisfactory application of Marxism would need to involve a sophisticated account of how people come to act and think the way they do, particularly in a capitalist society. Althusser's solution – his 'third way' between humanist and economicist Marxism – was to employ structuralist styles of explanation, such as those being applied elsewhere in the social sciences in the 1960s. In particular, structuralist analysis was being applied to human cultures by the anthropologist Lévi-Strauss. Structuralist approaches in the social sciences treat everything in their field of enquiry as interconnected – as part of some vast system. One outcome of this form of analysis is an emphasis on synchronic (structural) relationships and a neglect of change with time. As expressed by Shames, Saussure – the founder of modern structuralism – 'was able to study the complexity of the present only at the sacrifice of the study of its development'(Shames 1981: 4). Structuralism is hostile to developmental explanation.

Structuralism seemed to offer Althusser an objective, scientific form of analysis of social experience that did not make explanatory recourse to evolution or to human agency. Structuralism in the analysis of language and of culture was explicitly anti-humanist in the way Althusser wanted. It explained how human experience is constituted. Marxism had thus far lacked a proper theorization of social structure and its functions. Structuralism hailed Althusser, and Althusser recognized in structuralism the kind of rigorous, scientific analysis of social existence that he was looking for. His task was to synthesize it with Marxism.

The kind of causality recognized by structuralism involves complex and dynamic interrelationships of parts and wholes, rather than any linear sequence of cause and effect. Lévi-Strauss had indeed described myths in 'primitive' cultures as 'machines for the suppression of time' (cited by Leach 1974: 115). Althusser rejected any naively progressive view of historical movement (Jay 1984: 415). The totality of the knowable world and its history cannot, he argued, be reduced to a single genetic principle – not even a Marxist one. Althusser's reading of Marx emphasized that social reality is genuinely holistic and multi-determined. According to Althusser 'the Marxist totality was a decentred whole which had neither a genetic point of origin nor a teleological point of arrival' (ibid.: 406).

Althusser thus rejected any simple evolutionism in social theory. Evolutionism would involve the reduction of explanation to a single cause, rendering a social whole as the 'expression' of some single principle. In Hegel, for example, human social forms were sometimes seen as unfolding through a simplistic process of 'auto-development' (Althusser 1969: 198). If examples of such simplistic theorizing could occasionally be found in Marx's own writings, this could only represent the vestiges of a crude Hegelianism, for Marx (argued Althusser) had left genetic explanation far behind in working out the 'scientific' Marxism of *Capital*. There had been an 'epistemological break' in Marx's intellectual career, representing a total reorientation from a humanistic to a scientific perspective. With any traces of humanism, the 'mature' Marx had repudiated any notion of evolution in society. Structuralism, as adopted by Althusser, is hostile to the notion of evolutionary change, and Althusser's Marx is strenuously anti-developmental.

According to Althusser, human subjects owe their subjectivity not to developmental processes, but to the ideological structures in which they have their being. In becoming subjects, people come to certain false beliefs about their own status. For example, people come to the false belief that they are free agents. The false or imaginary nature of subjectivity is most clearly indicated by this particular delusion. In the belief that they are free, rational agents, able to comprehend and even transform the world around them – the belief encapsulated by humanism – subjects reveal most clearly the constituted nature of their subjectivity. What Althusser argued, was that people's consciousness is part of their oppression. Ideology can only function through its subjects, that is, through the activity and experience of people. Ideology is not some mysterious abstract force, but a characteristic of multiple actions and interactions.

Subjects are thus constituted by ideology. The forming of new subjects is crucial to the reproduction of capitalist society because those subjects it already has eventually become economically unproductive. An explanation of how these new subjects emerge is central to Althusser's account. People, initially as children, acquire subjectivity, and become smoothly-functioning members of the whole structure, by a kind of socialization process. People recognize and define other people as subjects, and learn about themselves by being recognized and treated in certain ways. But although it is people who do the recognizing of new subjects, they are merely acting as agents for various ideological 'apparatuses' or institutions in society. Such structures as family and church work through people who are already their subjects (mainly adults) in order to assimilate yet more subjects, including many who are presently children. Adults in capitalist society are like agents of a foreign power, enlisting more young people to become agents in turn.

This analogy is instructive. Becoming an agent for the USSR in the Cold War – the period when Althusser was writing – involved allegiance to a large and powerful external agency – the Central Committee of the Communist Party of the Soviet Union. In the days of Stalinism, this allegiance had indeed been personalized around the figure of 'Uncle Joe'. Personal belief and emotions were involved – the new agent desired to belong to this big agency that was recognizing and hailing him or her. Althusser also had the personal experience of attachment to the Catholic Church on which to base his analysis of this general process. Subjectivity is acquired by each individual through recognition by the apparatuses of modern life, working through adults. The growing child desires to be wanted by these apparatuses.

Althusser sketched out an anti-developmental account of subjectivity. His commitment to structural forms of explanation involved a rejection of developmental or 'genetic' accounts. He saw no reason to seek any kind of compromise such as Piaget's 'genetic structuralism' as favoured by Habermas. Althusser did however appeal to a psychological account of childhood – the account of the emergence of subjectivity provided by the psychoanalyst Jacques Lacan. A detailed examination of Lacan is to be found in Chapter 6. Althusser's assimilation of Lacan is perhaps at the level of terminology and imagery, and does not involve a reorientation at the theoretical level. Certainly, Althusser's image of subjectivity remains a striking one. The subject is but the support for a huge system, and is given personal meaning only by grace and favour of that system. To think one can do more, or be more, is to deceive oneself. We seem to see ourselves reflected in the mirror-glass facade of the corporate skyscraper, but we misinterpret the situation. *We* are the reflection, or the projection, of that powerful apparatus. Althusser's vision is a disturbing one, not made less so by his own life events (depression, the murder of his wife, and institutionalization up until his death in 1990).

Sève: the here and now

Althusser's structuralist account has not been the only recent attempt from within Marxism to identify the major processes and characteristics of human development. Lucien Sève was, like Althusser, a leading intellectual member of the Communist Party in France. Appearing slightly later than Althusser's key writings, Sève's *Man in Marxist Theory and the Psychology of Personality* was first published in 1968.

Sève distrusted structuralism for the reasons Althusser embraced it: its anti-humanism. Sève considered carefully Althusser's argument for an epistemological 'break' in Marx, before and after the rejection of a humanist approach. Criticizing Althusser, he argued that Marx's later writings represent a scientifically rigorous reformulation of humanist problems. The mature Marx, according to Sève, was a scientific humanist (Shames 1981). In *Capital* for instance, Marx was, according to Sève, trying to reconceptualize 'human nature' in entirely social terms. The sixth of the 'Theses on Feuerbach', written by Marx in 1845, is a central text for Sève (Burkitt 1991). Here Marx asserted that human nature (whatever is to be meant by that term) can be nothing other than a matter of social relations.

Sève's project is to identify and carry forward what he sees as the scientific humanism of Marx: a dialectical and materialist approach to human life, including what would normally be called human development. This approach would avoid universal statements about human nature or its development, because such statements imply that 'atemporal logical forms or norms underlie all development' (Sève 1978: 283). This would be idealism, which Sève rejects (Shames 1981). The search for general, abstract laws of human development is pointless, since laws are 'historically relative':

> The only general laws of development of personality . . . are dialectical laws stating the general forms of determination which make it possible to understand the concrete necessity of development in any particular personality; like the topology of the personality to which they correspond, such laws themselves are therefore historically relative.
>
> (Sève 1978: 356)

These 'dialectical laws' change with history, and their function is to explain the possibilities for what will be called development within some specific historical epoch. At most, there might be common 'topologies' in the life-histories of people growing up under the same economic circumstances. But even here, there could be no general statements of 'development'. One cannot talk about 'the child' in general but only 'children', not just in the plural but in the concrete.

This focus on 'the concrete' is central to Sève, and he is able to demonstrate its centrality to Marx also. For Sève this is an aspect of Marx's materialism. Quite explicitly, Sève is here rejecting a form of explanation that is often taken as the definitive Marxist approach to development. For Soviet psychology, and for Western psychologists who have appealed to it, a Marxist approach often consists in explaining what something is by tracing its history – 'how it came to be what it is'. Sève argues that this is a bourgeois, not a Marxist approach, however legitimated by Soviet science. In the context of developmental arguments this approach is a 'vulgar geneticism' (Sève 1978: 284). For Sève, a Marxist approach must focus on actual, present social relations. The adult personality must be seen as 'the effect of the singular insertion of an individual in a determinate system of social relations' (ibid.) – even if these social relations have been reproduced faithfully over many years. This argument is a radically anti-developmental one.

In the context of this issue, Sève makes some comments on Freud that should be noted (Sève 1978: 149, 214). In Sève's view, Freud was claiming that adult personality characteristics may be directly linked to early childhood experience. Sève rejects this 'geneticism' of explaining adulthood by appeal to infancy. He argues that adults are new people in comparison with their previous infant selves, because adults are involved in quite different social relations from infants or children. Adult personalities are to be explained by their current social activities, not by the causative effect of continuous personal history. The effect of earlier experience is at most to provide 'materials' which adult personality may rework (ibid.: 284). This reworking is unpredictable. To stress this, Sève refers to the notion of *bricolage* or 'tinkering'. Freud himself, Sève suggests, hints at a replacement of the theory of continuous development with an account of 'instances' – that is, an account based on concrete particulars (ibid.: 272). We return to Freud in Chapter 6.

The detail of Sève's account of personality is formulated in schematic terms (ibid.: 348). Sève categorizes human activity in terms of the Marxist notion of 'use-time'. Two dimensions of use-time are distinguished. The first dimension separates concrete from abstract activity, where 'abstract activity' means activity in social relations with others (such as wage labour). It must be emphasized here that this identification of abstract *activity* with the social is a technical one in which Sève departs from a more everyday sense of 'abstract'. The second dimension separates the *acquisition* of capacities (either concrete or abstract) from the *employment* of capacities. There are thus four sectors among which human activity can be distributed: acquiring concrete capacities; acquiring abstract (social) capacities; employing concrete capacities, and employing abstract capacities.

Different types of people, or people at different 'stages of life', may have their essential characteristics represented in terms of relative investment in each of the four sectors. The child of school age may, Sève suggests, be represented by a large commitment to the acquisition of concrete capacities, a somewhat lesser commitment to the employment of concrete capacities, a very small commitment to abstract acquisition, and minimal involvement in abstract employment (see Figure 5.1). The student differs from the school-child chiefly in the reversal of the amount of

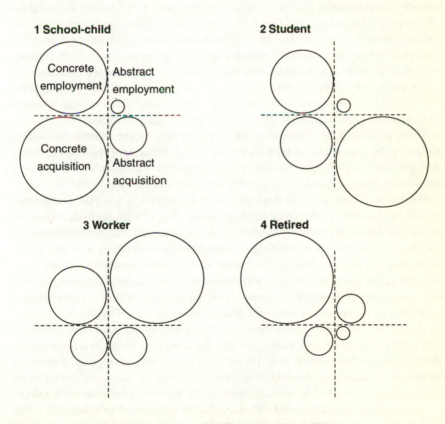

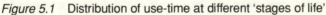

Figure 5.1   Distribution of use-time at different 'stages of life'

investment in the two acquisition sectors. That is to say, the student's major commitment of use-time is to abstract acquisition rather than the acquisition of concrete capacities.

In Sève's diagram, the student's investment in abstract employment is, like the school-child's, minimal. The student is more like a school-child than a worker. The (non-militant) adult worker, on the other hand, invests most use-time in abstract employment (wage-labour), along with moderate concrete employment and some very limited acquisition of both concrete and abstract capacities. The theoretical distinction between the student and the worker is fascinating in view of the political events of May 1968 in France, when the Communist Party of France declined to join the students' revolutionary activity on the grounds that the students were not real workers.

Sève emphasizes the 'extreme simplification' of his diagrams of the use-time distribution of the child, the student, the worker and the retired elderly person (whose major investment of use-time is in concrete activities). He suggests that the diagrams 'raise problems and suggest investigations' (ibid.: 349). Surprisingly, one investigation he thinks is suggested is into the question of 'the *stages of life* and the laws of psychological growth' (Sève 1978: 349). This suggestion, together with the categorical style of 'the child', 'the student' and so on, brings Sève's claims much closer to orthodox developmental psychology than he seems to realize. In employ-ing the term 'concrete' to mean 'non-social' activity (not part of a commodified exploitation system), Sève seems to neglect his earlier, materialist emphasis on the 'concrete'. The materialist claim is for the social significance of the concrete particular, but the use-time analysis seems to denigrate the concrete.

When presenting his diagrams of the 'personalities' of the student, the worker and so on, Sève restricts the term 'social' to the theoretically privileged category of waged labour. Only when surplus value is extracted from an adult's labour – as in classical Marxist economics – is that person's life really governed by social processes. Such activity is 'abstract' and requires theoretical analysis. Other kinds of activity, such as the kind that children are doing and learning to do, is *merely* concrete. Like the activities of animals, it can be observed and described in ways that do not require theory. Speaking through Marxist economics, Sève denigrates the activity of children (and by implication, that of women working in the home). In so doing, he compromises the concern with the everyday actualities of people's lives. Concrete particulars of everyday life, as theoretically important, have become concrete activity, of no interest to the Marxist scholar.

The re-emergence of developmental claims in the fine detail of Sève's account is not surprising in view of some developmental commitments on a larger scale. Throughout his book there runs the reference to social change as a form of development. Historical changes from 'lower' economic forms to 'higher' ones (ibid.: 325) are described by Sève in developmental terms. Communism is defined as 'full development' and as 'maximum' or 'unlimited flowering' (ibid.: 201, 325, 358). Sciences are themselves treated developmentally. Psychology is currently embryonic and it needs to 'mature'. Sève perceives his own scientific work as developmental: we must, he says, establish 'an epistemologically adult theory of the developed personality' (ibid.: 281).

These general evolutionist-developmental commitments, which stand in marked contrast to Althusser, undermine Sève's anti-developmental achievements. With such developmental attitudes to science and human history, Sève's account of individual lives can perhaps only gesture towards anti-developmental possibilities. Ironically, it is when Sève employs Marxist terminology most precisely that he loses sight of his critique of developmental explanation. That critique focuses on the importance of actual social conditions and relations. It is implied, I think, that all human activities are in a general sense 'social', and involve political and economic processes.

Sève's approach has been largely overlooked by critical psychologists of development, although it has played a minor role in the thinking of the *Kritische Psychologie* school (Elbers 1987; Holzkamp 1991: 51). It is possible that Sève's references to Soviet psychology (particularly to Leont'ev) have given rise to an impression of greater convergence with the Soviet work than is in fact the case. Althusser's claims have been examined fairly thoroughly by critical psychologists of development, but the work of Sève remains as under-utilized materials, not yet subjected to sufficient 'tinkering'. We now turn more directly to the employment of Marxism within critical psychology of development.

MARXISM IN CRITICAL PSYCHOLOGY

There have been several attempts by psychologists to incorporate Marxist theory in the context of human development. A number of versions of Marxist critical psychology of development have emerged, and these are examined in the remainder of this chapter. Marxist psychology has a considerable history, but the emphasis here is on current approaches. I first discuss the place of Marxism in the collection *Changing the Subject*. Consideration is then given to the *Kritische Psychologie* school of Holzkamp, Tolman and others, whose Marxism appeals quite directly to recent Soviet psychology. This leads into a discussion of Marxist versions of Vygotsky. Finally, versions of critical psychology most influenced by Critical Theory are discussed. That discussion focuses on contributions to Broughton's collection, *Critical Theories of Psychological Development*.

The Marxist critical psychology of development of recent years may be said to have started with the work of Klaus Holzkamp and of Klaus Riegel in the early 1970s. A broader historical account of Marxist critical psychology of development would first examine the 'Freud–Marx syntheses' attempted since the 1930s. Several figures associated with the Frankfurt School, including Herbert Marcuse and Erich Fromm, made attempts to articulate Freud and Marxism. The claims of earlier Marxist psychoanalysts such as Wilhelm Reich might be included in such an account. The influence of Marcuse, Fromm, and Reich on critical psychology of development has been too diffuse to justify detailed consideration of their claims in the present book. All three in fact receive mention in *Changing the Subject* – a book that gave new impetus to critical psychology and that incorporated Marxism into its project. Brief consideration of the treatment of Marxism in that book will serve as a point of departure for this discussion.

Changing the Subject

Changing the Subject (Henriques *et al.* 1984) is subtitled *Psychology, Social Regulation and Subjectivity*. Its aim is to establish a new account of subjectivity. Available accounts, it is argued, presuppose a dichotomy of individual and society. They either treat the individual as distinct from, and prior to society – explaining society in individualistic ways – or treat society as distinct from and prior to the individual – as in socialization theory. A satisfactory account must instead transcend that dualistic analysis.

Orthodox psychology is said to be individualistic and to neglect society. It is not enough to acknowledge the importance of communicative relationships between pairs of individuals such as mother and baby, or experimenter and subject. This shift from personal to interpersonal in the social context approach does not involve a shift from individualism. On the other hand, the classical socialization picture claims that 'society' turns a biological individual into a mature citizen. Developmental change, for the socialization approach, is simply a matter of the individual progressively adapting to the society. This adaptation process is treated as a natural process, giving rise to regular patterns of change through infancy and childhood. Such patterns are thought to exhibit a clear directional trend. This account is rejected by the authors of *Changing the Subject*. Socialization theory, they argue, treats 'the individual' and 'society' as distinct when in fact they must each be defined in terms of the other.

Changing the Subject takes as its starting point a consideration of the achievements and limitations of the social construction writers, who had challenged both traditional and social context accounts of psychology. To what extent did Shotter and Harré, in particular, succeed in breaking down the individualism of psychology? According to the authors of *Changing the Subject*, the social construction writers achieved very little in that respect. The perceived inadequacies of social constructionism centre on its humanism and its liberalism. The work of Harré and Shotter, for example, is seen as hopelessly liberal in its focus on a free, rational individual. The individual is still privileged over society. Marxism is in a sense the obvious answer to this situation, offering to provide a superior analysis of the individual and society. Marxism has presented itself as a distinct alternative to liberalism – as a method of analysis that reveals the illusory nature of the freedom presupposed in liberalism. For the authors of *Changing the Subject*, the corrective effect of Marxism is most important. However, an appeal to Marxism in the context of subjectivity may tip the balance too far in the direction of society. Societal structures may be privileged over individuals to an inappropriate extent, so that the individual–society dualism itself remains untouched.

What *Changing the Subject* sets out to do is to redefine the relations between the individual and society, not merely to shift the weight of explanation from one term to the other. Marxism plays a part in the process of redefinition of the dualism, but is not seen as offering a ready-made solution. The importance and the limitations of Marxism, in the context of subjectivity, are seen as being encapsulated in the work of Althusser. The authors of *Changing the Subject* stress the achievements of Althusser's anti-humanism in 'attacking as bourgeois any attribution of agency to the individual' (Henriques *et al*. 1984: 93). This critique of an individualist notion of agency was achieved, as they note, by the appeal to structuralist formulations. This appeal allowed Althusser to explain subjectivity in terms of social processes, especially in terms of the hailing of the individual by apparatuses of the state. Althusser is however presented as falling into various traps. His rejection of agency is seen as having gone too far. Agency is to be redefined, but not totally dismissed. The theoretical importance of continuity in subjective life is emphasized in *Changing the Subject* (ibid.: 204), and there is little place for such continuity in Althusser.

It is Althusser's structuralism that is blamed for his over-reaction to humanism. Althusser presented his structuralist Marxism as a scientific and objective worldview, validly representing social reality. *Changing the Subject* expresses doubts about the possibility of representing truth in anything like the objective sense of Althusser. Althusser's structuralism seemed to be making unfounded claims about patterns of correspondence by which scientific knowledge represents the social world. The authors consider the relationship between science and the world to be much more complex. The language of science (and language in general) produces the world we experience just as much as it reflects the world. In place of the structuralist emphasis on knowledge as representation, *Changing the Subject* favours the post-structuralist emphasis on 'signification'. Signification refers to the constitutive role of social practice – that is, to the ways in which social systems of meaning produce social reality. Such productive effects take place as a consequence of the social practices that go along with the meaning-systems. For example, educational psychologists actively intervene in the lives of children (and adults) when they carry out tests or other forms of assessment. The effects of their intervention have to be thought of in terms of organized professional practice. Meaning and reality are not just conjured up through interpersonal negotiation as claimed by the social construction approach.

The authors of *Changing the Subject* thus see both achievements and limitations in the Marxism of Althusser (and by implication, in Marxism in general). They claim that Marxism offers significant insights into the workings of contemporary society, and into the political functions of sciences such as psychology. Marxism must therefore inform the critique of psychology, including developmental psychology. However, Marxism remains trapped by the dualistic account of individual and society. In general Marxism emphasizes the societal side of this dualism. At times even Marxism can be individualistic, a problem illustrated by Althusser. For Althusser appears to be positing a non-social entity which has sociality bestowed upon it by the ideological apparatuses. Althusser's hailing process is too much like a version of socialization theory. Paradoxically then, according to *Changing the*

Subject, Althusser is both 'too social' and 'too individual' in his analysis of subjectivity. The paradox is to be resolved by rethinking the dualism of individual–society, and thereby going beyond Marxism.

Going beyond Marxism, for the authors of *Changing the Subject*, means appealing to Lacan and to post-structuralism. It was noted briefly above that Althusser had appealed to Lacan's psychoanalytic formulation of subjectivity. The appeal to Lacan is treated as Althusser's best move, but Althusser's Lacanianism is considered to be incomplete. These authors' own incorporation of Lacan is discussed in Chapter 6. As the authors of *Changing the Subject* perceive, Althusser runs the risk of recreating socialization theory in different terminology. Althusser places too much emphasis on the functional aspects of capitalist society, and how smoothly each new generation is incorporated into it. The authors of *Changing the Subject* demand a theoretical place for the possibility of resistance. Subjectivity, for them, must recognize this possibility. The position worked out in that book relies on Marxist traditions in a general way, and is sympathetic to the emancipatory aims of Marxism. For better or worse however, *Changing the Subject* effectively leaves Marxism behind. In doing so Henriques *et al*. may be thought of as having been somewhat ahead of their time, for Marxist critique was to retain a place in critical psychology for some while.

Kritische Psychologie

The writings of both Althusser and Sève described human development in ways derived from Western versions of Marxism. Closer to orthodox or 'official' Marxism was the continuing work of Soviet psychologists interested in development. Among those who followed Vygotsky in the USSR, Leont'ev has provided the most inspiration to contemporary critical psychologists. Leont'ev's work plays a particularly important role in the *Kritische Psychologie* school of Berlin and elsewhere, whose writings address issues of development among other areas of psychology. In the terms of this book, are their claims developmental or anti-developmental ones?

'*Kritische Psychologie*' is simply German for 'critical psychology', but it would be confusing to use the general term, in English, to refer to the specific programme of the Berlin group. *Kritische Psychologie* is a clearly-defined and technically rigorous approach to Marxist psychology (Elbers 1987; Tolman 1994; Tolman and Maiers 1991). It has been in the making for some 25 years, and recently has begun to make an impact on psychology outside Germany – particularly through the efforts of Charles Tolman. *Kritische Psychologie* was in many respects the reaction by German psychologists to the political upheavals of 1968, when student-led mass movements threatened the established governments of France and West Germany. Left-wing psychologists such as Klaus Holzkamp felt that either psychology had to be left behind – as being inherently oppressive of workers – or radically reformulated. *Kritische Psychologie* was an attempt to save psychology from irrelevance, by going 'back to Marx'.

Kritische Psychologie insists that psychology must be scientific. It must use Marxist theory to explain how certain conceptual structures have emerged in orthodox psychology – as reflections of economic reality. This would be a 'developmental' or historical approach to the analysis of present-day psychology and its object of study:

> The general approach of the categorical reconstruction of psychology's object is 'genetic' in the broadest sense of the term, that is, developmental, focusing on the genesis of psychical functions and structures. As such, it is modeled after the reconstruction of taxonomy resulting from the theory of evolution.
>
> (Tolman and Maiers 1991: 11)

The general approach to the criticism and the reconstruction of psychology is evolutionary and developmental (Holzkamp 1991: 51; Tolman 1994: 74). This brings *Kritische Psychologie* into contact with the psychology of development. Guidance on matters of development in the individual is sought chiefly from Leont'ev (Holzkamp 1991: 57; Holzkamp-Osterkamp 1991: 178). Leont'ev had placed greater emphasis than Vygotsky on the role of biological evolution in human nature. In line with trends in the more 'scientific' forms of Marxism which came to dominate Soviet thinking, Leont'ev sought to explain individual development by appeal to the supposed history and prehistory of the human.

Kritische Psychologie agrees with Leont'ev in treating this approach as consistent with Marxism. Marx, after all, had traced a kind of evolutionary progress in the forms of economy emerging in human society over several thousands of years. Feudal kinds of economy were replaced by industrial kinds, leading to industrial capitalism and eventually to communism. The evolutionary argument extends this kind of interpretation further back in time, into human prehistory and hence evolutionary ancestry. An account of the emergence of the human from the prehuman, and even of the origins of intelligent life in general, plays a key explanatory role in the arguments of *Kritische Psychologie*. This evolutionary account is used to define both the uniqueness of the human and the similarities between human and animal.

Human needs and motivation are inherently different, it is claimed, from what is found in animals. Human action is entirely structured by social (or more accurately 'societal') realities, rather than by mere physical features, and human activity is always mediated by social factors. Animals are in biology, humans are in society. This is an inherent difference in potential, illustrated by the failure of attempts to 'humanize' animals by rearing them like children. 'In short, human beings obviously have at their disposal a "nature", according to which they are, alone among living creatures, capable individually of participating in the societal process by virtue of their "natural" developmental potential' (Holzkamp 1991: 52). Holzkamp's scare-quotes do of course indicate an awareness of the problems of naturalistic analysis in this area, problems also recognized by Tolman (1994: 48).

As in all evolutionary accounts of human nature, claims about human–animal differences are only part of the explanation offered. For the appeal to a supposed evolutionary ancestry to be of any significance, some explanatory role for that ancestry must be posited with respect to the definition of the human of today. In general, evolutionary ancestry is treated as somehow still 'behind' or perhaps 'within' the human, manifesting itself perhaps in the characteristics of children (or infants at least). Human babies are biologically prepared for the societal life of *Homo sapiens* (Tolman 1994: 122), just as the societal nature of the species as a whole was prepared by evolution (ibid.: 92). The correspondences between the 'phylogenetic preparation' carried out long ago by evolution, and the biological preparation of each baby, are reinforced by common developmental terminology. The terms evolution and development are constantly combined and interchanged. Evolution (or 'phylogenetic development' (ibid.: 85)) is progressive (ibid.: 74): it gives rise to higher levels of development (ibid.: 76). Humans stand on the highest point of what appears to have been a single ascending path. If evolution is treated as progressive in this way, and if human nature is treated as the outcome of evolution, then the development of the individual human from birth to adulthood cannot but be treated as progressive also (Morss 1990). This is presupposed by Holzkamp when he asks:

> What is the *initial state of early childhood* from which the societalization process begins and what is the *necessary course governing the ontogenetic transition* from the initial state to the final result of individual societalization?
>
> (Holzkamp cited in Tolman 1994: 39, emphasis in original)

Tolman explains carefully (1994: 148) why the term 'societal' is preferable to 'social' and hence why the inelegant 'societalization' is preferable to 'socialization'. In particular, the term 'social' does not distinguish adequately between the ways bees or chimpanzees are social and the ways humans are social. 'Societalization', however, shares much with the more familiar term. Like 'socialization' it focuses on functional adaptation. This focus is illustrated by Braun's (1991) analysis of the 'ontogenetic preliminaries' of human development.

Braun stresses the immediacy of young children's activity. Young children learn 'the immediate meaning of signals, and with them to make themselves understood by adults with respect to their immediate needs, such as eating and drinking' (Braun 1991: 218). Such immediacy of experience and activity is more characteristic of animals than of humans, according to this approach; 'Whereas the individual prehuman animal's link to its world is a relatively direct one, the human's is a mediated one' (Tolman and Maiers 1991: 14). Children are working their way towards the human level of mediation through 'a series of qualitative stages' (Braun 1991: 218). They are developing from animal-like (biological) beginnings through to truly social levels – basically repeating evolution in its broadest steps. In the same way that evolution has exhibited progress in its production of the human, ontogenesis involves betterment of the individual. As observed by Braun in the context of children's social understanding of objects:

Providing the development is successful, the cooperative aspects become ever more important, the possibilities for influence are extended, the dependencies diminish, well-being is increased, and anxieties are overcome.

(Braun 1991: 219)

Functional adaptation is treated as the key to development. Children must come to recognize objective social meanings in the world, and thus become socialized. The child learns that 'a lot of experience has gone into available objects, that they have been constantly improved so that they were better suited for their purposes' (ibid.: 219).

This emphasis on functional adaptation is to be found throughout the writings of *Kritische Psychologie*. It provides a theoretical link between the biological and the social. The social or societal is treated as an evolutionary step above and beyond biology, and as it were standing on it. This formulation encourages an emphasis on children's development as natural regulation, or as the fulfilment of a quasi-natural potential. For all its merits, *Kritische Psychologie* is severely limited by its adherence to a developmentalist position. Functional adaptation is a major theme of the Soviet developmental psychology which has so influenced *Kritische Psychologie*. While critical of Western psychology, particularly for its collaboration with capitalist exploitation, *Kritische Psychologie* fails to establish an equally critical distance from the psychology of the East.

Vygotsky: revolutionary scientist?

Most appeals to Vygotsky in contemporary psychology of development downplay Vygotsky's Marxism. As described in Chapter 2, the Marxism in Vygotsky is usually identified in terms of some general theoretical commitments. Typically, Vygotsky's claims for the social origin of self and his emphasis on functional explanation are treated as the extent of his Marxism. More challenging Marxist possibilities may also be available however. The first of these to be discussed is the approach of Carl Ratner.

Ratner's (1991) book on Vygotsky's sociohistorical psychology appeals to Vygotsky (and Leont'ev) in order to arrive at a general social approach to psychology. As in Tolman's version of critical psychology, there is a general commitment to developmental forms of analysis, and much appeal to evolutionary explanation. More focused consideration is however given by Ratner to the implications for developmental psychology. Ratner's Vygotsky goes considerably beyond the notion of 'social context', and thus is to be distinguished from those applications considered in Chapter 2. Ratner also distances himself from the social constructionism of some other readers of Vygotsky. 'Things' may in the last instance be constructed socially, but we cannot make and remake the world around us merely at a whim. Thus, says Ratner, social acts 'are not purely intellectual or semiotic. Nor are they fanciful exercises in generating metaphors or narratives about things, as Ken Gergen and certain other social constructionists maintain' (Ratner 1991: 15). For Ratner, the social activities by which human experience of the world is created are activities that persist over time and thus have a history. They are underpinned, or at least made possible, by evolution. Evolution is as real as anything can be, and representing it scientifically is both valid and necessary. With *Kritische Psychologie*, there is a commitment to science as a truthful endeavour, and to psychology as a kind of science.

Ratner's account of childhood is concerned with socially-constituted characters. Once into childhood proper, development for Ratner is 'sociohistorical', not biological. From childhood onwards, children are wholly in society, at some historical time, and in many respects biology ceases to be of importance. Biological evolution provides the hardware for human development only in the sense that a TV set provides the hardware for the reception of a vast range of programmes. Thus Ratner emphasizes the wholly social nature of child and adult 'development'. In my terms, his account is anti-developmental because changes in activity are explained without reference to underlying, natural regularities. If there are similarities in children's thinking across cultures, says Ratner, then those cultures must be similar. Thus, advanced industrial societies might all create the kind of scientific thinking that Piaget called 'formal operations'. Dealing with abstract representations of information will be highly valued in a society that values technology. The US and the USSR might both generate this kind of thinking in its young people, irrespective of the political differences between those two societies. Ratner therefore avoids the identification of Piaget's 'formal operations' as a theory specifically of bourgeois development, treating such analysis as simplistic.

Ratner's analysis is a powerful demonstration of the inherently sociohistorical character of child development. However, Ratner's analysis of childhood relies on the assumption that children emerge from a biological state of infancy. In taking this position on infancy, Ratner's discussion of 'the development of psychology in the individual' is true to orthodox Soviet psychology. Babies are biological, children and adults are sociohistorical. Following Vygotsky in quite a literal way, Ratner describes such activities as smiling in the young infant as 'sub-cortical', natural activities. 'Higher' psychological functions are qualitatively different from those within the competence of the newborn and young infant. Only through interaction with more competent others does the baby acquire the ability to act intentionally. It must be noted, in summarizing Ratner's position, that many matters that affect infant development are seen by him as at the same time aspects of adult psychology, and hence sociohistorical. For example, attachment involves adult activity as well as that of babies, as do child-rearing practices in general. But infant development as such is for Ratner most definitely biological. As in all non-human animals, the human baby is governed by such psycho-biological processes as those controlled by the genes. Early development is, simply, developmental: it takes a regular course because it is determined by evolution (see Morss 1990, 1992a).

It is theoretically important for Ratner, as for Vygotsky (in my reading), and for Leont'ev and *Kritische Psychologie*, that human babies be treated biologically. It is the biological nature of the infant which makes possible the sociohistorical nature of the child. Ratner presents substantial empirical evidence for discontinuity between infant characteristics and child characteristics, but the matter is a theoretical and not an empirical one. Sociohistorical status is denied to the infant in order that it may be granted to the child, in much the same way that humans are defined as humans by the denial of certain attributes to other animals. In the case of Ratner, developmental explanation is enshrined in the account of infancy. Developmental explanation is good enough for inferior organisms, and the inferiority of those inferior organisms is itself defined in developmental terms. The compromises in Ratner's account are therefore general ones which transcend the issue of infancy itself.

Ratner's Vygotsky is, despite his developmental commitments, still quite a challenge to contemporary psychology of development. Newman and Holzman (1993) in their book *Lev Vygotsky, Revolutionary Scientist*, present a Vygotsky who threatens to overturn the whole discipline. Newman and Holzman's Vygotsky is a militant theorist who refuses to endorse the pragmatic adaptation to society that so many of his supposed followers describe. This revolutionary Vygotsky is committed to the kind of practical-critical activity that changes the world and makes history. Only such fundamental change, say Newman and Holzman, deserves the name development. Through their reading of Vygotsky, Newman and Holzman construct a persuasive case for the revolutionary possibilities in human activity (including that of children). Although they wish to retain the term development for 'good' change, they subject that term to considerable scrutiny, and employ it (for the most part) only with careful qualification. Development is to be seen as positive change of a collective nature, not the betterment of the capacities of an individual.

Newman and Holzman demonstrate the commitments to adaptation and functionalism in the contemporary Western Vygotskians, including those like Cole who recognize Vygotsky's Marxism. Vygotsky's often-cited discussions on tool-use as a paradigm for human cognition are reexamined. It is not the instrumental character of the tool – the 'tool-for-result' – but its dialectical character that is at issue, they argue. Tools are designed, used, refashioned, discarded, in contexts that involve complex and unstable interactions between people and nature. Tool-use is unpredictable: as suggested in the movie *2001: A Space Odyssey*, an opportunistic weapon in the hands of an ape can eventually lead to space technology.

In contrast, the tool as a means to a predetermined end is a conception which, when used as a general model of human activity, denies the possibility of change in the world. The world is taken as it is, offering only the possibility of greater efficiency in dealing with it. The things children and adults do, such as talk, are treated as behavioural tools the effectiveness of which has been honed by evolution. It is all too easy, as Newman and Holzman show, to assimilate Vygotsky to such a conventional, functionalist account – to turn the revolutionary scientist into an evolutionary scientist. The zone of proximal development is constantly threatened with closure, with colonization by particular interests. Instead of a space for emancipation, replete with possibilities, it becomes a prescription of what should happen next.

Babies and children are, at least potentially, revolutionaries. Unless prevented by circumstance, as is usually the case, their activity is creative in ways that threaten the social order. The ways in which babies and children imitate what they encounter are excessive rather than submissive. They imitate more than they 'need', and this excess is defined by the adult world as 'play'. Following a Marxist line of argument, child play can be seen as being appropriated and controlled by the adult world (by the production of toys for example). Imitation itself is progressively controlled, some kinds being proscribed (as 'cheating', at school) and some kinds becoming mandatory (copying from the board). These matters are not discussed in detail by Newman and Holzman, and the naturalistic tendency of their argument should not be overlooked. It would be possible to present infants and children as natural revolutionaries in a romantic sense. A natural impulse towards freedom would be set against the constraining processes of society, forcing the child ever more precisely towards acceptable adulthood. But this would be yet another version of socialization – of the regularized taming of the natural (a-social) child. Newman and Holzman insist that their Vygotsky is 'unnatural' (1993: 173) and that he contests the closure implicit in any use of the term 'natural'.

In the typical school, say Newman and Holzman, human development is 'instrumentally and pragmatically misorganized' (ibid.: 153). True development would be endless, a continual revolution. Conventional views of development are therefore rejected. Regular, predictable changes only make sense within a functionalist attitude. As they are careful to point out, Vygotsky's own writings are frequently genetic in style, presenting an explanation of some aspect of human activity in terms of its determinate 'history'. Newman and Holzman contrast such developmentalism (the 'having a history') with a Marxist approach of 'being in history'. For 'having a history', the past is an enormous weight pressing on the present, like the immense pressure on the ocean floor. The analysis of such history, or evolution, requires correspondingly immense expertise. 'Being in history', on the other hand, situates itself on the ocean's mobile surface (ibid.: 88).

Even Marx, Newman and Holzman observe, slips into functional language from time to time. An example would be the well-worn quotation from Marx on the superiority of the worst human architect in comparison with the best bee or spider. For this supposed superiority is expressed in terms of the architect's mental purpose (he 'raises his structure in imagination before he erects it in reality'). This formulation presents human work as merely pragmatic – an end is visualized, and means are devised to achieve that end. Moreover, primacy seems to be accorded to mental processes in the individual, an assumption that contravenes Marx's arguments for the social production of consciousness. This bee-and-architect account of human labour is Marx as cracker-barrel anthropologist.

Newman and Holzman have presented us with a new Vygotsky – an anti-developmental Vygotsky in all but name. Most emphatically, they reject individualist accounts of development. Some traces of a naturally good development remain: a crypto-romantic notion of self-actualization perhaps. This may be inherent in the emancipatory objectives of their work. But what they mean by development is radical in its implications.

Broughton and company: dialectical psychology and Critical Theory

We have seen how critical psychologists of development responded to Althusser, and how Marxist critical psychologists have attempted to carry forward the work of Soviet psychology. The most substantial area of Marxist critical psychology remaining to be discussed is that influenced by the Frankfurt School. Contemporary appeals to Adorno and Habermas, in the context of the critique of developmental psychology, are particularly well represented in Broughton's *Critical Theories of Psychological Development*.

Critical Theories of Psychological Development (1987) is a rich and varied collection of essays in critical psychology. The contributors attempt to look behind the claims of developmental psychology. In doing so, they raise serious questions about the concept of developmental change. In this section, a selection of the contributions to Broughton's collection will be examined. What I will suggest is that anti-developmental directions are quite clearly signposted in that book, but that these directions are not (in general) followed through with sufficient clarity of focus.

The intellectual approach most characteristic of the collection derives from the 'dialectical psychology' of Klaus Riegel. Riegel's dialectical psychology may be thought of as a fairly eclectic combination of Marxism and of various non-Marxist traditions of social analysis, especially the sociology of knowledge. Sociology of knowledge concerns itself with the impact of social structures and processes on systematic forms of knowledge such as science. Typical concerns of dialectical psychology thus include the ways in which the theories, methods. and claims of psychology in the West reflect the political reality of modern capitalism. For Broughton and his colleagues, as well as for Riegel before them, developmental psychology is of especial interest and significance within this more general investigation.

Riegel's own work had included critical writings on developmental psychology. In line with his Marxist version of the sociology of knowledge, Riegel had described the ways in which alternative theories of (child) development might be seen as direct expressions of economic conditions. Riegel's analysis was based on a fairly straightforward economicist reading of Marxism. Thus, the individualist capitalism of Britain could be seen as producing harsh, competitive interpretations of childhood, in which each struggles with each to acquire adult forms of knowledge. On continental Europe, a more liberal 'mercantile' form of capitalism is perceived to have emerged, generating a more organismic and 'child-centred' attitude such as that of Piaget.

According to this approach, the science and profession of psychology might be said to be 'ideological', and in the introductory chapter to the edited collection, Broughton refers to Riegel's work as 'ideology critique'. What must be stressed here is that 'ideology critique' is a broad and fairly flexible term, used in the Broughton collection to refer to a general attitude rather than a single technical method. Marxism is only one of its sources of influence, drawing as it does on a variety of traditions in the social sciences. The appeals to Critical Theory – in the persons of Habermas and Adorno – and to Weber's notion of rationalization, must be seen in this context.

In general, developmental psychology is treated by Broughton and company as 'serving the best interests of maintaining social stability' (Broughton 1986: 157). The claims and theoretical formulations of developmental psychology are often treated as distortions or incomplete representations of reality. Developmental psychology is seen as typically treating change which is 'actually' produced socially as if it were natural. This general characterization of developmental psychology is endorsed by a wide range of critical psychologists (Burman 1994a; Morss 1992b; Stainton Rogers and Stainton Rogers 1992; Tolman 1994; Walkerdine 1993). The Broughton collection perhaps expresses greater confidence than some other writings that the actual processes may be readily discerned by the critical eye.

The true processes and the real alternatives are concealed by the formulations of developmental psychology. At the same time, developmental psychology is itself seen as produced by larger social forces and hence as exemplifying or representing those forces. Psychology's claims about the self and the development of the self, for example, may be seen as truly reflecting large trends of rationalization in society. Psychology is both false and true at the same time.

This form of critical psychology therefore consists of the recognition of the complex interplay between the scientific discipline and the realities of modern society. As focused on issues of development, critical psychology investigates the ways that developmental change is defined within the orthodox discipline. It examines the functions and implications of these 'official' definitions. Critical developmental psychology, as conceived by Broughton, 'construes development itself as social, in every respect'. Broughton continues:

> Rather than conceiving of social effects on individual development, the very possibility of development and of individuals is premised upon a particular social formation. . . . The very conditions of possibility of development, as we know and experience it, are constituted by society.
>
> (Broughton 1987: 14)

Broughton's critical scrutiny of the notion of development, and his insistence that what we call development is produced by social processes, points us towards the idea of anti-developmental psychology. However, Broughton's chapter is no more than an introduction to these issues and these possibilities. To evaluate this approach, attention must be directed to other chapters in the collection and in the case of Broughton himself, to a more detailed presentation of his argument.

To focus on the latter first, Broughton's analysis of the 'psychology, history and ideology of the self' (Broughton 1986) includes an account of parallels between theories of development of the self and features of modern social life. The latter is defined on the basis of a social history of civilization that derives from Habermas. It also employs Weber's notion of the trend to rationalization in modern industrial societies. The account has an evolutionary flavour, perhaps inevitable when such large social trends are being discussed:

> The rationalization of work and authority comes to pervade life simultaneously at macro- and microsociological levels. It comes to shape not only the broader political, social, and cultural forms, but also the manifold life tasks of the enterprising individual. Thence, rationalization penetrates the psyche to modernize consciousness itself.
>
> (Broughton 1986: 149)

Since Weber, analysis of society has had to take account of mass-consumption and its related forms of consciousness. In this connection, Broughton refers to Adorno who had observed that 'even personal relations and the self become objects of consumption'. Like the stereotyped consumer housewife, comparing the (optical) whiteness of her sheets with that of her neighbour's, the subject of consumer society constantly compares its own inner qualities with those of others. In Broughton's words, 'the consuming glare of the inwardly turned eye permits a self-monitoring that cybernetically anticipates comparative judgements of rival consumer peers and makes the appropriate corrections in behaviour' (ibid.: 150).

This practice of self-examination makes a cult of 'self-awareness'. In so doing, it actually creates the inner qualities, including whatever passes for 'personal growth'. Development in oneself, as perceived by oneself, involves an internalization of the demands and emblems of consumer society: every day one seeks to make of oneself a better product – new, improved, the best and brightest yet. The technological advancement is tied to a rhetoric of nature, such that the development is treated as organic growth. Like all good products of the 1990s, the self is friendly to the environment.

Here and elsewhere, Broughton has made provocative suggestions concerning the significance of this 'ideological' analysis for the critique of development. He suggests a number of ways in which aspects of modern, rationalized life manifest themselves in theories of the self and its development. It is not clear, however, that the analysis proceeds far enough beyond the programmatic. Statements tend to remain at a high level of generality, as a diagnosis of 'the self in today's world'. Coupled with this is a reluctance to relinquish the notion of development in its more personal applications. At the end of his introductory chapter, for example, Broughton writes about development as being a felt aspiration towards 'a collective union of internal and external freedoms'. Thus, he notes, 'we are perhaps entitled to speculate that a critical approach to the field [of critical developmental psychology] both requires and guarantees a real act of human development on the part of the psychologist' (1987: 23).

Broughton thinks it inappropriate, therefore, to carry the critique of 'development' all the way through to its more personal implications. Developmental statements may it seems no longer be ideological when they are made about oneself. Broughton's defence of developmental discourse seems inconsistent with the analysis of the modern, rationalized self reviewed above. It sets up a point in the psyche (his own at least) beyond which rationalization has not yet penetrated. This point is not a facetious one. If the appeal to personal development were intended to establish the sanctity of the inner self, then the force of the rationalization argument would be seriously compromised. The spirit of Broughton's writings is certainly anti-developmental, but from the perspective of the agenda of *Growing Critical*, the achievement is limited in important respects.

If we look elsewhere in the Broughton collection, we find the most focused version of the anti-developmental argument in the contribution by Lichtman. In his incisive treatment of 'the illusion of maturation in an age of decline', Lichtman argues that the notion of individual development derives from and reflects political ideologies of progress in the expansion of capitalism:

> As we accumulated wealth and opportunity, the ideology of continual progress appeared self-evident; the progress of individual lives through an isomorphic development seemed equally obvious.
>
> (Lichtman 1987: 145)

More specifically, 'developmental' treatments of death and dying – such as stage-sequence accounts of dying – serve ideological functions. Such treatments imply that death is not only necessary, but in some sense functional for the community as a whole. It must be accepted as the proper end of a productive life. But as Lichtman says, 'the truth is that death extinguishes what is of potentially infinite value'. He continues:

> There is no more truth than in Dylan Thomas's 'Do Not Go Gentle into That Good Night'. A society that exploits and disfigures so many of its members and then counsels acquiescence in the final destruction of their emaciated existence is worthy only of contempt.
>
> (Lichtman 1987: 147)

Developmental theory, Lichtman asserts, is complicit in this process. To define maturity in terms of resignation is to 'efface' individual suffering. Likewise, he argues, 'isolation, estrangement, and loneliness' – the inevitable features of subjective life under capitalism – are redefined, in developmental terms, as 'autonomy, independence, and self-reliance' (ibid.: 128). Such processes of falsification are, he argues, characteristic of 'the illusion of "growth" and "development"'. Lichtman's is a powerful anti-developmental statement, and its power derives in large part from the Marxist legacy.

In Broughton's collection the most detailed appeal to Adorno is found in the chapter by Buck-Morss. With Riegel, Buck-Morss had (in the 1970s) identified the Piagetian glorification of abstract modes of thinking as an ideological position. The kind of (ostensibly) content-free mental manipulation that Piaget called 'formal operations' and set at the apex of intellectual development is more readily found in industrialized than in non-industrialized cultures. For Buck-Morss, this is entirely predictable: formal operations simply codify the favoured modes of interaction of a money-based economy. Buck-Morss notes that the abstract formalism of Piaget is itself a cultural-ideological product, the outgrowth of a particular era in capitalist development.

As well as restating this argument, Buck-Morss extends her appeal to Adorno. Adorno's 'negative dialectics' is brought together with Riegel's 'dialectical operations' in order to redefine the Piagetian project. The objective is to study 'the development of children's thinking in terms of negative, dialectical operations' such as the understanding of contradiction and irregularity ('advanced levels of negative dialectical operations'). What emerges is very close to a stage theory of cognitive development; indeed, 'Piaget's developmental perspective on consciousness . . . provides a necessary correction of Marx' (Buck-Morss 1987: 270). This developmental appropriation of Adorno has, I think, to be seen as a retreat. It brings the argument closer to Habermas, to whom Buck-Morss refers 'with some misgivings' in this context (ibid.: 262). Her misgivings arise from Habermas' incorporation of Piaget and Kohlberg into his developmental account, an incorporation carried out 'with rather less criticism' than she would advocate. Moreover, in contrast to Buck-Morss' own position, Habermas has 'rejected Adorno's relentless negativity', in working out a 'positive dialectical theory of ego development' focusing on identity, and characterized by parallels between ontogenesis and phylogenesis. Buck-Morss' analysis of Habermas is consistent with my own characterization of Habermas as developmentalist.

Considering Buck-Morss' status as interpreter of Adorno, her own developmental claims in this chapter can only be considered disappointing. In many ways, the application of Adorno to the critique of development still remains to be done. One possible avenue is suggested by Adorno's comments on philosophy, as summarized in Buck-Morss' more technical writings on negative dialectics. For Adorno, philosophy is restless and unending. It is not possible simply to unmask ideology and then march on. Definitive understandings of the way things are, are not to be anticipated. In an enigmatic style that resonates with the 'deconstruction' of more recent writers, Adorno tells us that philosophy

> persistently, and with the claim of truth, must proceed interpretively without ever possessing a secure key to interpretation; nothing more is given to philosophy than fleeting, disappearing traces in the riddle-figures of that which exists and their astonishing entwinings . . . thus it must always begin anew.
>
> (Adorno cited in Buck-Morss 1977: 52)

Buck-Morss' comment on this claim is that 'history [is] constructed backwards, like Proustian remembrances, or Freudian screen-memories'. Here the connection to developmental theorizing is made – for both the Proust and the Freud references are to the reconstruction, through an active kind of memory, of a life-story.

Broughton's collection is very successful in bringing together a coherent critique of developmental psychology. The coherence derives in the main from the common intellectual background of Riegel's dialectical psychology – Critical Theory and related forms of social analysis. For some contributors, whose work has not yet been discussed, these traditions are brought into contact with psychoanalytic theory and its claims in the developmental area (see Chapter 6). Most generally, Broughton and company insist on the political dimension to developmental psychology. This emphasis should in many ways be seen as a Marxist one. The diversity of ways in which the political dimension is understood by different contributors is itself an illustration of the complexity of the Marxist influence on the critique of development.

The Marxist influence does not in itself guarantee that the pitfalls of developmental explanation have been avoided. Even the most clearly-focused of the critiques of developmental explanation in the Broughton collection – that of Lichtman – does itself appeal to that form of explanation in the context of some comments on infancy:

> One finds constant reference to the infant's omnipotence long before it can be credited with any meaningful conception of causality, hatred of the other before any conception of the other has emerged, primary narcissism when it is acknowledged that the infant still lacks a conception of its self, relations to other objects before any self–object relation can be conceptualized.
>
> (Lichtman 1987: 147)

Lichtman's characterization of the incapacities of the infant is quite dogmatic. The limitations are presented as natural, developmental ones. Ironically therefore, the freeing of the elderly from the chains of developmental explanation is achieved at the cost of the developmental imprisonment of the baby.

These are complex issues, and point us forward to the matters raised by psychoanalytic traditions, which have had much more to say about infancy and early childhood than has Marxism. The essential point is that developmental explanation is very difficult to eradicate. The difficulties, as well as the possibilities of that project, are well illustrated by the Broughton collection.

PROGRESS SO FAR

A spectre is haunting developmental psychology: the spectre of Marxism. Orthodox psychologists are afraid of it, and many critically-minded psychologists take care to distance themselves from it. These days, with the demise of state communism, Marxism seems to some like a ghost that has been busted. If that were so then Marxism could pose no challenge to the theories and practices of orthodox psychology. Yet Marxist and post-Marxist traditions continue to generate critical positions that trouble the established order. Among these are challenging articulations of the critique of developmentalism.

The plot thickens: in some forms it congeals and solidifies, threatening to block the arteries of a critical psychology of development. To 'stop fooling ourselves' turns out not to be quite so easy. If we want to endorse the emancipatory impulses of Marxism, we must choose which of the many Marxist voices to listen to. The strength of Marxist anti-developmentalism lies in the insistence on people's real, concrete conditions of social life, that is, the politics of human development.

Abstract accounts of development can only suppress and mystify such considerations.

To get some grip on the realities of human life under capitalism we have to read Marx and those he influenced. Of course, capitalism has changed since the time Marx was writing. It has become more international, more oriented to consumption and the service industries, more technologically efficient. But the realities remain. Capitalist economies are exploitative of their citizens – of us. Our daily lives are profoundly shaped, even determined, by our functions within the capitalist economy. Human development is not a matter of freedom, choice and equality; to pretend it is so is to collaborate with the oppressive system.

The Marxist commitment remains to human emancipation. Perhaps this commitment is itself unavoidably developmental. Certainly there is an optimism in much Marxist thinking, if only a grim and long-term optimism. If even this kind of optimism is developmental, then we should also look at more pessimistic lines of thinking about human nature. In this context, our century's greatest intellectual pessimist has been Sigmund Freud – to whom we next turn.

Chapter 6

Psychoanalysis and the subversion of development

> [Freud] cannot find the slightest tendency towards progress in any of the concrete and historical manifestations of human functions. . . . All forms of life are as surprising, as miraculous.
>
> (Lacan 1988b: 326)

Does the psychoanalytic approach to development represent a critical approach to human development? Should Sigmund Freud and Jacques Lacan, in particular, be thought of as developmental or as anti-developmental writers?

These questions have to be faced by those critically-minded psychologists who have employed Freudian terminology, or that of Freud's follower Lacan (see, for example, Urwin 1984, 1986; Walkerdine 1984, 1987, 1991). Critical psychologists of development who are interested in psychoanalysis have had to make choices between various readings of Freud or of Lacan. Alternative readings may be made of the original texts, and there are numerous subsequent and secondary commentaries. Several different approaches to change and its regularities in human life may be identified within Freud's own writings and in those of Lacan. Some converge with orthodox developmentalism as that term is being used in this book. Others present challenging alternatives to that orthodoxy. Whether these critical psychologists have made the correct choices or not is an issue to which I return towards the end of this chapter, after clarifying these alternatives.

Freudian theory is anathema to many orthodox psychologists of development, particularly those who value experimental findings most highly. An appeal to Freud is by itself a critical gesture in many contexts, in the sense of representing a challenge to the mainstream. As far as claims about the course of human development are concerned, however, appeals to Freud are not necessarily critical in a substantial way. The employment of psychoanalytic terminology may rephrase developmental claims rather than challenge them. It is a mistake to treat Freud's work as entirely in opposition to scientific orthodoxy either of his own time or of ours. The relationships between Freud's writings and the mainstream of psychology, psychiatry or medicine are complex, since Freud's claims converged with the mainstream at some points and diverged from it at others. If the complexities of these relationships are ignored, it then becomes difficult to appreciate the significance of Freud's more innovative claims. The significance of the divergences can only be appreciated if a contrast is made with the convergences. Freud's claims and counter-claims concerning regularity in human change exemplify this issue.

From before the beginning of this century up till his death in 1939, Freud wrote and rewrote accounts of human development. Many of his claims challenged orthodox beliefs. However, some aspects of Freud's approach to development were consistent with the scientific orthodoxy of his time (Sulloway 1979). For example, he treated sexuality as central to development, but so did the other medical 'sexologists' of the end of the nineteenth century. Many aspects of children's development, as well as the characteristics of adults, were being described in the scientific literature as being connected in some way with sex and the sex organs. Again, Freud sometimes treated development in the individual as closely prescribed by evolution – as did most other developmentalists in the decades after Darwin (Morss 1990).

This chapter explores in some detail the developmental and anti-developmental readings of Freud, and then discusses the more recent writings of Jacques Lacan. It then examines the ways in which critically-minded psychologists have sought to apply Freudian or Lacanian ideas to the consideration of development. The appeal to psychoanalytic formulations within critical psychology of development is rarely made wholesale or in isolation from other considerations. For Urwin and for Walkerdine, in particular, the employment of Freud and Lacan is selective, and is balanced by appeals to more recent intellectual approaches. The role of post-struc-turalism in critical psychology of development is discussed in Chapter 7. Here I focus on the appeals to Freud and Lacan as such. What I will suggest is that these applications of Freud and Lacan have paid insufficient attention to the distinction between developmental and anti-developmental explanation in their claims. If that is the case, contemporary writings in the critical psychology of development may fail to make full use of the psychoanalytic resources. Moreover, Freud may provide a back door through which developmental argument can enter critical psychology.

CONVERGENCES: FREUD AS DEVELOPMENTALIST

For much of his career Freud seems to have taken it for granted that developmental regularities are indeed there to be discovered. Freud as developmentalist was attempting to delineate those regularities and to synthesize this information with clinical observations. He was formulating developmental ('genetic') explanations for adult disturbance and for adult personality in general. The text-book Freud of today is usually presented in this way – in terms of a stage theory of development and a causal model for the effects of early experience. This reading of Freud is firmly rejected by critical psychologists (Urwin 1986: 258). The developmental Freud cannot be identified with this simplified and popularized Freud however. The developmental Freud is to be found throughout the technical writings, and also in various of the post-Freudian psychoanalytic traditions. The attempt is now made to summarize Freud's most long-standing developmental claims. This will make it possible to clarify the distinctiveness of his anti-developmental formulations.

Seduction and its aftermath

Sigmund Freud's accounts of regularity in human development were an important part of a lifelong research programme, and went through various revisions. At the beginning of his research career, in the early 1890s, he treated the adult personality as significantly determined by specific early experience. In particular, at that time, Freud focused on the consequences of exposure to adult forms of sexuality (Forrester 1990). This experience he termed 'seduction', although Freud thought of the adult involved as foolish rather than depraved. For example, the baby's genitals might be played with by the nurse.

In a number of cases, Freud was able to show that adult patients could be helped to recover a memory of such a traumatic event. The seduction theory was part of a systematic genetic account of adult personality: specific early experiences cause specific adult characteristics and problems. These effects are not entirely direct; they require the mediation of memory in adulthood, and only become traumatic as a consequence of unconscious processes. As a developmental form of explanation, however, the scheme is fairly mechanistic; what happened then is the cause of what is happening now.

Quite soon after formulating this scheme, however, and for the rest of his career, Freud came to see this situation rather differently. His explanatory framework began to focus on general changes rather than on particular events. Rather than the regularized development of the personality being explained in terms of actual experience, Freud came to treat a sequence of development itself as basically natural. This pattern of regular change comprised 'psychosexual development' – the oral stage, the anal stage, and so on. Personal experience was now conceptualized in terms of deviations within the preset pattern of developmental stages of libido.

As defined in various revisions of the *Three Essays on the Theory of Sexuality* (first published in 1905), psychosexual development involves a sequence of ways of interacting with the world (Freud 1979). Libido is focused on a different part of the body in turn. In each case, characteristic desires and fantasies are generated and experienced by the growing child. Experiences that he had earlier attributed to 'seduction', and explained accordingly, Freud now attributed to these natural, developmentally appropriate fantasies. Adult memories of 'seduction' experiences were not real memories at all, but a reflection of universal childhood desires. Freud thus discounted the testimony of those of his patients who claimed to remember, in therapy, that they had been 'seduced' by an adult. As he later stated, almost all of his adult women patients made this claim in connection with their fathers.

The interpretation of this theoretical move by Freud is controversial, particularly in terms of its implications for the status of memories of abuse. Questions have also been raised about his personal motivation in making this theoretical move. What must be emphasized in the present context is that Freud's theoretical move was a move from one form of developmentalism to another. The very early Freud was developmental in a somewhat low-level or 'bottom-up' way: in the seduction theory, considerable explanatory weight was placed on actual, diverse personal experience. This was the closest Freud got to an environmental form of explanation for adult disturbance. The move to a universalist theory of psychosexual development reversed that distribution of explanatory weight. Individual experience was now seen as a very minor contribution to long-term personality, which was largely governed by a natural progression of stages – a high-level or 'top-down' approach to explanation. In effect, Freud replaced a low-level, proximal explanation of regular change with a high-level, distal explanation of regular change. He thus retained and perhaps consolidated a commitment to developmentalism.

It is important to note other continuities between Freud's earlier stance (the seduction theory) and the later work. Freud's early position was already a stage theory of sorts, for he was presupposing general, natural changes as the context for specific effects. The early Freud presupposed characteristic types of vulnerabilities in infants and young children – sensitive periods of growth in which seduction would be particularly harmful. Even Freud's most 'environmental' model for neurosis thus involved commitments to universal regularities in psychic growth. In his writings of the late 1890s, Freud explored the notion of an alternating sequence of two kinds of periods – 'event' periods in which the child was open to influences of certain kinds, and 'repression' periods in which the child was relatively closed (Laplanche and Pontalis 1973: 236). The necessary and normal progression from one kind of period to the next (open to closed, or closed to open) entailed the retranscription of remembered material. Such material was 'remembered' by the psychic mechanism, whether available to consciousness or not. Revival of certain memories in a later period – particularly in adulthood – would give rise to particular neurotic consequences.

The later Freud, commencing with the first account of 'pre-genital' (child) sexuality in 1905, emphasized above all the differences between childhood and adulthood. The chief characteristics of mental life were now defined in terms of sexuality. Whereas adult sexuality is efficiently focused on the genitals, according to one's gender, child sexuality is untamed – exploding wantonly in all directions, obtaining pleasure from and with every part of the body. It is 'polymorphously perverse'. Increasingly, in Freud's accounts of the necessary transition from the infantile to the adult form of sexuality, infancy and childhood became sub-divided into identifiable stages. Each stage comprised the dominance of a different part of the body in sexual terms. The focus of libido was seen to shift around the body surface, in the oral, anal, and phallic (pre-genital) stages, after which a period of 'latency' was discerned. Finally, from adolescence onward, libido came to be focused on the genitals, by now experienced as distinctly male or female.

Such a periodic or stage theory fits in well with a biological framework. Sulloway (1979) has argued that this high-level form of explanation – the theory of universal psychosexual phases or stages – was Freud's response to discovering evolution as a scientific doctrine. Freud's account of natural phases of childhood, claims Sulloway, can be shown to be closely linked to widespread scientific assumptions about an historical sequence of phylogenesis (through 'lower' animals and 'higher' animals to humans). For example, the period of 'latency' which divides pregenital from genital sexuality in the growing person reflects, for Freud, a real period of human prehistory, something like an Ice Age.

Whatever significance is placed on Freud's biological appeals, Freud's 'mature' theory of psychosexual experience is undeniably a developmental one. Freud's claims were sometimes expressed rather rigidly in terms of stages, sometimes more fluidly in terms of phases and processes. His writings of the 1920s are full of such phrases as 'at the very beginning, in the individual's primitive oral phase' (Freud 1974: 19). There is little theoretical point in making reference to such a phase unless the phase is set in a developmental framework. Freud's point is not that newborns feed by mouth, because children and adults do too (usually), but that newborns experience the world through their mouths in ways that children and adults have left behind. It will be inappropriate, but informative (therapeutically and theoretically) for a child or an adult to interact with the world in a newborn-like way. Freud's is a statement about newborns in general – which gains its explanatory force from what it implies about subsequent stages of development. In effect, Freud is telling us the basic sequence of changes through which humans must go.

Oedipal situations

Together with the oral, anal and phallic stages of development, Freud's most influential developmental claims relate to the Oedipus complex (Benjamin 1987, 1988). Here Freud addressed issues of gender differentiation. I will indicate some important features of this formulation, without attempting a comprehensive summary.

Men and women, Freud argued, change gradually (that is, develop) towards the appropriate end-point of sexuality in each case. Freud was convinced that female behaviour and development are different in important ways from male behaviour and development. Human development, for Freud, therefore consists of male development and female development. Each has a proper path, but each also has numerous pathological alternatives and deviations. Freud's account of human development therefore consists of a complex landscape or map, with two broad groupings of pathways – a male and a female – diverging from a common root. All the possible forms of adult mental state are represented on the map, and each can be traced back to a particular deviation from the true path. In each grouping there is one straight track, the high road that leads to appropriate adult sexuality in each case. As it turns out, Freud finds it much easier to delineate the male track than the female track. To caricature Freud somewhat, the male track follows a clear path, goes up and down various mountains and fords a number of streams. It requires strength and endurance, and the heights can be dangerously exhilarating. The female track – the proper route for young ladies to take – is much less clearly defined. Deviations from the male track tend to go into ravines or over precipices. Deviations from the female track are not always easy to distinguish from the track itself.

Despite some undeniable sexism in Freud's descriptions of gendered development, he was not content with easy answers as to *why* men and women grow up differently. He was emphatic that male attraction to women, and female attraction to men, cannot simply be in-built. He was struggling very seriously to find an intellectually satisfactory explanation as to how this normative adult state comes to emerge so regularly. The Oedipus complex was a major component in this explanation.

When expressed as a stage theory, Freud's account describes both the boy and girl infant moving through an oral and an anal stage prior to any awareness of sexual differentiation. It is during the next, 'phallic', stage that anatomical differences become salient. The having or not-having of a penis now dominates the mental life of both sexes. The boy's greatest fear is castration, which he fantasizes as a punishment at the hands of his father. This fear is linked with the boy's feelings of antagonism for his father, whom he treats as a stronger rival claimant for his mother's affections. This is the male version of the Oedipal situation. For Freud it guarantees that the boy will develop properly, that is, like his father. The fear of castration shows the boy the solution to the Oedipal problem, that is, the problem of the choice of a love object. It shows him that he must yield to his father, identify with him, and become as like him as possible, including the eventual selection of a similar mate.

The boy identifies with his father to such an extent, according to Freud, that he takes into himself the elements of strength, dominance and decisiveness perceived in his father. What the son interiorizes is an attitude of moral rectitude, of the objective, rational and impersonal delivery of justice. For Freud, this reproduction of paternal authority is itself the reason for the Oedipal process. He believed it to have become innate in contemporary male development only because of generations of ancient (prehistoric) experience. Having solved the Oedipal problem, the boy has arrived at a near-adult version of male sexuality. Only one step further is required. The boy must decide that his mother is specifically inappropriate as a love object. He is then enabled to start looking elsewhere.

This change of target from 'mother' to 'someone like mother' is made possible by a kind of developmental moratorium, a period in which sexual feelings go 'underground' for several years. This 'latency' period lasts approximately for the school years. Not only does it allow the boy to be diverted away from his mother as a sex object; it also permits the build-up of the sexual energy that will be released at puberty. Indeed this release is what puberty is, from a psychological point of view. At last, the boy's sexuality is of a mature male kind: focused on his genitals, and directed towards a mother-like person who is not his mother. All of this is achieved by the correct functioning of a natural developmental process.

While the boy is striding ahead on his developmental pathway the girl is making much less progress. The girl, according to Freud, does not have either motive or opportunity to confront her mother in the same way that the boy has to confront his father. The girl may treat mother as a rival for father's affections but there is no equivalent for the castration threat. If anything, the girl may consider herself to have already been castrated. Further, the girl's antagonism towards her mother is undermined by her continuing attachment to the mother, as the girl's first love object. The girl's relationship with her mother is therefore not nearly so traumatic as the boy's with his father. The effects of this apparently less confrontational experience are actually deleterious for the girl. The severity of the boy's rivalry with his father, coupled with the superiority perceived in the father, give rise to a dramatic and effective solution to the boy's Oedipal problem. According to Freud, the little girl's experience of the phallic stage (and especially the feeling of having been castrated) gives rise to chronic inadequacy. A long-term set of drives is set in place in the growing girl, referred to as 'penis envy'. As an adult woman, said Freud, she seeks for a penis, most ideally by giving birth to a male child. So the castration-complex in the boy is the dramatic solution to a set of psychic problems. In the girl it is merely the start of a lifetime's anguish and unhappiness.

The girl's attitude to her mother is hence ambivalent. Mother was her first love object, as for the boy, but she must repudiate love for a woman (whereas the boy must simply redirect that love). Although the girl may come to treat her father as the more appropriate love object (because he is of the opposite sex to herself), this object is a distant and impersonal one, never perhaps as true a love object as her mother used to be. Further, narcissism in the girl – love directed towards herself – is likely to be retained longer because it overlaps with love for the mother (both being same-sex relationships). In the case of the boy however, love for his mother (a female) runs directly counter to narcissism and hence helps to displace it more effectively.

The sexual development of the boy is thus clear-cut and dramatic; the sexual development of the girl is messy and uncertain. With hindsight, at least, it is hard not to see this asymmetry in explanation arizing at least in part from gender bias. Freud's account combines the taking of male sexuality as the prototype with a conventional male view of the messiness and noisiness of women. But a recognition of this bias must not be allowed to conceal deficiencies in Freud's account of male, as well as of female sexuality. As described here, Freud's is a straightforwardly developmental theory: '*the* boy' develops like this, '*the* girl' develops like that. A universal sequence is prescribed in each case. Whenever Freud, or any of his followers, discusses sexuality in Oedipal terms the discourse is a developmental one. As summarized by Grosz, psychoanalysis

> regards the body as a developmental union or aggregate of partial objects, organs, drives, orifices, each with their own significance, their own modalities of pleasure which, through the processes of Oedipal reorganization, bring these partial objects and erotogenic bodily zones into alignment in the service of a higher goal than their immediate, local gratification.
>
> (Grosz 1994: 169)

Pleasure, reality and regression

As well as indicating a series of developmental stages, and linking these with sexual differentiation, Freud discussed some general psychic processes in developmental terms. His combined account of the pleasure and reality principles and his discussions of the various kinds of regression all appeal to developmental forms of explanation.

The notion of a pleasure principle had played a central role in Freud's thinking since the 1890s. It was thought of by Freud not so much as a motivation to seek pleasure, but as a neurophysiological mechanism for the reduction of unpleasant stimulation. Any stimulation, whether from outside (environmental) or from inside (instinctual) was thought by Freud to make a demand on the psyche. Thus 'the greatest pleasure it is possible for us to attain, that of the sexual act' (Freud 1922: 81) is a negative rather than a positive pleasure. The pleasure comes from the discharge of excitation. Pleasure and sexuality are closely related in Freudian theory, but not in a hedonistic way. The pleasure principle copes with sexuality rather than promoting it. The pleasure principle was sometimes thought of by Freud as a quasi-physical law, directed to the avoidance of pain defined as stimulation. Getting rid of such demands was, for Freud, a natural objective of the mental system. True to his upbringing in the great, bureaucratized Habsburg empire of Austria-Hungary, Freud saw the urge to keep a clean desk as entirely natural.

There is nothing developmental about the pleasure principle as such, unless it is combined with a developmental account of the emergence of specific drives (Freud 1922). Pleasure – in the sense of the discharge of stimulation or excess energy – might be thought of as a constant goal of mental activity at whatever age. In fact, Freud treated the pleasure principle as something of an abstraction, never totally manifested in real life. In any event, it could not maintain its hold on mental life beyond infancy. Developmentally, a reality principle sets in as the baby discovers that seeking pleasure directly just does not work. The contents of the mental 'in-tray' cannot always be simply swept on to the floor. The reality principle is a set of compromises by which pleasure is deferred or redirected.

The picture that emerges from the combination of the pleasure and reality principles is a straightforwardly developmental one. Much of the infant's mental life is composed of the hallucination of desires, whereas the adult has learned that hallucination is unsatisfactory. The broad developmental picture here – autistic thinking in the baby, realistic thinking in the adult – is familiar through the laborious works of Piaget, for example (Morss 1990: 118). Within psychoanalytic theory, Freud's developmental account of a sense of reality plays a major part in the 'ego-psychology' that dominates psychoanalysis in the US. Therapy then comes to focus on the strategies of a relatively coherent ego, as it seeks – with some hope of success – to maintain a balance between internal drives and external constraints. To be working in accordance with the reality principle is a sign of the mature ego. Failure to accept the necessity to adapt to reality is itself a developmental delay.

When discussing the relationships between the reality and pleasure principles, and elsewhere, Freud not infrequently refers to a process of 'regression' to an earlier stage of organization (Freud 1975: 124). This use of the notion of regression is a direct expression of developmental commitments. Freud was careful to distinguish three different senses of regression as a process: not only temporal, as above, but also formal and topographical. Temporal regression involves the reinstatement of some earlier psychical state in the individual. Formal regression involves a 'lower' (less complex or advanced) mode of representation taking the place of a 'higher' one. Topographical regression involves the working backwards of a normal process: for example, the perceptual experience of dreams results from unconscious activity in sleep, a reversal of the 'forward' process from perception through to motor activity. The normal, forward process of discharge, in accordance with the pleasure principle, is not available to the sleeper.

Having made these distinctions, Freud emphasizes that the different kinds of regression usually coincide, 'for what is older in time is more primitive in form and in psychical topography lies nearer to the perceptual end' (Laplanche and Pontalis 1973: 387). There is a hierarchical view of evolution at work here, in which the higher or more advanced kinds of thinking of the human adult rest (rather precariously) on the lower, older levels of primitive thinking found in children and animals. This is the picture of evolution which dominated the human sciences at the end of the nineteenth century.

Therefore, not only is Freud endorsing the straightforwardly developmental notion of temporal regression, he is also bringing the formal account (of levels of thinking in the waking adult) and the topographical account (of neuroanatomical process in the sleeping adult) into the developmental domain. Here, in a particularly focused way, Freud's claims converge with orthodox developmentalism. Stages of libidinal development, the Oedipus complex and regression, show us a Freud who placed considerable weight on developmental forms of explanation. But there is more to Freud than this. However strong Freud's commitment to developmental explanation may seem to have been, alternative readings are also to be found.

DIVERGENCES: FREUD AS ANTI-DEVELOPMENTALIST

> It is often merely a question of our own valuation when we pronounce one stage of development to be higher than another.
>
> (Freud 1922: 51)

Freud undercuts his developmentalism in a number of ways. He seems, for example, not to have been hopeful of achieving a comprehensive, unified stage theory. Thus we find separate accounts of the development of libido, of the development of the love objects of the ego (narcissistic, homosexual, heterosexual) or of its defences. These separate accounts were themselves subject to frequent revision. Attempts at grand synthesis of these plural developmental schedules were made by Freud's colleagues rather than by Freud himself. Abraham and Ferenczi, in particular, each attempted to formulate a comprehensive Freudian stage theory of development (see

Sulloway 1979); as Lacan observed, 'Ferenczi is the one who started to put the famous stages into everyone's heads' (Lacan 1988a: 127).

Freud's lack of confidence in his developmental analyses ran deeper than the matter of plurality. The problem was not just that a large number of schedules had to be described, but that each made a theoretical impact on the others. Freud's accounts of different developmental schedules are not contemporaneous in his writings. Each new or revised account constituted a form of criticism of his previous claims. His account of narcissism, for example, did not just provide an additional stage schedule to be placed alongside the theory of libidinal stages. At the same time it indicated limitations in that earlier formulation. In rather the same way, Freud constantly redefined and redivided the different types of instincts which he thought must be acknowledged. Each new categorization was a critique of the previous ones. However confident Freud's statements about specific developmental schedules may appear to have been, they were always subject to future revision – sometimes within the same piece of writing.

Freud's developmental stage claims were thus heavily qualified. Another aspect of this was his treatment of the different schedules as having some degree of independence from each other. His treatment of temporal regression offers an example of this. Temporal regression is a complex notion, for regression may be treated in terms of libidinal stages, or stages of object relations, or stages of some other process. Rarely if ever does he mean by regression that a person has gone back to some previous state in its entirety. Indeed, as suggested by Laplanche and Pontalis (1973), it is in the asynchronies of the various schedules – in lags between one and another – that Freud often finds explanatory footholds.

Freud's developmentalism must thus be seen to be heavily qualified at least. The issue is whether the developmentalism is qualified, undermined, or overturned by his alternative arguments. Certainly, he explored some distinctly anti-developmental possibilities for explaining human experience. The discussion of Freud's alternatives to development focuses in turn on the role of therapy, on repetition, and on the death drive.

Instead of development: therapy and the life-story

Freud's writings contain anti-developmental as well as developmental formulations. To some extent this is a matter of his therapeutics, or rather what he wrote about therapy, as against what he wrote about human development in a more abstract sense. His developmental schemes are presented most dogmatically when they are farthest removed from the therapy context. His interpretation of actual patients and their symptoms involved a highly flexible use of these developmental schemes.

Freud's accounts of therapy are certainly not to be completely divorced from his larger accounts of human nature in general. It might be said that there was a tension in his writings between a straightforward, nineteenth-century evolutionism – an optimistic framework for describing human development – and a more pessimistic awareness of human frailty. The evolutionism is to be found more in the general statements on regularities in development. The descriptions of actual cases (although surprisingly few are described in any detail) are largely free of such scientific self-assuredness.

Freud's descriptions of therapy seem to undermine developmentalism in several ways. For example, the patient's relationship with the therapist may turn out to involve a replay of her relationship with a parent – an example of transference. In this sense the patient might be said never to have grown up. All of us, it is implied, carry our childhoods within us as an active and dynamic part of our adult selves. Stated more strongly, Freud's claim is that we accumulate all our memories and experiences – and that they are subject to continual, non-conscious reprocessing. Memory is an active process in this formulation and is not to be thought of as mere 'storage'. There are significantly anti-developmental aspects to Freud's notion of memory, which must therefore be distinguished from more orthodox appeals to the retention of 'lower' levels of thinking.

Traditional views of development typically involve progress through a sequence of levels, each in some way higher than the previous one (Morss 1990). Although there are numerous hierarchical versions of developmental theory which allow for some kinds of regression, they tend to be committed to the assumption of progress in ways that Freud's therapeutic analysis is not. The developmental approach may well find a place for the retention of previous states, but the inferiority of such states is considered self-evident. A good example is Jean Piaget's remarks about adult problem-solving. Given some problem like a car that will not start, initial attempts to be scientific and to test out hypotheses may, if unsuccessful, make way for such 'lower' strategies as randomly hitting something. Previous states are lower states, and remain inferior even if in some way reactivated.

The reality of therapy, then, might be seen as requiring a major correction of the linear and progressive view of development. The continued activation of earlier stages may be more marked or more troublesome in a neurotic individual, but Freud insists that this is a general situation. We do not grow 'up', says Freud; we grow 'along' (or around in circles, perhaps). In *Civilization and its Discontents*, Freud himself makes an analogy with the earlier phases of a city (Freud 1961). One could imagine, says Freud, that every earlier state of the city of Rome, for example, still existed within or alongside its present state; every building or column since demolished or built over is still somehow 'there'. This archaeological metaphor was not an accidental one, for Freud frequently treated his investigations as a form of archaeology of the mind. But it is important to note that the Rome analogy does not involve digging down to find actual remains – the hearths and middens which may still lie below present buildings – but the imaginative leap into multiple worlds.

Freud used to refer to representational gadgets such as the 'mystic writing pad' (from which writing disappears when the top layer is lifted up), and surely he would have appreciated the power of the word-processor to store every version of a text alongside every other version as each is made. Certainly, the computer can label each version and keep them in time order so that the latest is in a sense the 'best' or most mature. In terms of the software, such matters of status are little more than arbitrary. The human operator may decide, on a whim, that the version previous to the most recent editing session was in fact the best for some purpose, or the very first version may have a freshness that subsequent revisions lack. As with most machine analogies, the presence of the human operator is essential to the argument. Whereas human brains 'keep editing themselves' (Trevarthen, personal communication 1993), different versions of a text in a word-processor do not interact with each other except by human intervention. But a human writing a book on a word-processor – or even revising a manuscript already annotated by different hands – is giving life to past states or past events in ways that go far beyond simple recovery or salvage. Remembering may have immense consequences – raising the *Titanic* is at the same time lowering the Atlantic.

Freud's argument can be taken further in the anti-developmental direction. As Forrester (1990) has shown, Freud is claiming a significantly constructive role for memory. If all of the patient's past is still part of her present psychic structure, then that past is still in some sense negotiable. 'Remembering' a past event is not like playing back a piece of film. It is much more interactive – more like making a film perhaps. A patient's personal history, which might be called her/his 'development', is in important respects a retrospective interpretation. The patient's development becomes something like a creative act by the patient herself (see Shotter 1993c: 128). Rather than seeing Freud (as therapist) uncovering the patient's actual personal history, we see him assisting the patient to reinterpret that history. Such processes of interpretation are, presumably, subject to all sorts of constraints and limitations. The point, however, is that the possibility of reinterpretation (however limited) frees up the gridlock of prescribed developmental stages.

Freud is here rendering problematic the temporal role of original or source events in a person's life. He is questioning whether symptoms can be traced back to an actual event. The construction of a developmental account for the patient – the identification of supposedly actual historical events, together with their developmental sequelae – is cast into doubt. Freud appears to have eliminated progressive development from his theoretical system. But if people do not develop, then what do they do?

Instead of development: repetition

The suggestion above is that the patient in therapy may (perhaps with help) come to reinterpret herself in more positive terms. This would be an optimistic reading of psychoanalysis. Characteristically, however, this optimism is undermined elsewhere in Freud's writings both on therapy and other issues. For as suggested by the example of transference, the patient's present actions and thoughts may be no more than repetition. The past may exist in the patient's head not as a resource for personal growth but as a tyrannical compulsion. The significance of this possibility is that such a compulsion to repeat may not be confined to the patient in therapy. Repetition may be the truth behind the illusion of development.

Throughout his career, although in different ways, Freud emphasized the theoretical and practical significance of repetition (Bradley 1989: 46). To some extent, of course, this is an aspect of the persistence of earlier states. The process of interpretation of one's past can also be brought under the domain of repetition. A particular episode may be constantly revisited and worried at, in a way that does not allow it to be truly 'past'. Further, particular kinds of interpretation may themselves have compulsive force. Depressive states may be characterized by a repetitive and almost ritualized compulsion to reinterpret a range of previous experiences in a particular, negative way.

Freud attempted to work out the theoretical implications of repetition in one of his most closely-argued and difficult books, *Beyond the Pleasure Principle* (first published in 1920). Some comments on the pleasure principle (and its complement the reality principle) were made above. The 'beyond' in Freud's title is ambiguous. Most generally, the title may be glossed as 'dealing with issues beyond the explanatory scope of the pleasure principle as previously defined'. In *Beyond the Pleasure Principle*, and in apparent conflict with the pleasure principle model, Freud identifies a compulsion to repeat unpleasant experiences as a feature of both normal and neurotic behaviour. For example, World War I veterans were found constantly to revisit the trenches in their dreams. Such long-term effects of war trauma had also been observed in soldiers of the American Civil War, when the condition was called 'nostalgia'. Similar effects have been found in some Vietnam veterans. In what sense, Freud asks, could the repetition of severe trauma be regulated by the pleasure principle? Why should people continually recreate painful relationships – moving on to another partner but replaying the same script? Why should a small child throw away, and keep throwing away, the things he most loves?

Freud suggests several different explanations for these kinds of observation. One explanation relates to a hypothetical primal destructive tendency or death drive (discussed in the following section). Before entering this explanatory framework, however, Freud outlines an account of repetition that relies on the notion of trauma (1922: 29). Sentient organisms, Freud claims, have an evolutionary history that has involved them in structural change as a result of external stimulation. Eventually, such change has resulted in an effective defence against most external stimulation – what is allowed through is already selected and controlled. In the normal course of events impulses press towards expression (the discharge of excitation) in accordance with the pleasure principle. Trauma, for Freud, involves the invasion of massive stimulation into the psychic system, either from outside (the environment) or from inside (instinctual drives).

More significant than the invasion of energy as such is the response of the psychic system to the invasion. The system's own energy is withdrawn from various sites and activities in order to 'bind' the incoming stimulus, giving rise to strange side-effects from trauma. This binding is, at least, the way the system attempts to deal with trauma. The process can be assisted by the presence of anxiety, which supplies extra energy to the defences. If the defensive manoeuvre fails however, the system simply tries again. And again, and again. It is a simple feedback mechanism – only the successful outcome will terminate the activity. If the attempt is unsuccessful first time, it may never be successful. This is the link between trauma and repetition.

In the case of traumatic dreams, in particular, the psychic system is simply stuck in hopelessly cyclical activity. Treated as a prototype of human mental life, this image is entirely hostile to any conventional account of developmental change. For all dream and fantasy is, in a sense, traumatic. Instinctual drives confront the psychic system with the same kind of potency as external shocks, but even more frequently. There is even less defence against this 'fifth column'. A hopeless rearguard war is fought in which the same attempts to master the insurgence are made and remade. The same patterns of thought reemerge time and time again in different forms, whether hallucinatory (in dreams) or actual (in conduct or speech). Because of the nature of psychic activity, humans are condemned to repetition. They are continually trying to do something right that it is impossible for them to do right. What might look like progress in a human life is simply the replacement of one doomed strategy with another.

Throughout *Beyond the Pleasure Principle*, Freud raises the question of the relationship between the pleasure principle and the repetition of painful experience. In asking this question, Freud includes an observation on his grandson. By 18 months of age, the child had accepted separation from his mother, 'as the result of which he could let his mother go away without making any fuss' (Freud 1922: 13). At the same time, the boy was observed repeating a ritualistic piece of play. He continually threw away various toys into hidden corners, saying 'o-o-o-oh', and also continually threw away and retrieved a reel on a string, saying 'o-o-o-oh – Da'. In Freud's analysis (for which he has some supporting observational evidence), the child was compulsively reenacting separation from his mother, such that 'o-o-o-oh' represents the German word 'fort', meaning 'go away'. 'Da' means 'there' so that 'o-o-o-oh – Da' represents something going away and reappearing, like his mother.

Like the soldier's reenactment of wartime trauma, this does not look (says Freud) like the repetition of a pleasurable experience. Freud offers several interpretations of the child's actions, including the idea of the child 'mastering' the separation experience by repeating it under his own control. This interpretation is a developmental one, which emphasizes the adaptive functions of repetition. But Freud argues more broadly that the obsessively repetitive nature of this child's game illustrates a general instinctual tendency to repeat, rather than some special characteristic of childhood. The anecdote of the 'fort-da game' plays a rather limited role in the theoretical exposition of *Beyond the Pleasure Principle*. What it does, however, is provide supportive evidence for the idea of an urge to return to a former state – what will be revealed later in the book as the death drive. Significantly, Freud's discussion of 'fort-da' concludes with the suggestion that the instinctual tendencies at work here must be seen as 'beyond the pleasure-principle, that is to say, tendencies which might be of earlier origin' (ibid.: 16).

Alternatives to development: the death drive

Freud's account of repetition as a failed response to trauma explains repetition in terms of the supposed functioning of the psychic system. Repetition is something of a side-effect of the traumatic situation. But Freud wishes to make a stronger point about repetition in *Beyond the Pleasure Principle*, during the later parts of which repetition comes to be treated as an inherent tendency in psychic life. This enables Freud to introduce his notion of the death drive.

Both repetition and death are interpreted as the return to a former state. Death, for an individual organism, is a return to the inorganic state from which it once emerged. In Freud's analysis, living beings are inherently conservative. Changes that appear to be progressive ones (including 'development') must therefore be attributed to external causes. Development is unnatural, in comparison with the inner urges of the organism. What we call development must be seen as so many 'circuitous paths' as in a maze. Development is a distraction, a grand irrelevance, and the 'higher' the organism (Freud implies) the greater the irrelevance. There is only one goal which all organisms could share, the search for which could constitute the instinctual drive common to all forms of life. '*The goal of all life is death*' (Freud 1922: 47, emphasis in original).

Freud's death drive is presented as a surprising but logical implication of a series of theoretical claims. The notion of the death drive is here 'beyond' the pleasure principle in the sense of taking the argument beyond the former understanding of the pleasure principle – an understanding now seen as rather narrow. For death can be treated as an objective of the pleasure principle. A general tendency to return to a former state (of lower energy level) is consistent with Freud's more general accounts of the pleasure principle itself. Quite early on, Freud had noted that the pleasure principle can be treated as an extension of the physical laws relating to energy. All physical matter, it can be said, seeks lower levels of energetic state. Hot things cool down. Highly organized things decompose into less highly organized things. Dead or inorganic matter is at lower levels of energy than live matter. Hence death is a return to a former state of lower energy. Freud's notion of death drive or instinct is a kind of nostalgia, a yearning to return. *Beyond the Pleasure Principle* is thus one step in a long process of redefining and qualifying the pleasure principle, and hence refining the energetic account of human mental life that Freud and his colleague Breuer had initiated in the 1890s.

Having identified pleasure with death, Freud feels it necessary to balance the death drive against an opposing life-force. Towards the end of *Beyond the Pleasure Principle*, Freud identifies a general instinctive tendency to build up and combine. This drive he calls Eros. What might appear to be regularity in development would thus be, in reality, little more than a series of side-effects of the conflict of these larger forces. Rather like tectonic plates, the large forces governing organic life clash and shift, giving rise to rather transient landforms on the surface (see Curt 1994). Consistent with this kind of analysis, Freud's general discussions of inherent tendencies in life processes have rather little to say about developmental regulation.

Developmental change is secondary, almost incidental to the great plot of life. We must not, says Freud, be deluded by the appearance of progress in developmental change. People may repeat previous experiences, may seek to reinstate previous situations, but it would be misleading to say that people 'develop'. Once situated beyond the pleasure principle, we see that development is no more than an illusion.

LACAN: THE NAME OF DESIRE

One name that frequently appears in critically-minded accounts of early development is that of French psychoanalyst Jacques Lacan (see, for example, Boothby 1991; Forrester 1990; Frosh 1987; Macey 1988). It is therefore important to decide whether Lacan's own writings constitute a critical psychology of development, and whether more recent applications of Lacan do so. Lacan moved in and out of official Freudian psychoanalysis in France during the decades after World War II (that is, the decades after Freud's death). His most influential claims were those presented in his *Seminars* during the 1950s (Lacan 1988a, 1988b).

Due perhaps to their exotic style, the significance of Lacan's writings for critical debate is sometimes rather taken for granted. What I will suggest is that Lacan's writings do contain clear indications of an anti-developmental attitude. Indeed, Lacan has stated that Freud's 'inclination . . . to have repeated recourse to a genetic view of things' is 'the shakiest aspect of his work' (Lacan 1988b: 211). At the same time, and as is the case with Freud, developmental statements can also be extracted from Lacan. This is particularly so with respect to infancy. Some of the critical psychologists who have referred to Lacan have endorsed that developmentalism. The careful dissection of Lacan's anti-developmentalism is therefore essential. Some general and introductory remarks are made first, followed by more detailed consideration of the 'imaginary' and of the 'symbolic'.

Lacan's version of psychoanalytic theory is couched as a return to Freud, in order to correct what he perceives as the deviations of post-Freudian theory. He returns to Freud's emphasis on the importance of the unconscious in determining human life. He believes this to have been submerged by subsequent developments in Freudian therapy, particularly in the US. Psychoanalytic techniques and theory had come, after Freud, to focus increasingly on the conscious control available to the patient. Therapy was seen as requiring a trained expert assisting the patient to confront his or her problem, to deal with it rationally, and to achieve a more stable and healthy mental life. The patient's ego is thus assisted to restructure itself and recover control over the unconscious forces. This 'ego-psychology' approach to therapy is essentially a developmental approach; the therapist is assisting the patient to reestablish a normative developmental pattern.

According to Lacan, this developmental approach to therapy is deluded and is not Freudian. People do not have the kind of control over their own lives that is presupposed by such an approach. There is no such coherent, well-defined ego either before or after therapy. What in fact is happening is not that the patient is being helped to reassert control, but that the therapist is exerting control over the patient. The control is exerted through the application of the therapist's supposedly expert knowledge. To call the result 'development' is to suppress the actual processes and motivations. By implication at least, Lacan makes us suspicious of any professional (or parental) claim to be selflessly assisting the development of another person.

In his return to Freud, Lacan is therefore returning to the recognition of the power of unconscious forces. These forces split the subject apart. Lacan rejects the notion of a coherent, unified subject. The human subject is not coherent but fragmented, deeply divided within and against itself. It is simultaneously part of many different relationships, each of which is ever-changing. Neither the self nor the ego are any more than constructed and transitory entities. Their apparent cohesion and stability, the apparent demarcation of their boundaries, are mere illusions.

Lacan's rejection of ego-psychology and its therapeutic implications cannot be over-emphasized. Ego-psychology is a humanist enterprise, in which coherence and integrity of the personality are treated as both desirable and attainable. Coherence and integrity are, in this approach, the proper outcome for early development. They are the foundations for autonomy. Threats to coherence can be withstood if development is healthy. This commitment to positive, healthy development in the direction of personal autonomy is also a humanist one. Generally, humanism is set up on the assumption of coherent and individual selves, knowing themselves and knowing their own freedom. Lacan's approach has been described as 'virulently anti-humanistic' (Forrester 1990: 130). Lacan saw the anti-humanist possibilities in structuralism, but it was not until the 1950s and 1960s that Lacan explored the consequences of such a structuralist world-view for psychoanalysis. His own approach was already defined.

As David Macey (1988) has shown, Lacan's brand of psychoanalysis was constructed on the basis of classical (pre-Freudian) French psychiatry, and surrealism. Strange bed-fellows perhaps, but the surrealist writers of the 1920s employed 'random' or nonsense techniques for generating poetry, and they held that such techniques draw directly on unconscious processes. This was the basis for Lacan's linguistic view of the unconscious, later redefined by him in terms of the structuralist linguistics of Jakobson. Symbolic systems, for Lacan, came to be thought of as networks of signification. Words do not carry meaning by virtue of their connection with objects, or with concepts, but by virtue of their systematic relationships with other words. Any word is but one alternative among many other possibilities, in a given context. Without those alternatives being present in the system, no word or string of words could mean anything. For the structuralist linguists this approach was a formal, scientific one. The meaning of each and every utterance in a language depends, they claimed, on the structure of the totality of the language – a totality their approach alone could grasp.

While employing this approach, Lacan gave it a characteristic twist, hinting somehow that the coherence of structuralism was the coherence of paranoia. The best example of a well-structured, total language, said Lacan, is the language of the unconscious – the language of dreams and fantasies. This subversive, surrealist attitude in Lacan should never be forgotten, for Lacan's appeals to scientistic formulations always involve an element of play or of teasing. Total, comprehensive systems of explanation are always susceptible to Lacan's irony. This surely applies to his own claims, to the extent that they constituted a system (for example, a system of developmental claims). As Lacan insisted, 'You can be Lacanians; as for me, I'm a Freudian' (Forrester 1990: 125).

As noted above, claims concerning developmental sequence are undeniably present in Lacan's writings. The status of such a developmental sequence for Lacan himself is however difficult to ascertain. Often, he employs statements about genetic phases or sequences only to undercut them. He emphasizes the theoretical importance of regression in Freud, but redefines regression in such a fluid manner that its developmental import is virtually erased. Lacan seems to distance himself from the more conventional developmentalism of psychoanalysis:

> The idea of the regression of the individual to the initial stages of his develop-
> ment dominates, as you know, much of our conceptions of the neuroses as well
> as those of treatment. The entering into play of this notion, which now seems so
> familiar, is however not a matter of course.
>
> (Lacan 1988b: 132–3)

The mirror stage and the imaginary

If any developmentalism is to be attributed to Lacan, it must certainly include the normative sequence of the imaginary followed by the symbolic order. Lacan as developmentalist has presented us with an account of how babies change and mature. He describes the very young infant as psychically fragmented (Lacan 1977). Partly through encounters with reflected images of itself, the baby accedes to an imaginary realm of experience, through which the ego is constituted. Because of the mediating role of the mirror, the ego is not unitary but divided. Finally, in terms of normative achievements, the young child is cast into the realm of symbolic discourse in the form of a subject who speaks.

The 'mirror stage' provides the most concrete instantiation of imaginary functioning. The mirror stage has become the most widely known of Lacan's theoretical claims, yet its status in his overall account is difficult to establish. In his *Seminars*, Lacan describes the mirror phase as 'this turning point in development, in which the individual makes a triumphant exercise of his own image in the mirror, of himself. We can understand that what occurs here for the first time is the anticipated seizure of mastery' (Lacan 1988a: 146). Despite such claims, it would probably be a mistake to take the mirror stage too literally, as a claim for the normative developmental progression of the infant. It is at the same time an illustration of ageless features of subjectivity, and perhaps of the psychoanalytic encounter. In Lacan's words, 'the mirror stage is not simply a moment in development. It also has an exemplary function' (ibid.: 74).

Treated developmentally, the mirror stage is said to emerge some time during the first year of life. The newborn, for Lacan, has a minimal awareness of self. It lacks clear boundaries between its own body and the world, and its body is experienced as fragmentary, anarchic. As Lacan describes it, the young infant's experience of seeing a mirror reflection of itself is a crucial developmental step. The reflection is in some sense recognized as being the self, but also recognized as being something other than the self. The reflected image is a more complete or better integrated image than the directly perceived self, an ideal image of the self. For example, the baby may need physical support in order to stand upright, but its image in the mirror appears to be able to stand up by itself. Its awareness of its own physical body is an awareness of incompetence, a sense of being pulled back down to earth. From the time of the mirror-stage onwards – that is, from the latter part of the first year of age – the child's world is structured by a divided awareness of itself. The most basic form of personal experience involves a mediated relationship with oneself – a relationship mediated by the mirror. 'This means that the human ego is founded on the basis of the imaginary relation' (Lacan 1988a: 115). For the infant by itself could no more construct an ego for itself, from its own resources, than could the image in the mirror. Both need the other, and both are needed by the other.

In some respects Lacan's mirror stage is a reformulation of Freud's notion of infant narcissism. For Freud, the infant can be thought of as being in love with itself, that is, directing love towards itself as object. Lacan's baby has, similarly, fallen in love with its own reflection. Identification with this image is so complete, according to Lacan, that this relationship takes over the whole of the infant's psychic apparatus. It is now possible for an ego to emerge, but its very nature is constituted by the split self. 'It is in the nature of desire to be radically torn' (Lacan 1988b: 166). The ego is experienced only as set over against something else. There is a distance within the ego, represented by the spatial distance necessary for the perception of a mirror-image. An eye pressed flat against the silvered surface would be blind. There is a sense of detachment or difference, perhaps alienation, built into the ego. It was never unitary.

For Lacan, then, the ego does not 'emerge' as a natural feature of developing personhood. It cannot be thought of as the manifestation of some inherent quality, or as the expression of some potential. Such accounts presuppose unity and coherence to the ego. Instead, Lacan insists, the ego is constituted over time and over space. This historical constitution of the ego implies, for Lacan, a 'radical contingency' rather than any stage theory. Erikson's stage theory of ego development thus goes 'against the very spirit of Freudian theory'. Lacan asks:

> Can you really, you analysts, in all honesty bring me testimonies of these splendid typical developments of the ego of subjects? These are tall stories. We are told how this great tree, man, has such a sumptuous development, how throughout his existence he overcomes successive trials, thanks to which he achieves a miraculous equilibrium. A human life is something entirely different!
>
> (Lacan 1988b: 155)

Everything that can be said about the ego is thus for Lacan a statement about the imaginary domain. The imaginary is governed by perception, especially visual perception, and perceptual activity (including dreams or hallucinations) remains linked to it. It is imaginary processes that give to human perception the kind of structure that in other animals is in-built. But the imaginary does not function with complete autonomy. The fragile coherence which it sustains is under constant threat from the anarchic activities of the body. Rather like the baby's first steps – that are more like running than walking – the imaginary is inherently unstable.

Castration and the symbolic

Lacan's ego is a house divided against itself. The imaginary world of the infant involves no more than a vision, an illusion, of coherence. The nearest that the baby comes to a coherent self or self-image is in the perception of a mirror-image. This situation will follow, perhaps inevitably, the earlier state of fragmentation in the newborn, but can hardly be thought of as a better state. Even when Lacan appeals to a sequence of stages – itself a developmental move – later stages are rarely treated as 'higher' than earlier ones. The transition from imaginary to symbolic involves a total change in the world of the infant, and gives rise to subjectivity, but is defined by Lacan more as a fall than as an achievement.

Living in the world of the mirror cannot be sustained for ever. Such an existence may indeed be no more than glimpsed, seen just long enough perhaps to be longed for thereafter. In developmental terms it is accession to spoken language that signifies the loss of imaginary innocence. Entering into one's adult native language is to enter a most complex and perhaps self-defining system. Once in language there seems to be no way out again – words just lead to more words. If one seeks anything more then one is doomed to disappointment. Nothing that one can apprehend through language is outside of it. One's own self can only be apprehended through language, so that subjectivity is inextricably bound up with the structural and symbolic properties of language. Subjectivity is no more than a place in the language system. For Lacan, the subject is that which speaks in language: subjectivity arises only through speech, and 'development only takes place in so far as the subject integrates himself into the symbolic system' (Lacan 1988a: 86). Any sacrifices that have to be made to enter language will remain bound up with subjectivity. In entering language one is going under the knife.

In infancy, says Lacan, both boys and girls live in an intense relationship with a mother. This relationship is not so much with a real flesh-and-blood mother but with a mother as perceived by a baby, that is, an imaginary mother. With the ending of the mirror stage, all babies become cut off from the mother – just as their umbilical connection was severed some while earlier. Lacan is not talking about physical separation from the actual mother, or about working mothers or childcare arrangements; he was no more interested in such mundane details than was Freud. What he describes is, it appears, an inevitable aspect of early development. Its consequence is an experience of lack in the growing child. What has been lost is felt as having been some powerful agency. This something remains with the child as a focus of thoughts and feelings, and as a kind of peg on which to hang any more coherent meaning-systems that may come along. This sense of loss thus comes to define the inherent disappointments of language – this is what I am looking for as I discover, again and again, that language is inadequate to my need. Although it is an absence, it is an absence that is felt so strongly that it enables positive constructions to be set up.

For Lacan, the language system has crucial links with gender. The entry into a world of language – that is, a symbolic world – is also an entry into a gendered world of subjects. The 2–3-year-old child is already beginning to grapple with Oedipal problems alongside the entry into language. Following Freud's account of the Oedipal process, Lacan places great emphasis on the notion of castration. With Freud, he claims that little boys fear castration at the hands of a father, as a consequence of rivalry over possession of the mother. Little girls believe themselves already castrated. If language is a system of signifiers, of codings of difference, then foremost among the signs of difference is the presence or absence of the penis. This differential status, thought of by Lacan as fundamental to the operations of language, is termed the phallic.

The phallic is thus a function rather than a thing. It is not the penis itself that matters for Lacan, but the systems of signification that give meaning to its presence or its absence. If little boys (and even big boys) fear its loss, and if little girls fear that it has been lost, then it is this symbolic role that is of significance. Indeed, 'presence versus absence' is an inadequate representation of the phallic function. Presence as confident possession is denied to both sexes. Lacan's distinction is, rather, the more subtle distinction between types of absence. Absence, for Lacan, is interrelated with lack and desire. So is language – for the self-referential character of language is an admission of its failure to grasp what lies beyond language. Try as they might, words can only refer to other words. Thanks to its symbolic structure, language makes possible a systematization of lack. Desire becomes articulated in linguistic terms and hence the unconscious comes to be structured like a language.

Most important for Lacan is the process by which the symbolic first intrudes upon the imaginary – first opens up the intense and intimate world of baby and mother. It is the father who inserts himself between them, and his voice that breaks in on the silent contemplation of mother and baby. The word which the baby hears, the pa's word, is a password that opens the door to a symbolic world of socially shared meanings. That word is, at least symbolically, 'No'. The father's presence is, for Lacan, a forbidding one, since the social world that he represents is a world of law and of morality. This is a codified social world, a world of prohibitions.

Lacan is following Freud at this point, although in his own style. According to Freud, the father's moral sense is interiorized by the son as a result of the Oedipal situation. For Lacan, it is the father's stern 'No' that effects this interiorization. Father may deny, refuse, contradict – this is his legitimate role. This is the Law of the Father. Capitalization alerts us to an abstract claim. The 'No' of the Father is, in French, 'Non' which for Lacan slides in and out of 'nom' (name) – hence we arrive at the formulation 'Name of the Father'. The Name of the Father is somewhat akin to the Name of God, in that the Name itself is an expression of its own power. It is a holy mystery, as in the Old Testament where the nearest that human understanding was allowed was such terms as 'I am'. This is Lacan's way of expressing the power of patriarchy and of patrilineage, and it is with entry into the symbolic that these systems come to constitute the subject. For the boy, entry into the symbolic is something like an initiation. He has entered into the same terms of reference as his father.

The symbolic realm – which is all that can replace the unstable imaginary realm of infancy – therefore has special connections with masculinity. As for Freud, it is only the boy who can be fully drawn into the codified world of justice and morality. The girl will always remain something of an outsider. More broadly, however, both boys and girls remain cut off from an earlier satisfaction, a half-remembered time of ecstatic joy ('jouissance'). For both boys and girls, symbolic language is a constant searching and yearning for what has been lost: a something that will not require a symbolic system to endow it with meaning. The loss of the imagined mother is transformed into a symbolic structure in which loss is not redeemed but recuperated. Language involves loss and absence, but it works.

Lacan's account of the entry into the symbolic is vivid and powerful. But Lacan undercuts the normative developmentalism of this account:

> If you look at it closely, this domain of the symbolic does not have a simple relation of succession to the imaginary domain whose pivot is the fatal intersubjective relation. We do not pass from one to the other in one jump.
>
> (Lacan 1988a: 223)

Elsewhere, Lacan notes that the anterior status of the imaginary 'is not chronological, but logical' (ibid.: 170). Even this claim seems excessive when the imaginary and symbolic realms are compared, for the differences between them are immense. The imaginary is an intense, narcissistic universe where psychic processes are condensed and compacted. The symbolic is an extensive, articulated universe, in which everything is defined by difference within an arbitrary code of signifiers. It would seem implausible to construct a simple genetic scheme of 'growing up' from the former to the latter.

Lacan may not have believed in such a scheme, although he made use of it when it seemed appropriate. My suggestion is that Lacan did not endorse developmental arguments so much as play with them. This 'entering into play' gave him a way of commenting on developmental explanation – and in so doing, distancing himself from it. Perhaps it is sarcasm that best reflects Lacan's attitude to developmentalism:

> One may want to fit man in to a harmonious, natural mode of functioning, one may want to get him to connect the stages of his development, allow him the free blossoming of what in his organism, reaches, in its own time, maturity, and to give to each of these stages its time for play, then its time for adaptation, time for stabilization, until the new living feature makes its appearance. An entire

anthropology can be ordered around this. But is that the anthropology that justifies psychoanalyses [sic], that is to say, sticking them on the couch so that they can tell us a lot of bloody nonsense?

(Lacan 1988b: 85)

CRITICAL USES OF PSYCHOANALYSIS: DEVELOPMENTAL OR ANTI-DEVELOPMENTAL?

Normalizing, regulation, and development

A variety of appeals to Freud and to Lacan have been made within recent writings on critical psychology of development. The authors of *Changing the Subject* treat psychoanalysis in general as an important ally in the undermining of a humanist notion of the subject (Henriques *et al*. 1984: 205). Freud, they argue, demonstrated that a rational, unitary self is little more than an illusion. He made the case instead for treating the self as contradictory and governed by irrational processes. Psychoanalysis therefore offers a more adequate approach to 'the continuity of the subject', that is, 'a view of development which is in direct contrast to . . . over-simplified social or biological determinisms' (ibid.). Psychoanalysis recognizes the complexity and indeterminacy of the effects of particular life events 'on the psychic development of individuals, particularly in the early years through the family constellation'. It can therefore contribute to a revision of developmental theory.

A further reason for the general endorsement of psychoanalysis in *Changing the Subject* is its attempt to link up the unconscious with society. This project was initiated by Freud himself (see also Ingleby 1987) and carried forward by Fromm and Reich, among others. Also, Freud is commended for having indicated some of the unconscious processes, such as splitting, that must be recognized in examining subjectivity. Issues such as power, desire, and violence, argue the authors of *Changing the Subject*, require the attention to personal motivation that only psychoanalysis supplies, so that 'the examination of the unconscious is an essential precondition for understanding our resistances as well as the possibilities for change' (Henriques *et al*. 1984: 225).

Careful distinctions are drawn in *Changing the Subject* between the positive contributions of psychoanalysis and the pitfalls associated with some versions of it. The most general danger is identified as a tendency toward normalization – that is, the normative prescription of particular forms of relationship or patterns of change. Developmental explanation, as I am defining it, might thus be seen as one kind of normalizing technique. Normalizing and regulation, it should be stressed, are considered by the authors of *Changing the Subject* to be endemic to traditional psychology as well as being widespread in psychoanalysis. The question is whether psychoanalysis has freed itself from such features.

Freud's own privileging of the position of the father in the family is an example of normalizing (ibid.: 206), and the general tendency is found to be widespread in post-Freudian theory. Erikson's stage theory of 'ego development' prioritizes functional adaptation of the individual, so that 'under ideal circumstances child-rearing practices produce the personality characteristics which the smooth running of the particular society requires' (ibid.: 209). The claims of Melanie Klein concerning the significance of young children's play have also served a normalizing function (ibid.: 180, 199), as have the formulations of the Object Relations school. Object Relations theorists, such as Winnicott, claimed that the forming of relationships with others is a primary motivation in the infant. Winnicott's account of mothering was thoroughly normative, appearing to prescribe for the mother a total dedication to meeting the psychic needs of the baby. This normative move has the effect of blaming the mother for any undesirable consequences in the growing child (see also Bradley 1989: 162):

> It is now relatively easy to place the source of all pathology onto the mother for failing to meet the baby's needs. More than any other psychoanalytic account, Winnicott's emphasis has contributed to the normalization and regulation of motherhood, through social work and medical practice, in the arguments used against providing nursery provision, and so on.
>
> (Henriques *et al.* 1984: 211)

More recent versions of Object Relations theory, such as that of Chodorow (1978), have not resolved this problem of normative regulation (Henriques *et al.* 1984: 226). The Object Relations approach insists that some forms of development are better than others, even if social arrangements may conspire against ideal development. For Chodorow, the gendered division of childcare under patriarchy gives rise to unbalanced development in both boys and girls. This is a normative account, as is that of Benjamin (1987) which appeared subsequent to *Changing the Subject* (see Appignanesi and Forrester 1992: 469). Benjamin's version of Object Relations theory defines a 'true differentiation' as the proper goal of development, characterized by a balance of attachment and autonomy. According to Benjamin, Freud's account of the male Oedipus Complex represents a 'one-sided or false differentiation' (1987: 227) in which dependency and attachment are repudiated. Benjamin follows a line of argument already rejected by the authors of *Changing the Subject*, as they demonstrate the inadequacies of normative psychoanalysis.

For the authors of *Changing the Subject*, it is the work of Lacan, among all the post-Freudianisms, that offers the best chance for departure from the normalizing and functionalist tendencies that linger in psychoanalysis. Of all the appeals to psychoanalytic theory within critical psychology, those articulated by Urwin and Walkerdine recognize most clearly the problems with developmental explanation with which this book is concerned. Their work therefore provides the focus for my discussion. Have these critical psychologists succeeded, with Lacan's help, in establishing a non-normative role for psychoanalysis? To do so, according to the argument I am presenting, would involve a comprehensive rejection of developmental forms of explanation.

Cathy Urwin has explored Lacanian claims in relation to more orthodox approaches to infancy (Urwin 1984, 1986). These explorations have been guided by commitments to the concrete realities of mothering in contemporary life. Valerie Walkerdine has employed Lacanian and Freudian vocabulary in several contexts, including the acquisition of mathematics (Walkerdine 1988) and girls' responses to popular fiction (Walkerdine 1987).

Both Urwin and Walkerdine have treated Lacan's work as the most useful of the many revisions of Freudian psychoanalysis. Lacanian psychoanalysis, above all, places personal motivation in the context of a socially constituted self. Neither Urwin nor Walkerdine, it should be stressed, thinks of Lacan's claims as entirely satisfactory. With their colleagues, they identify serious deficiencies in Lacan (Henriques *et al.* 1984: 216). These deficiencies include a tendency towards universalist explanation in Lacan – a neglect of cultural and historical specificity. Both Urwin and Walkerdine have attempted to synthesize the psychoanalytic approach to subjectivity with other approaches. The synthesis with post-structuralism is discussed in Chapter 7, so my examination of their claims is by no means concluded here. What I will suggest in the present chapter is that the appeals to Lacan and Freud tend in themselves to involve developmental appeals, and that it is the influence of psychoanalysis that enables developmental forms of explanation to survive even in the writings of these contemporary critical psychologists. Critical psychology has not paid enough attention to the anti-developmental possibilities in Freud and Lacan.

Urwin's Lacan

Urwin's chapter in *Changing the Subject* (Urwin 1984) is concerned with a re-conceptualization of infant development, with particular reference to the development of language. It attempts to bring together a number of diverse approaches: psychoanalytic theory (including Lacan's mirror stage), recent empirical research on infant development and communication, and some elements of a post-structuralist analysis. Various strengths and limitations are identified in these approaches and a synthesis attempted. Here I focus on Urwin's treatment of Lacan and of the more orthodox developmental accounts of infancy.

Urwin emphasizes that a synthesis of psychoanalytic and traditional (empirical) psychology of infancy requires accommodation on both sides. She stresses the inadequacy of traditional psychology's view of development as upward progress (Urwin 1986: 257), contrasting this simplistic view with the subtle complexities of the psychoanalytic account. Also in contrast to traditional psychology of infant development, psychoanalysis has always discussed affect and motivation as well as cognitive processes. For its part, Urwin argues, contemporary empirical research has revealed competencies in the infant and complexities in early interaction that psychoanalysis has not recognized. Urwin's objective therefore is a social revision of contemporary infant research, to be informed by psychoanalytic insight. Where, and why, does Lacan fit into this programme? Urwin explains that Lacan's emphasis on the fragmentary nature of the self represents an essential contribution. She presents her account of development as a revision of Lacan's mirror stage. In fact very little of Lacan remains after Urwin's revision, because her changes are major ones. Examining them will help to clarify Lacan's own claims as well as Urwin's.

Urwin presents a clear outline of a Lacanian developmental scheme, in which the mirror experience takes the baby from initial fragmentation through to an imaginary stage. This in turn leads on to entry into language and the symbolic order, with its Oedipal problems. The limitations of Lacan, for Urwin, are several. Lacan's treatment of language, and his notion of the phallic function, are dismissed. To treat language as a complete system, that in some way depends on the difference signified by the phallus, is for Urwin at the same time universalist and culture bound. It is to treat one cultural position as universal and inevitable. Urwin thus rejects Lacan's analysis of the symbolic realm as a stage subsequent to the imaginary.

In addition, Urwin criticizes Lacan's account of infant behaviour at the commencement of the mirror stage. She suggests that Lacan has failed to explain how and why the infant immediately recognizes herself in the mirror. This competence at self-recognition seems to imply some earlier developmental achievement of self-identity – empirically plausible, in terms of modern developmental psychology, but quite inconsistent with Lacan's overall account. This inconsistency is only a problem, however, for a developmental form of explanation of the mirror stage. If Lacan's aims are different from this then a question of the form 'what must come first?' may be inappropriate. As this point illustrates, Urwin's critique of Lacan is not designed to separate out developmental from anti-developmental readings as I am advocating. Urwin's objective is to employ a revised Lacan in order to arrive at a more adequate developmental account.

For Urwin, Lacan is working with an inadequate account of the newborn and very young infant. Thus Lacan's description of what developmentally precedes the mirror stage, as well as what follows it (entry into the symbolic order), is rejected by Urwin. The mirror stage floats free from its moorings. But this is not all, since Urwin also wishes to revise the mirror stage itself. As Urwin notes, Lacan's mirror stage involves a conflict between the apparent wholeness of the 'ideal' self as reflected, and the fragmented self as experienced. Urwin reinterprets this conflict in terms of the baby's sense of control over the world. For Urwin, the conflict is between apparent control on the baby's behalf – if she moves her hand, so does the reflection – and the lack of control experienced in social communication with adults. This emphasis on social interaction in the mirror stage has no counterpart in Lacan. Urwin follows Lacan in placing a conflict at the heart of the stage, driving it forward in some respects, but the nature of the conflict is entirely different. Urwin emphasizes that the notion of viewing oneself in a mirror can only be metaphorical. Rather, it is parents' activity that actually performs the mirror's function of showing the baby a more competent version of itself. Urwin's mirror is not Lacan's. What we must ask, in due course, is whether Urwin's revision of Lacan is more or less developmental than the original. More detail is necessary in order to answer that question.

Urwin's formulation of the central problem for the mirror-stage baby relates to the incompleteness of the baby's communicational activity. The baby's activity, she argues, is only meaningful as a result of adult interpretation and completion. This notion of communicational disparity is in itself a fairly orthodox one (Burman 1994a: 39). In other accounts, this notion of infant 'incompleteness' is expressed in terms of Vygotskian processes, or as an example of the 'symbiotic' relationship between infant and mother. Such more orthodox accounts tend to treat the disparity as the inevitable consequence of natural deficiencies on the child's part. It is also treated as natural for adults, especially mothers, to make good the baby's deficiencies. A harmonious picture emerges of the adult helping the baby to communicate. In this orthodox view, any frustration experienced by the baby is more than compensated for by the experience of positive social interaction. In this respect Urwin's account differs dramatically from orthodox descriptions of communicational disparity and its consequences. For Urwin the communicational disparity is a source of tension and conflict for the baby; 'these ambivalent and contradictory feelings in babies show how inadequate are accounts of "mothering" which presume that this task is simply a question of meeting the baby's "needs"' (Urwin 1984: 302).

Urwin's account focuses on the implications of communicational disparity for the baby's experience of power. The baby gradually becomes aware of its communicational insufficiency, and this awareness is one motivation for the emergence of language. Language offers a way out of the state of inferiority experienced by the baby, since it makes possible an evening-up of the balance of power. It offers the baby some genuine control over its social environment. Babies have to work out that their own communicative power is insufficient, and they have to establish ways of remedying that situation. There is something of a functionalist flavour to this account, since it seems to be presupposed that babies will indeed acquire language and that it will be adaptive for them to do so. The emphasis on functional adaptation is also seen in Urwin's references to Freud's 'fort-da' example. In Urwin's summary, the child's repetitive game is explained as a means of working through or mastering 'problems in separating from his mother' (Urwin 1984: 277; 1986: 279). This account simplifies that of Freud, who had in fact noted that the boy 'could let his mother go away without making any fuss' (Freud 1922: 13) and for whom the explanation for the game is somewhat open ended. Freud's is not a normative account of how 18-month-old children deal with separation.

Urwin explicitly rejects any stage theory of development (Urwin 1984: 319). She insists however that some general developmental trends are to be discerned, and that we should not be misled by the appearance of early competence. During the first six months of life, for example, interaction between infant and adult becomes increasingly balanced as compared with its initial asymmetry. Very young babies may appear to be communicating on something like an equal basis, but this is only because of their mothers' 'phasing, timing and preparedness to make concessions to the babies' developmental level' (ibid.: 294). Imitation can occasionally be observed in the 2-week-old baby, but only a limited model of other people is yet available to the small baby. Likewise, what may look like intentionality in the young baby's activity is merely a form of learning, driven by the anticipation of pleasure or control 'in the here and now'. Any apparent ability to represent in young babies is likewise illusory; intentionality and the ability to represent cannot be expected to emerge until six months or so (ibid.: 295). Such claims are in themselves rather orthodox ones. Urwin's appeal to such empirical facts is therefore of interest. It is essential to her argument that communicative and cognitive competences do not emerge too soon, for the communicative inferiority of the young baby is central to her revision of Lacan. On the other hand, 'pretend play emerges much earlier than is usually believed' (ibid.: 307). Urwin is driven to make developmental claims: in effect, to endorse a normative account of infancy.

Having taken this step into a normative framework, Urwin is able to incorporate such developmental notions as stranger anxiety into her account. This is the claim that infants demonstrate a particular, fearful response to strangers at a particular stage of development (Bradley 1989: 110). Urwin notes that Lacan's account, in contrast with Freud's, deemphasizes a 'maturational and normative theory of stages in libidinal organization' (Urwin 1986: 276). Her extended discussions of infancy demonstrate however how difficult it is to avoid normative formulations, especially if any kind of synthesis of empirical findings and psychoanalytic theory is attempted. In the context of infancy, normative statements readily take developmental form ('first they do this, and then they do that'). But we should not be overpowered by the apparent affinities between infancy and developmental explanation. The tables can always be turned. An interaction between a baby and an adult need not be analysed in terms of the needs of the baby. As Urwin observes:

> The mother, for example, may conjure in fantasy the potential lover who controls or entices her, or project herself as the passive recipient of the desires of another, or as active and potent, a positioning which may not be available elsewhere. As for the baby in the mirror stage, these kinds of interactions act as a support to the adult's own narcissism. This is one of the reasons why relating to babies can be so pleasurable.
>
> (Urwin 1984: 294)

Walkerdine's Lacan: mastering mathematics

Valerie Walkerdine has made extensive use of a Lacanian analysis of desire in the context of childhood. Like Urwin, she emphasizes that normative versions of psychoanalysis are to be avoided. Lacan's account, if treated with care, can be thought of as existing 'outside the framework of normative models' (Walkerdine 1991: 42). One major area of interest for Walkerdine – conceptualized by her in Lacanian terms – is mathematics education with particular reference to gender. Walkerdine's research involved the detailed study of mathematics teaching and of the ways achievement in mathematics is perceived.

In *The Mastery of Reason*, Walkerdine (1988) emphasizes that mathematics is the most focused vehicle of rationality in the primary school curriculum. It represents Western knowledge in its most crystallized form. Fundamentally, 'mathematics is seen as *development* of the reasoned and logical mind' (Walkerdine 1989: 25, emphasis in original). Succeeding in mathematics thus has far-reaching consequences, and so does failure. Walkerdine rejects the treatment of mathematics learning as simply a pure form of cognitive development – as assumed by Piaget for example. 'Mastery of mathematics is not the end point of a naturally achieved maturation, or a developmental sequence which is universally human, as in all theories of cognitive development' (Walkerdine 1988: 200).

Indeed, Piaget's account of mathematics learning, with its emphasis on the young child's engagement with the physical universe, is now cast in a new light (ibid.: 190; see also Burman 1994a: 157). The element of control is highlighted, and Piaget's account revealed as a fantasy of omnipotence. To achieve understanding in mathematics, as evaluated by one's school-teachers, one must treat the universe as subject to mathematical formulae and to one's manipulation of those formulae. Achievement in mathematics is a matter of mastery over the universe. Mathematics expresses 'the dream of a possibility of perfect control in a perfectly rational and ordered universe' (Walkerdine 1988: 187). To be achieved, this mastery has to be expressed in symbolic, abstract forms. Appropriately, the front cover of *The Mastery of Reason* has William Blake's 'The ancient of days' setting a right-angled framework on the world He has created. Achievement in mathematics involves power, not just knowledge.

Mathematics, then, which purports to be entirely rational, is in fact caught up in functions of which both teacher and learner are unaware. Walkerdine argues that the achievement of mathematics is at great cost, because the 'dream' of rational control demands the suppression of value, emotionality, and desire. The consequences of this suppression can only be understood, she argues, by reference to Freudian or post-Freudian theory. More specifically, the case of mathematics learning calls for a Lacanian explanation because of the symbolic nature of mathematics as a sign system. Lacan had highlighted those aspects of Freudian theory that deal with structured systems of signs (for example, the way different images can be substituted for each other in dreams). Lacan's account of a symbolic realm focuses precisely on this issue of the sign system and how it enables desire to be suppressed. Walkerdine therefore treats mathematics as a symbolic system in Lacan's sense – as a realm of experience analogous to language, entry into which involves analogous processes.

The appeal to Lacan enables Walkerdine to make sense of her findings on gender effects in teachers' perceptions of mathematics achievement. Even when girls can manipulate formulae as well as boys, Walkerdine (1989) reports, they are treated by teachers as having less of an understanding of mathematics – that is, less of a mastery over the physical universe. Put in stereotypical terms, the girl is seen as having worked hard and learned the routines whereas the boy is seen as having a natural aptitude which has developed appropriately. This gendered dichotomy seems to be a powerful one. Measured proficiency may fail to distinguish the sexes, or may even indicate superiority in girls, but 'girls have to be proved to fail or to be inferior at mathematics, despite the extreme ambiguity of the evidence' (Walkerdine 1991: 61). Lacan had suggested that entry into language, as symbolic, involves Oedipal processes and the articulation of desire within the unconscious. 'Desire' here refers in particular to the infant's desire for the mother (or rather, its desire to be the object of desire of the mother). For Lacan, the realm of the symbolic has particular connections to the phallic function. The symbolic realm of Lacan allows desire to become controlled: never satisfied, and never acknowledged. Boys' relative success at mathematics, as judged by their teachers, must therefore be seen as bought at a high price. 'The proof of masculine superiority and female failure has constantly to be remade and desperately reasserted' (Walkerdine 1988: 200). There is a terrible black hole in the psyche of the mathematics achiever.

For Walkerdine, specific issues relating to mathematics learning, and the specific issues of gender that arise there, are to be explained by appeal to Lacan's account of the imaginary and the symbolic. Walkerdine's use of Lacan here would appear to be a developmental one, in which what seem to be universal developmental processes affecting all boys and all girls are set out. She notes that the mastery of mathematics is 'a specific and powerfully created discourse' (ibid.: 200) – not an ahistorical process – but the Lacanian interpretation tends to undermine that specificity. Walkerdine's account describes the achievement of mathematics as a consequence of the symbolic control of desire. Mathematics is subsumed under the symbolic realm in general.

Walkerdine's analysis of mathematics emphasizes its deluded pretentions to universality, to 'a rationality devoid of any content which can describe and therefore explain anything' (ibid.: 187). Looked at this way, mathematics expresses a desire for a world that is 'regular, ordered, controllable'. It defines itself quite precisely as being content-free, and hence value-free. Surely there is a danger of Lacan's developmental scheme becoming another mathematics: an account that puts desire firmly in its place. Lacan's theoretical system should perhaps instead be thought of, like mathematics, as a 'discourse . . . produced within a specific set of practices and purposes which guarantee its applicability and its effects. These ensure the "suppression" of its constructednesss and the articulation of its generalizability as the basis of the nature of "mind"' (ibid.).

I have already suggested that Lacan undermines his own apparent developmentalism. Walkerdine undermines that developmentalism as well. In her discussions of mathematics education, Walkerdine treats everyday practices in the home or classroom as forms of discourse, within which children's knowledge is produced. In her chapter in *Changing the Subject*, she describes how children were produced as subjects for education within a child-centred mathematics curriculum. Children's 'development' in mathematics – treated in a Piagetian tradition as basically natural – is therefore controlled by social practice, including the curriculum. In that chapter Walkerdine finds it unnecessary to make an explanatory appeal to psychic characteristics in children; the analysis of social practices subsumes the analysis of desire. Similarly, in *Democracy in the Kitchen*, Walkerdine and Lucey emphasize the significance of an 'examination of the psychic dimensions of violence *within* an understanding of power, oppression and exploitation' (Walkerdine and Lucey 1989: 138, emphasis added). Psychoanalytic claims should not, it is implied, be granted too much autonomy. The consequence of studying children and mathematics should perhaps be the discounting of Lacan.

Walkerdine's Lacan: reading magazines

Children's learning of mathematics is a long-standing interest of Walkerdine. The function of cultural products such as children's reading materials is also a major concern. In her chapter in *Critical Theories of Psychological Development*, Walkerdine (1987) discusses school-girl magazines and their place in the production of adult female sexuality. A detailed anaysis is given of typical plots from the British girls' comics *Bunty* and *Tracy*. As in *The Mastery of Reason*, the appeal to psychoanalysis is driven by a combination of factors.

Walkerdine wishes to avoid what she sees as several pitfalls in discussing the effects of school-girl fiction on its readers. The pitfalls she identifies are exemplified by three available approaches to the analysis of these effects. First is a totally cognitive, rational account, in which girls are seen as using the material to guide their freely-chosen, enlightened decisions (a humanist interpretation). Second is the classical socialization account, in which the reader's mind is moulded by the materials, leaving no space for resistance or diversity in response. Third is a 'discourse determinism' according to which social practice, as represented by the magazine stories, imposes itself on the subject in a way that closely mirrors socialization.

For Walkerdine, a more adequate account of the role of subjectivity in the response to fiction is offered by psychoanalytic theory. Earlier psychoanalytic analyses of fiction (specifically of fairy-tales) are considered insufficient, but Walkerdine's is a revision rather than a rejection of that approach. In this chapter in *Critical Theories of Psychological Development* Walkerdine appears to endorse a standard psychoanalytic account of female development. Although Freud is read through Lacan here, the account is (in comparison to *The Mastery of Reason*) more Freudian than Lacanian. The appeal of school-girl fiction, such as romantic comics, is seen to lie in its portrayal of the successful resolution of girls' psychological conflicts (Walkerdine 1987: 87). These conflicts are to be thought of in terms of unconscious desires, as stressed by Freud's Oedipal theory. Freud's emphasis on the unconscious has been eroded, as Walkerdine notes, by more recent versions of psychoanalytic developmental theory. Object Relations theory, in particular, has described development in terms of coherent needs that might in principle be satisfied through interaction. The role of Lacan in this context is to refocus attention on unconscious desires of a Freudian kind: desires that are impossible to satisfy, except in fantasy.

The deepest and most significant desire (according to Freud) is desire for the mother. The little girl 'can never possess the mother. Freud therefore postulates the struggle for the transfer of desire from the mother to the father to account for female heterosexuality' (Walkerdine 1987: 91). This move away from desire for the mother 'accompanies the recognition that she, originally perceived as the omnipotent Phallic Mother, does not, in fact, possess the phallus' (ibid.: 121). This formulation of the claims of 'modern psychoanalytic theory' emphasizes the aspects of Freud to which Lacan has been most faithful. It is a much less technical employment of Lacan than that found in *The Mastery of Reason* however. The Phallic Mother is a Freudian notion: the Oedipal girl's idealization of a super-mother endowed with male power. Walkerdine is in danger of endorsing Freud's Oedipal theory as a developmental account – a normative statement of psychic growth (first young girls think mother has a penis, then they realize that she does not). Like the Lacanian account of girls' attainment of mathematics, then, the approach to girls' reading materials takes a developmental story from psychoanalysis. Psychoanalysis provides the framework for developmental continuity in the same girl who first struggles with sums and later relaxes with *Bunty* and *Tracy*.

In both contexts, Walkerdine insists on the inadequacy of her own analysis of these cases in terms of social practice. Her general argument is that an account based entirely on social practice can never be adequate. This would be to throw the baby (of subjectivity) out with the bath-water (of orthodox psychology). Some account of subjectivity is required, but the subject must not be endowed with an unrealistic level of integrity or autonomy. Lacan's is the best available account because it describes a fragmented subject. Through Lacan, Freud can be reread as an account of desires. In this way, for Walkerdine, Freud's account of fantasy may be salvaged. The effect of this move is to reinstate a developmental reading of Freud.

Walkerdine's use of psychoanalytic theory must be scrutinized carefully. It runs the risk of reducing a potentially anti-developmental framework to a developmental one. Specific and concrete social practices and their effects might then be submerged in a normative scheme, either Freudian or Lacanian. Elsewhere, Walkerdine has emphasized the fragility of the knowledge-systems erected by the drive for mastery (Walkerdine 1993). An appeal to psychoanalysis risks serving the same drive – in this case, for mastery through total explanation. Totality and closure are obtained by appeal to the developmental claims of Freud and Lacan. These claims provide a comfortably linear narrative with which to make sense of the fragments. But the closure may only be imaginary. Development makes sense because the scientist sees him/herself reflected in the world: 'You shall become like me' (Morss 1995: 17). As Freud himself may be said to have remarked, 'Where *it* was, there *I* shall be' (Freud 1975: 112). For Freud this is narcissism, for Lacan it is the mirror stage.

Walkerdine acknowledges the unstable nature of this developmental appeal to psychoanalysis. Cultural practices give rise to the 'channeling' of psychic conflicts and of desire ('fueling its flames'), as if desires emerge in some autonomous fashion; but at the same time it is 'the cultural practices that produce phantasies' (Walkerdine 1987: 117, 90). It is implied by the latter statement that psychoanalytic descriptions must be grounded in the analysis of social discourse, not allowed to be self-validating. A similar situation thus emerges from the consideration of girls' reading as from the case of the learning of mathematics. Walkerdine seeks a synthesis of psychoanalytic explanation with one based on the analysis of social practice, while recognizing that such a synthesis is unstable. What I am suggesting is that the psychoanalytic commitment threatens to reveal itself as a developmental one (although alternative uses of Freud and Lacan are possible).

In moving from psychoanalysis to social practice, Walkerdine might be seen as distancing herself from Lacan. Walkerdine's analysis of social practice has only been hinted at so far since this chapter has focused on critical psychology's appeals to psychoanalysis. This aspect of Walkerdine's work – constituting some of the most successfully anti-developmental achievements of critical psychology – is taken up in Chapter 7.

PROGRESS SO FAR

This chapter has attempted to distinguish the developmental from the anti-developmental claims of Freud and Lacan, and to look at critical psychology of development against this background. In terms of the critical application of psychoanalysis, attention has been focused on the writings of Urwin and Walkerdine because of their recognition of so many of the problems of developmental argument. As they emphasize in *Changing the Subject* and elsewhere, psychoanalytic accounts of childhood have tended towards the normative and the regulatory. Among those who have appropriated Freud or Lacan into a critical agenda, it is Urwin and Walkerdine who have made the most serious effort to avoid the pitfalls of normative and functional analysis. In order to avoid those pitfalls altogether, however, I have argued that it is necessary to identify the developmental arguments in the psychoanalytic accounts. Alternatives might then become available.

The progress achieved by psychoanalysis is the critique of progress. For, despite his quite frequent reliance on developmental argument, Freud provides the means to question its every manifestation. He challenges us to see any occurrence of regularity as, instead, repetition or reinstatement. We are therefore challenged to ask 'why?' Why should children go through the same sequences of change as their parents did? Why should children regularly become transformed from 'them' into 'us'? Why should we continually search for simplistic causal sequences in people's lives?

Among critical psychologists of development, it has been those most influenced by Lacan who have recognized the force of these kinds of question. It is the same writers, for related reasons, who have turned to post-structuralist arguments (especially those of Foucault) as well as to psychoanalysis. Some aspects of this post-structuralist move have necessarily found their way into the present chapter. More detailed consideration will now be given to the implications for developmental psychology of the post-structuralist enterprise. As we shall see, Foucault, rather like Lacan, seems to raise a quizzical eyebrow at the term development.

Chapter 7

Post-structuralism and the deconstruction of development

> The scientific object of developmental psychology, namely the developing child, is a product of a particular kind of discursive enterprise and not an independently pregiven object about which psychologists make 'discoveries'.
>
> (Henriques *et al.* 1984: 101–2)

Marxist and psychoanalytic approaches to development have attempted to be scientific. Psychologists adopting any of the many versions of these methods have sought definite answers to their questions concerning childhood or developmental psychology. The developmental claims derived from Marxism and from psychoanalysis are positivistic claims: this is how things are. This assumption of definitiveness even applies to the employment of Lacan by critical psychologists.

What distinguishes the more recent, post-structuralist work in critical psychology is a loss of faith in this positivistic approach. Science is no longer treated as the search for answers to problems that arise outside science. Nor can science – even Marxist science or psychoanalysis – be seen as generating objective forms of knowledge that can be used to inform practice. Instead, scientific procedures are seen as playing a part in producing the objects that they study and the interventions that they sanction. Science is treated as a set of social practices, of organized procedures and ways of talking – that is, science is a 'discursive enterprise'. What sciences study is not entirely created by the procedures of the science, but what comes from outside those procedures is itself the product of social practices. A science such as developmental psychology, or a scientific version of Marxist psychology or of psychoanalysis, overlaps and interacts with numerous other social practices in constructing the object of its 'gaze'. These social practices include teaching in all its forms, family life in all its variations, and so on. We, as researchers, parents, or students of psychology, are ourselves constituted in part by our involvement in these practices. Subjectivity, and any changes in subjectivity to be associated with age, must be seen as constructed in this manner. However critical we may think ourselves, we cannot simply stand back from the social world and analyse it in a detached manner. It is us.

In attempting to articulate the complicated ways in which subjectivity and social practice are intertwined in modern life, contemporary critical psychology is paying increasing attention to the work of Michel Foucault. This chapter attempts to summarize some of the ways in which Foucault's writings are relevant for a critical examination of developmental psychology, and to evaluate some of the appeals that have already been made. Towards the end of the chapter I discuss some writings that are influenced by post-structuralism in general, rather than by Foucault in particular, and briefly consider the related issue of deconstruction.

What I will suggest is that Foucault, and others such as Derrida, present us with unambiguously anti-developmental arguments. Unlike Marx and Freud, broadly speaking, post-structuralism is uncontaminated by developmental claims. It is not necessary to separate out the developmental from the anti-developmental strands in Foucault. Work is still required, however, as Foucault himself has indicated:

> All my books . . . are little toolboxes, if you will. If people are willing to open them and make use of such and such a sentence or idea, of one analysis or another, as they would a screwdriver or a monkey wrench, in order to short circuit or disqualify systems of power . . . well, all the better.
>
> (Foucault cited in Eribon 1991: 237)

Foucault's antagonism towards 'systems of power' extended to over-systematic forms of analysis in the social sciences and humanities. Although his writings of the early 1960s made considerable use of structuralist styles of analysis, Foucault increasingly distanced himself from structuralism in his later work. Having defined Foucault as a post-structuralist, an attempt should therefore be made to clarify what this term means in relation to structuralism.

The distinction between structuralism and post-structuralism is not easy to define, but the differences are important. One general feature of structuralist formulations within the social sciences is a positivistic scientific style, characterized by certainty in its analytic claims. If properly carried out (it is assumed) analysis will lead to firm knowledge. Structuralism approaches an area of human social experience with the objective of comprehensive description. For example, semiotics is the attempt to give a total and coherent descriptive system for the use of signs in human interaction. The clothes that people wear and the food they eat may be analysed in terms of systematic 'codes' that give meaning to specific items of dress or of food.

Structuralism involves a search for meaning, carried out with the presupposition that meaning is there to be found. For example, a structuralist notion of text would involve the assumption that definitive analysis can be carried out on any book, comic, or television programme. '*The*' message of a text is revealed by appropriate analysis. Structuralism assumes that there is always some 'code' to be cracked, or some form of language to be understood. In the hands of an expert, any cultural product can be 'decoded'. It is this confidence in the effectiveness of its methods that most distinguishes structuralist styles of analysis. Marxist versions of structuralism are confident that a scientific form of critique can be articulated, through which the truth about social life will be revealed. Althusser's approach is the most severely structuralist approach to Marxist critique. Like other forms of structuralism, Althusser's is highly complex and explicitly rejects simplistic explanations of social life. But hand-in-hand with the complexity of the analysis is an insistence on the scientific validity of the method. Indeed structuralism involves a redefinition of what it is for a social science to be scientific.

Althusser's structuralist Marxism highlights some general features of Marxist critique. The 'ideology critique' derived from the Frankfurt School shares Althusser's assumption that correctly informed analysis will lead to correct identification of the functions of some particular cultural product (television advertising for example). Emancipatory intervention is then made possible. The disagreement between Althusser and Habermas is more concerned with means than with ends – with the form of analysis rather than its objectives. Critical psychologists who have adopted ideology critique have likewise assumed that correct analysis will give rise to true statements about the social world. Critique will reveal what is really going on under the surface of developmental psychology (Broughton 1987). The self-certainty of the critical psychologist can be as great as that of the traditional, 'positivist' psychologist. All critique is not structuralist in a technical sense, but structuralist kinds of critique bring into focus the general characteristics of critique. The conditions for the possibility of critique include the belief in a true method.

A structuralist account presents us with a complete picture: a place for everything, and everything in its place. Tables and diagrams take the place of texts. The system is closed, having become fully known. A body of knowledge has been opened up to the detached gaze of the (prototypically male) scientist, pointing out the form and function of this organ or that to his audience. This is a style adopted by Lacan in his analysis of the unconscious as being 'structured like a language'. The work of Foucault and other post-structuralists challenges the authority of structuralist social science. One important feature of this challenge is the denial of structuralist notions of coherence. Integrated systems of thinking are treated with suspicion, in a style that reaches back to Nietzsche's writings of a century ago. Foucault rejected Marx and Lacan (Eribon 1991: 266, 272) in this spirit. To the structuralists' claim that everything is connected (if properly analysed), post-structuralism responds that everything is unconnected. The emphasis is on diversity and fragmentation rather than coherence. In terms of the scrutiny of texts, for example, a diversity of conflicting messages is likely to be uncovered rather than one hidden meaning (Parker 1992). If this situation is taken seriously, then the writings of the post-structuralists must themselves be treated in this way. A neat summary of 'what Foucault meant' would represent something of a contradiction in terms. However, the attempt must be made to highlight some of the themes that have been discerned and endorsed by critical psychologists.

FOUCAULT AND THE HISTORY OF SUBJECTIVITY

If Marx and Freud are taken as the founders of two great intellectual traditions in the analysis of human social life, Michel Foucault should perhaps be accorded similar status as the founder of a third. His work is certainly the most visible and striking of what is referred to as post-structuralism. Foucault's work presents challenges to developmental psychology in a number of ways and on a number of levels. Some of these challenges have been recognized by critically-oriented writers in psychology (Henriques *et al.* 1984; Parker 1989; Richer 1990; Rose 1985, 1990).

More generally, Foucault has caused psychologists to rethink the status of their discipline. It has usually been taken for granted that psychology is directed towards benevolent ends – in terms of intervening helpfully in people's lives in various ways. The more successful psychology is as a science – the more it is enabled to carry out research in its preferred ways – the more effective this benevolence will be. But such sanguine assumptions about the role of scientific knowledge in human affairs are seriously questioned by the kind of investigation that Foucault carried out and inspired.

Foucault's writings cover a range of topics in social life – madness, health, punishment, sexuality. Often carried out through an historical examination, Foucault analyses the 'administration' of public and private life in both modern and ancient times – the ways in which people's lives are regulated by themselves or by others. Scientific disciplines, and professional practices which intertwine with them, are for Foucault to be seen against the background of such administration. Sciences and professions are seen as generating bodies of knowledge that are sets of statements, practices, expectations and definitions, allowing people to control themselves and each other. The boundaries of such bodies of knowledge are not always distinct. Some aspects of a science may be formalized in text-books, but the everyday activities of the people embroiled in the science are just as much part of the knowledge system. Any discussion of a science must refer not only to its research practices, but also to the institutional and personal infrastructures of research such as laboratories, journals, conferences, and careers. Knowledge is secreted by such distributed networks of activity.

Foucault shows that governmental and scientific scrutiny has, over the last two centuries (at least in Western Europe), come to focus on matters of population surveillance and control (Rose 1990). Scientific and medical studies of populations – including the measurement of samples and the establishment of norms – have been closely related to changes in the regulatory role of the state: to education, welfare, health provision and so on. Foucault is careful to avoid the suggestion that all these state systems work together in a smoothly functional way, as a Marxist analysis might assume. Further, he makes clear that the deliberate manipulation of the population by some person or persons in government – as portrayed in a conspiracy theory of society – is not the typical situation. This is not to say that in certain times and places people's lives are not indeed controlled in such a totalitarian manner. Foucault's point is that we must not be misled by this particularly striking situation (the *1984* scenario as it were) into overlooking the more subtle ways that power typically functions in society. It is easy for a liberal-minded science or profession to express quite genuine horror at a totalitarian exploitation of their expertise. It is harder, perhaps, to recognize the connotations of power and control within the everyday discourses of those disciplines themselves (see Parker 1992).

These cautionary aspects of Foucault's work – and Foucault is indeed something of a moralist in that respect – have been employed in the more general critiques of psychology as a science, such as those of Nikolas Rose. Psychology and its history are illuminated in striking ways by the kind of analysis Foucault has initiated. Foucault's own work on mental illness and on the punishment of criminals, focuses attention on discipline – both mental and physical. For Foucault, such matters are closely interconnected with the constitution of the modern human subject. As social practices are established to incarcerate or otherwise mark out the mad and the bad, those not so marked become defined as voluntary agents who have elected to remain on the right side of madness or of the law. People can define themselves only in terms of the administrative arrangements (in the widest sense) to which they are exposed. Nowhere is this more true, according to Foucault, than in the case of sexuality.

Childhood, sexuality and subjectivity

A good example of the direct relevance of Foucault arises from issues of children's rights in the context of sexuality. In a discussion of sexual morality and the law, Foucault makes the observation that adult perceptions of childhood serve to disempower children in the context of violence and abuse by adults (Kritzman 1988). Foucault points out that children are thought to be asexual (or to be sexual in ways that are entirely distinct from the sexuality of adults). Hence children are incapable of talking about adult sexuality, and their testimony is therefore discounted. In such a situation, the legal and professional frameworks of meanings serve, among other things, to differentiate what is truth from what is not. What a child says cannot be the kind of truth in which the law deals.

It is made clear in Foucault's discussions of the family, as well as being implicit elsewhere, that childhood is itself constituted through social processes. People are after all treated like children in a variety of circumstances, with chronological age not always the most critical factor. 'Treating someone like a child' may involve special locations such as schools, and special professions with their own expertise, or more subtle discriminations in a common space. The same person who is treated as a child in some circumstances may be treated as an adult in others: in an emergency, for example, a young child may be given responsibility usually withheld. It seems impossible to pin down 'what' childhood is, or what a child (or an adult) is, in any definitive sense. Such matters appear to be consequential on social practice – on organized activity and participants' reflection on that activity. In a general sense, at least, Foucault insisted that human subjectivity is socially produced.

Sex and sexuality were of abiding interest to Foucault. Apparently so intimate and so personal, and apparently so naturally determined, Foucault insisted on the inherent contestability of sexual knowledge. Scientific discussions of sexuality, including discussions of its supposed development in the individual, must therefore be looked at in a different way. The historical significance of Freud's claims concerning sexuality is a case in point. It is commonly held that Freud's writings scandalized a society conditioned by a 'Victorian' repression of sexuality. This account presumes that human sexuality was suppressed in the nineteenth century and that sexuality in children was not even acknowledged. It is often thought that Freud's work was resisted precisely because it revealed what had been hidden. But as Foucault (1981) and others (for example, Sulloway 1979) have shown, Freud's early work was carried out at a time of intense scientific interest in human sexuality, including the sexuality of children. Freud's psychoanalytic claims can be seen as a contribution to the regulation of sexuality. Children's sexuality was defined by Freud as having been hidden but now revealed to medical science. The occult nature of sexuality – standing in need of scientific illumination – was, for Freud, itself an illustration of the necessity of repression. For civilization to be possible, sexuality must be repressed. A Freudian knowledge of sexuality (whether of children or of adults) carries with it the presupposition that sexuality must be controlled in certain ways.

The very notion of nineteenth-century sex being 'underground' is itself a Freudian account, for it parallels the supposed path of sexuality in the Freudian child. Repression of sex in the nineteenth century is taken to have followed on from the public celebration of sex in previous times. Boisterous and innocent sexuality – at the same time, rough-and-tumble and slap-and-tickle – characterizes early childhood, for Freud. Similarly, the conventional account of the history of sexuality treats the eighteenth century (in Western Europe) as a period of bodily freedom (with images of *Tom Jones* in mind, perhaps, or half-remembered bawdy folk-songs). The happy, natural time of early childhood is banished by 'latency', in which the sexual urges get repressed – hence building up pressure to explode at adolescence. Similarly, sexuality 'goes underground' in the nineteenth century, only to emerge even more powerfully once the sources of repression are removed.

The point is that Freud's own work, as it was received and understood by its audience, gave rise to a new way of understanding the history of sexuality. Science, Foucault would say, produces knowledge: Freud, among others, produced sexuality as the twentieth century knows it. The role of repression is vital to this account, and our post-Freudian perception of 'Victorian' attitudes to sex epitomizes repression. For this notion of repression to make sense, some natural and powerful force must be presupposed to *be* repressed. Sexual desire must be treated as incorrigible, as essential (natural, universal, biological). But examination (by Foucault and others) of the characteristics of sexuality in the eighteenth century and earlier, has shown that this naturalistic explanation just does not work. Sexual life was just as much subject to techniques of regulation in the eighteenth as in the nineteenth century, however different the actual techniques might have been. What people did with their bodies, what they expected, allowed or forbade others to do with their bodies, was subject to as many complexities and cultural constraints as in 'Victorian' times. People's knowledge about bodies arises from the same complexity of social practice that generates regulation and the distribution of power.

The example of sex demonstrates forcefully that people's lives, identities and experience are produced and maintained through social discourse. By constituting and regulating subjectivity, such discourses manifest both knowledge and power (Curt 1994: 54). Thus, for Foucault, sexuality refers to definitions of bodies as well as of minds, and is not reducible to essential human desires:

> Sexuality must not be described as a stubborn drive, by nature alien and of necessity disobedient to a [repressive] power which exhausts itself trying to subdue it and often fails to control it entirely. It appears rather as an especially dense transfer point for relations of power: between men and women, young people and old people, parents and offspring, teachers and students, priests and laity, an administration and a population.
>
> (Foucault 1981: 103).

Foucault was not especially interested in developmental psychology as such; as a lecturer in psychology (his first teaching post) he delegated the teaching of child psychology to an assistant (Eribon 1991: 138). Psychology in general he considered to be backward, 'a sort of absolutely inevitable and absolutely fatal impasse in which western thought found itself in the nineteenth century' (cited in Macey 1993: 158). Psychology, he felt, needed to abandon its commitment to naturalistic objectivity and to study 'what is most human in man, namely his history' (ibid.: 62). Foucault was to define this history in his own terms. His work is important for the study of human development for several reasons. It investigates the ways people define each other and themselves, whether child or adult. It refuses to accept naturalistic explanations at face value: it does not believe that anything in history or development can usefully be called 'natural'. Foucault treats people's interactions with each other as the intersection of systems of knowledge and power. Such a project, however flawed or incomplete, cannot but be of significance for the critical reexamination of developmental psychology.

'Big' development: Foucault and history

By looking at specific social practices and institutions – such as the prison, the 'medical gaze', sexuality – Foucault sought to trace the emergence of present forms of knowledge of ourselves as subjects. This form of analysis he came to call 'genealogy' – to distinguish it from the 'archaeology' he had employed earlier. 'Archaeology' came to seem rather too structuralist a notion, so that in describing the method of *The Birth of the Clinic*, what he had called in 1963 'a structural analysis of the signified' he called in 1972 (in the revised edition) 'an analysis of discourses' (Macey 1993: 171). Bodies of knowledge cannot simply be unearthed; they can only be discerned in action, which means action through time and change. These considerations relate to Foucault's larger-scale interests in history.

The issue of continuity versus discontinuity in history is important here. For Foucault, a body of knowledge attains a certain kind of cohesion and identity, but this is fragile. What may look like continuity and persistence over time actually involves the reproduction or maintenance of the social practices involved. Change through historical time, Foucault emphasizes, must not be treated as if it is natural or transcendental (1972: 12). History is not 'development' as that term is often used; there is no natural or default condition in the world such that entities or intellectual frameworks grow and change of themselves. To treat history in such a 'developmental' way is to flirt with idealism. According to Foucault, therefore, 'the traditional devices for constructing a comprehensive view of history and for retracing the past as a patient and continuous development must be systematically dismantled' (Foucault 1977: 153).

Foucault is quite aware of the difficulties involved in simply dismissing continuity in the historical past. But he always treats continuity as problematic and contestable (Foucault 1972: 176; Smart 1985: 56). What Foucault identifies in developmental or evolutionary accounts of history – in any form of history that presupposes patterns or trends – is reductionism. The vast complexity of historical events, their over-determination by numerous ongoing factors, is suppressed by developmental accounts. One simple explanation is set in place instead of an account so complex that the term explanation might be inappropriate. Foucault implies that such simplistic explanations mystify and mislead, for example giving the impression of inevitability to historical change. Any sequence treated as natural is surely implied to be inevitable. In recent times, for example, the dominance of European nations over others has been treated as natural, inevitable, and therefore correct. Consistent with Foucault's general claims, such developmental discourses must be seen as being imbued with relations of power. At least in the context of history, developmental accounts must be seen as mystifying and perhaps oppressive. Marxist approaches to history are rejected by Foucault, for 'Marxism exists in nineteenth-century thought in the same way a fish exists in water; that is, it stops breathing anywhere else' (Foucault cited in Eribon 1991: 162). Developmental accounts of history, like all sciences, do produce a form of knowledge, but it is knowledge of which we should be wary.

The notion of progress itself is frequently a mystifying and deceptive one – an unexamined core of commitments, treated as natural and inevitable. Few historians have been able to describe the past without discerning progress in it. Foucault denies progress, evolution, and development as they conventionally pertain to the description of human history. These terms connote a realm of being above and beyond everyday concrete reality. There is always an appeal to a higher level of reality – a plan, a direction, a trend, or a natural process. Foucault wishes to eradicate this developmentalism from history, no matter what the consequences might be. Importantly for us, he also (if only by implication) wishes to eradicate developmentalism from the study of human development: for he is concerned not simply with the context of human lives, but with their substance. Subjectivity in today's world has emerged through history not through some natural process. It cannot now be natural – to be natural would be to be outside of any body of knowledge, to be true in an absolute sense – and Foucault has denied this possibility. To be consistent, he must reject any naturalistic account of development in the person. He must treat human development as an entirely social matter. Neither bodies nor the knowledge they embody can be said to develop. Any apparent continuity within a person's development can itself only be a matter of discourse. Foucault has fragmented history, as treated by more orthodox academics, but has also reconnected elements previously treated as distinct. A parallel has been drawn with the geophysical notion of plate tectonics (Curt 1994: 59). Not always explicitly, but always implicitly, Foucault has done the same for human development. He has broken up the developing body, but has joined its parts to a social world.

Foucault has not directly addressed the matter of developmental psychology's accounts of the person. But it seems to me impossible to avoid the consequences of his general critique (Morss 1992b). In any case, Foucault's investigations of human subjectivity – in terms of sexuality, for example – break down accepted notions of developmental continuity and natural-ness in the person, in just the same way as they break those notions down in the historical context. If there is no generic human condition across time and place (as humanism had contended), then human life-span change cannot consist in the unfolding or the realization of such a condition. There could not possibly be universal stages or sequences in development. Universal stages could be no more than bodies of knowledge, forms of scientific, professional and lay discourse. The human life-span cannot be outside of history in the sense that it is portrayed in the conventional text-book of developmental psychology. There is no such thing as 'the' life-span or 'the' life-course.

Foucault's critique of development in the context of history converges with his analysis of subjectivity. Both represent a rejection of humanism; in Foucault's words, 'our task is to completely free ourselves from humanism' (cited in Macey 1993: 171). He thus attempted a method for defining human subjectivity which avoids the limitations of humanism. Subjectivity, for Foucault, is produced by and within socially maintained discourse. In many respects he dissolved the commonly assumed identity or continuity of the human subject across time and place. For the mere emphasis on social context does not in itself challenge humanism. The impact of social situations and of historical frameworks can be acknowledged within a humanistic analysis, so long as some constant human condition remains in operation. The historical setting becomes a backdrop to some universal human drama. For Foucault, and in contrast to this, continuity or identity of the human personality is treated as merely contingent. It is treated as something which only occurs if it is being produced – not through fixed laws of the economy, as for Marx, nor through the law that constitutes desire for Lacan, but through shifting discourses of the administration of the body (Eribon 1991: 272). This is a challenging proposal.

FOUCAULT IN THE CRITIQUE OF DEVELOPMENT: *CHANGING THE SUBJECT* AND AFTER

The first large-scale exploration of Foucault in the context of critical psychology was in *Changing the Subject* (Henriques *et al*. 1984). Hollway, Urwin, Walkerdine and their colleagues argued that a post-structuralist analysis is essential if the dualism of individual versus society is to be overcome. The individualism of traditional psychology endows that individual with a spurious kind of agency, a freedom to make rational choices in terms of its own best interests. Even the social construction work of Harré and Shotter, they insisted, had failed to move the discussion out of this liberal-humanist framework. The social constructionists' assumptions about people's agency and voluntary decision-making were in need of correction. Marxism was a good antidote to this liberalism, they suggested, but went too far (at least in Althusser's structuralist version) in denying the importance of human subjectivity. Althusser's account 'slides' into functionalism (ibid.: 107) because it underplays the clashes and contradictions between discourses. Because of these contradictions, and because discourses are not necessarily coherent among themselves, 'the relation of, say, psychology and pedagogy to practices of the social (for example, schooling) is complex, mobile and to some extent indeterminate' (ibid.). This insistence on conflict and indeterminacy rules out any kind of socialization theory, a point emphasized by the authors of *Changing the Subject*. The recognition of conflict in social life works against the functionalism of socialization theory – a position that presupposes the smooth and relatively predictable uptake of individuals into a social world (see also Dannefer 1989: 5).

Foucault's post-structuralist analysis is crucial to *Changing the Subject* because it is concerned with subjectivity, considered as produced through the clash of discourses:

> In brief we use 'subjectivity' to refer to individuality and self-awareness – the condition of being a subject – but understand in this usage that subjects are dynamic and multiple, always positioned in relation to particular discourses and practices and produced by these.
>
> (Henriques *et al.* 1984: 3)

The authors of *Changing the Subject* are emphatic that science, truth, and subjectivity must be considered in terms of their production through social and historical processes. Knowledge – as generated through a discipline such as psychology – cannot be adequately examined except in relation to its regulatory power. Walkerdine's chapter in *Changing the Subject* is directed towards such an examination of the specific case of developmental psychology. This chapter, with other writings of Walkerdine, represents a rigorous application of post-structuralist styles of analysis to the critical psychology of development.

Walkerdine and an anti-developmental Foucault

Valerie Walkerdine has studied the production of subjectivity in a number of contexts and has argued that desires are formed, or at least transformed, within discourse. Throughout her work, Walkerdine has explicitly challenged the notion of development as being outside social life – as being natural. She insists that what we call development – what parents and teachers, for example, may treat as inherently regulated change – can only be an effect of normalizing and regularizing practices (Walkerdine 1993). Examples abound in her various writings on young children's conversations with adults, children's mathematical experience, and school practices. The anti-developmental, Foucault-influenced style of analysis, which remains of major significance in her writings, is best illustrated by her chapter in *Changing the Subject*.

Walkerdine's chapter on 'Developmental psychology and the child-centred pedagogy' (Walkerdine 1984) starts off by examining the process of 'progressive' primary education as a liberal, humanist enterprise. Walkerdine describes the methods of surveillance of children (and indeed of teachers) that are associated with 'active' forms of learning in the classroom. The informal classroom layouts that are employed may be less obviously controlling than the rigid rows of desks in the 'old-fashioned' schoolroom, but control is still being exercised. Teachers' recording of 'developmental' achievements of the individual child is a more subtle kind of regulation. In discussing the function of such recording procedures, Walkerdine observes that development 'is produced as an object of classification, of schooling, within these practices themselves'. She concludes:

> It is in this sense that developmental psychology and the child-centred pedagogy form a couple: the apparatuses of the pedagogy are no mere application [of 'scientific' findings] but a site of production in their own right . . . . Central to the practice therefore is the *production* of development as pedagogy.
>
> (Walkerdine 1984: 162)

'Child development' is thus a form of expert knowledge partly constituted by teaching practices. Teachers' observations go to make up the expert knowledge about a particular child's achievements, defined as developmental achievements.

Less directly, schooling practices call for certain kinds of expert knowledge about children in general – that is, for knowledge of 'child development' on which to base the curriculum. Causal influence runs in various directions here, and the beliefs and expectations of parents and of children themselves also play a part in the constitution of development. Walkerdine's point is that children's 'development' cannot be described except by reference, explicit or not, to certain social conditions and practices. No school can honestly claim to treat children according to their 'natural' development, for 'we would find no classroom which stood outside the orbit of some constellation of discursive and administrative practices' (ibid.: 162).

Teaching practices, in general, relate themselves to accounts of human nature and its supposed development (Singer 1992). Child-centred pedagogy treats children as unfolding naturally along a certain developmental path, but in a way that requires certain kinds of interactions with the world about them. In this account, children learn for themselves, but they learn the right things if their development is natural. At the same time – the teacher-training rhetoric continues – each child is treated as an 'individual'. Children are treated in certain ways by educational systems, and this treatment has the effect of regulating those children, their parents, and their teachers. Part of the regulation is the treatment of children as representatives of 'the child', who develops in certain universal ways. Text-books of developmental psychology play a major part in this process of normalization. These regulatory processes are concealed, and the talk about 'natural' development is part of that suppression.

The interest in regulation is a direct influence of Foucault, as is the focus on social practices as such. Also, the treatment of truth as always a production (never a discovery) is central to post-structuralist argument. Development, as truth, must be seen as produced. Walkerdine's general point, in her own words, is that 'developmental psychology's object is constituted in such a way as to reduce all problems to "the child's acquisition of . . . ", "the development of . . . "'. The developmental approach can be no more than one of many alternatives. Walkerdine undermines the developmental account in a number of ways in this chapter and in subsequent writings.

Walkerdine is following Foucault very closely when she argues that 'in so far as it constitutes individuals, in this case children, as objects of its gaze [psychology] produces them as subjects' (Walkerdine 1984: 197). Walkerdine's work is the closest and most sustained examination of developmental psychology from a Foucauldian viewpoint. Its identification of developmental knowledge as produced, situated, and entirely relative to social practice – however institutionalized such practice may be – is one of the best examples yet available of an anti-developmental formulation.

The Lacanian Foucault of *Changing the Subject*

Critically-minded psychologists who have explored the implications of post-structuralism have at times felt it necessary to extend or revise Foucault. Having emphasized the achievements of Walkerdine's appeal to Foucault, it is therefore important to note that Walkerdine and her colleagues consider Foucault's formulations to be limited in vital respects. These limitations are mentioned in the earlier sections of *Changing the Subject*, but are put to one side in Walkerdine's own chapter, as described above. The inadequacies perceived in Foucault give rise to the attempt to synthesize post-structuralism with aspects of psychoanalytic theory.

The authors of *Changing the Subject* are, it must be emphasized, extremely enthusiastic about Foucault. They consider the emphasis on social practice and discourse to be essential. They argue, however, that this emphasis can give rise to a position that would be too relativistic. Foucault's writings (at least as available in 1984) did not seem to address the demands of a radical interest in subjectivity:

> Now in displacing the individual as a simple agent the post-structuralists achieved a massive and important step. However . . . in this view the subject is composed of, or exists as, a set of multiple and contradictory positionings or subjectivities. But how are such fragments held together? . . . What accounts for the continuity of the subject, and the subjective experience of identity?
>
> (Henriques *et al*. 1984: 204)

These concerns almost seem humanist ones, but the authors of *Changing the*

Subject insist that a rejection of humanism (as in post-structuralism) does not solve the problem of subjectivity. People's lived experience remains to be dealt with. Foucault's analysis is therefore treated as partial, although essential. A revised version of Lacan is employed to fill what these authors see as something of a gap in post-structuralist argument (ibid.: 237; see also Curt 1994: 49).

The appeal to Foucault in *Changing the Subject* is thus heavily qualified. Certainly, the Lacanian claims are themselves interpreted and revised in a post-structuralist direction. Emphasis is placed on the social production of the kinds of effects that Lacan described and that the authors of *Changing the Subject* wish to endorse. The synthesis of Lacan and Foucault is best illustrated by the writings of Walkerdine's colleague Wendy Hollway. In *Changing the Subject*, and more recently (Hollway 1989), Hollway has attempted to bring together a post-structuralist discourse analysis with some elements of Lacanian theory. The analysis of discourse is considered inadequate by itself, particularly in connection with motivational aspects of heterosexual relationships. Hollway's chapter on 'Gender difference and the production of subjectivity' (Hollway 1984) immediately follows the introduction of Lacan within *Changing the Subject*. Hollway presents an analysis of adult heterosexual relationships in terms of alternative discourses. Discourses 'make available positions for subjects to take up' in their interrelationships (ibid.: 236). For example, Hollway identifies a 'male sex drive discourse' that locates women as the object of men's biologically driven sexuality. Other competing discourses include the 'have/hold discourse' and the 'permissive discourse'. Hollway illustrates these different discourses with extracts from interview material.

Discourses are general social practices, but they 'do not exist independently of their re-production through the practices and meanings of particular women and men' (ibid.). People do not have voluntary choice over which discourse to position themselves within, or how and when to switch from one to another, but neither are people's actions determined by discourses in a mechanical fashion. Foucault, according to Hollway (and her colleagues) strays too far in the direction of 'discourse determinism'. Foucault's approach must therefore be balanced with a sensitivity to the subjectivity of individuals, that is, to 'the histories of individuals' (ibid.: 238). Individual history is to be thought of in Lacanian terms. Hollway chooses the Lacanian discourse within which to position herself. I will suggest that her Lacanian discourse is a developmental discourse.

Hollway claims that 'desire for the mother is repressed but never extinguished. It reasserts itself in adult sexual relations' (ibid.: 247). In the individual, a 'historical chain runs from mother (the first Other) to woman/Other' (ibid.: 262). Thus, the signification of 'woman' for her informant 'Jim' 'has a history going back to his desire for the mother. The argument is an illustration of Lacan's slogan "the desire for the Other is the desire for the mother"' (ibid.: 249). It should be stressed that Hollway is not uncritical of psychoanalysis. Freud's Oedipus scenario, in particular, is treated as in need of a social reading. But the Lacanian formulation somehow escapes this stricture. Initial desire for the mother is a universal condition that drives the development of sexual identity and gives rise to irrational aspects of adult relationships. This claim is an explicitly developmental application of Lacanian theory. For Hollway, Lacanian claims are immensely privileged. Since those Lacanian claims are developmental ones, in my analysis, the anti-developmental force of Foucault is thereby compromised. The Foucault approach may indeed allow for the kinds of analysis of subjectivity and desire which critical psychologists are rightly demanding. As Walkerdine's own work demonstrates, it is not limited in the ways described in *Changing the Subject*.

There are both developmental and anti-developmental possibilities in Lacan, but the Foucault–Lacan synthesis of *Changing the Subject* tends to obscure this distinction. Having distanced themselves from conventional developmentalism, its authors' position is somewhat compromised by an appeal to a developmental Lacan. The forced marriage of Foucault and Lacan threatens to compromise the advances made through the analysis of discourse. Indeed, the authors of *Changing the Subject* themselves recognize the limitations of Lacan and indicate the need for post-structuralist appropriation:

> One of the implications of using a structuralist paradigm is that Lacan's theory tends to collapse into an account of a universal, albeit contradictory, subject who is not situated historically, who is tied and bound by pre-existing language, and is incapable of change because of it. This, of course, is precisely the position which we wish to avoid. . . . What we are proposing is to replace Lacan's emphasis on a universal and timeless symbolic order with an emphasis on discursive relations, viewed in their historical specificity.
>
> (Hollway 1984: 217)

This project is not fully carried through by the authors of *Changing the Subject*. Their Lacan remains insufficiently reconstructed, and what emerges is an unsatisfactory amalgamation of Foucault and Lacan. Indeed, the 'limitations' discerned in Foucault may be misconceived. It is Walkerdine's own work (in *Changing the Subject* and elsewhere) that indicates most clearly that Foucault is more adequate than they have judged.

The main objection made to post-structuralist approaches is that a focus on social and cultural practice might give rise to a 'discourse determinism'. People would be described as being 'made' by discourse or cultural practice in a kind of back-door socialization theory. The human subject would be conceived of as passive – as an object rather than a subject. Socialization theory, in its familiar psychological form, had been dismissed very early in *Changing the Subject*. Althusser's structuralist approach was identified later in that book as itself a kind of socialization theory – in which the smooth functioning of society 'as a whole' seemed to override all other theoretical considerations. But the accusation of 'discourse determinism' may be misdirected. As Walkerdine observes, it is 'some structuralist accounts' that claim that the readers of comics are 'simply constituted by the relations of signification within the text' (Walkerdine 1987: 117). Therefore it is the structuralist rather than post-structuralist approaches that give rise to this problem of reinventing socialization. In terms of an analysis of girls' comics, a structuralist analysis might claim to reveal what the comic is 'really' saying. This dogmatic approach would imply that the readers of the comic have little choice but to assimilate this true (but hidden) meaning.

A post-structuralist approach to such cultural products would break down the simplistic theory of the subject required by any socialization theory. If a text is thought to contain a single message – delivered to the subject as it were subliminally – then the subject is being treated simply as the receiver or 'decoder' of a stimulus. The message somehow crosses the divide between the objective world of the stimulus material and the mental world of the human subject. Neither Foucault nor Walkerdine would accept this account of subjectivity – an account that Walkerdine would consider dualistic. Post-structuralist thinking, including that of Walkerdine, treats subjectivity in the same terms as it treats social reality. The subject is not on a different level of being, but belongs to the same social world as the texts it encounters. Readers of school-girl magazines are not entirely above or 'outside' the texts that they are reading. The discourses carried by the texts are not confined to the covers of the magazine. Discourses relating to girls' activities and possible experiences at school are at the same time part of the magazine and part of the real life of the reader. So the polarity of textual material (as object or even stimulus) versus reader (as subject) is not one that any post-structuralist account would sustain (Curt 1994: 42). Post-structuralist accounts, including those of Walkerdine, quite precisely critique that object – subject polarity.

I am suggesting that the limitations Walkerdine and her colleagues have seen in the post-structuralist approach are, if anything, problems that post-structuralism is best equipped to overcome. The limitations they identify are characteristic of a structuralist approach, not a post-structuralist one. Walkerdine's negative justification for her emphasis on 'desire' is therefore unsatisfactory: desire in a Lacanian sense is not an answer to limitations in the post-structuralist account. Foucault has at least offered a way of trying to get to grips with these issues of 'power–knowledge–pleasure' (Foucault 1981: 11). Walkerdine's aim has been to bring the psychic and the social together within one explanatory framework, and she finds Lacan's semiotic version of psychoanalysis uniquely relevant to that project. Walkerdine emphasizes that desires are channelled by social practices, and ultimately produced by them. Desires are, as it were, social in the last instance. But Freud and Lacan seem to intrude in the immediate context, and their normative, developmental claims attain a solidity that they do not deserve.

The focus on desire is meant to allow individual experience to be recognized, but desire insists on becoming abstract. Walkerdine says in her paper 'Breaking the law of the father', that 'we can move forwards, not backwards, to expose the historically specific modes of our regulation and subjugation' (1991: 130). My suggestion is that Foucault, rather than Lacan, represents 'forwards' in this context. Walkerdine's work is a most incisive and challenging application of post-structuralist style to the matter of 'development'. Development, as a supposedly natural progression – an unregulated regulation – is instead seen to participate in a complex web of social expectations and personal positionings. None of these features should be thought of as fixed, or as universal. They are concrete, but not individual. Walkerdine's analysis makes it possible to gain enough distance from the notion of development to see around it and behind it. Indeed with Walkerdine's help we may learn to see right through it.

LIFE AS TEXT? DECONSTRUCTIVE READINGS OF DEVELOPMENT

The authors of *Changing the Subject* approached post-structuralism through Marxism and increasingly through Lacanian psychoanalysis. One reason for their unwillingness to endorse Foucault in a whole-hearted manner was a worry about what they perceived as relativism. Foucault seems to undermine all truth claims, treating all forms of knowledge as the ephemeral product of shifting social processes. Critique – uncovering what is really going on – now seems impossible. Although they had rejected Marxism, Henriques *et al.* retained an attachment to some aspects of the materialism of Marx. They did not want a recognition of the realities of oppression and exploitation to get dissolved away in some relativistic analysis. One aspect of the appeal of Lacan, also, was the anchoring of post-structuralism in something more solid (the actualities of early development). Consistent with such views, Walkerdine and her colleagues have been wary of the textual forms of analysis explored by Derrida and others, even though such forms of analysis do share some common ground with post-structuralism.

Others, however, have been more willing to explore the relativistic implications of post-structuralism. In terms of critical psychology of development, this has involved a focus on the role of interpretation – of the processes by which one of many possible alternatives is selected, in the actions and the claims of developmental (or critical) psychologists. The focus on multiple interpretive possibilities is central to those versions of post-structuralism that concern themselves with 'texts'. Writers such as Rex and Wendy Stainton Rogers and Ben Bradley have been more receptive to these textual versions of post-structuralism than were the authors of *Changing the Subject*. This receptivity reflects the influence of the social constructionist work of Harré, Shotter and Gergen in their earlier thinking, since the social construction writers had themselves emphasized the importance of interpretive and textual processes. This attention to text, and hence to literary forms of analysis, is sometimes indicated by the use of the term 'deconstruction', although this term is to be found in many kinds of critical writing (Morss 1992b).

The 'critical polytextualism' of the Stainton Rogers (1992; Curt 1994), discussed below, involves an acceptance of the multiplicity of interpretations that are in operation in any social practice. There is a recognition of the rhetorical nature of science, including any science of developmental psychology, in pressing its claims. Any one interpretation involves the suppression of others. The relativistic attitude of post-structuralism – its disbelief in any absolute grounds for any particular moral or philosophical stance – is therefore accompanied by concerns that are of a moral nature. At the same time as the Stainton Rogers are insisting that developmental psychology is 'only' a set of stories, they also insist that it matters very much what stories are told by whom and about whom. The present discussion will summarize the 'critical polytextualism' of the Stainton Rogers, and will then look briefly at Derrida before illustrating some Derridean features by reference to Bradley.

Critical polytextualism

> We are not interested in trying to improve developmentalism by correcting its errors. What we are arguing . . . is that the whole enterprise of developmentalism needs to be abandoned altogether!
>
> (Stainton Rogers and Stainton Rogers 1992: 42)

Developmental explanations for issues concerning children are placed under intense scrutiny in *Stories of Childhood* (Stainton Rogers and Stainton Rogers 1992). Above all, developmental explanations are treated as suppressing alternative accounts; 'until very recently, virtually everybody working in any area concerned with children assumed that the findings and the theories of developmentalism were *the* knowledges, and the *only* knowledges worth considering' (ibid.: 7–8). Developmental explanation should instead be seen in much more relative terms. What scientists say about children reflects larger discourses available to them, within which the scientists' work is positioned.

The relative (rather than absolute) status of psychology's claims gives rise to complex effects across time. Psychology's accounts of childhood show paradoxical changes and continuities. For example, in the penultimate chapter of *Stories of Childhood*, the authors set alongside each other a series of statements about child sexual abuse and its effects (from the late 1980s), and a series of statements about children's masturbation and its effects (from 1909). As the following alternating extracts suggest, the scientific claims concerning these phenomena are strikingly similar (material from the 1909 source is in brackets):

> Other common behavioural characteristics of sexually abused children . . . include . . . withdrawal from group activity; depression . . . (Perhaps the most constant and invariable, as well as earliest signs of the masturbator are the downcast, averted glance, and the disposition to solitude). Fear of disclosure . . . may completely prevent that child from putting a sexually abusive experience into words. . . . (The art with which they elude watchfulness and evade questions is often inconceivable).
>
> (Stainton Rogers and Stainton Rogers 1992: 168–9)

Similar parallels are illustrated between the scientific accounts of the incidence and the long-term effects of these two kinds of activity. It is almost as if the old text has simply been updated.

What are we to make of such parallels? It would probably be a mistake to treat the early claims as simply 'wrong' and the recent claims as simply correct. It would also be a mistake to use the similarities in scientific observation as a justification for denying that a real and serious problem may presently exist. But the similarities are indeed worrying. For example, contemporary treatment of sexual abuse some-times treats sexual interference itself as of more significance than any physical injury that accompanies it. It is the *knowledge* of sexuality that presents the greatest danger to the child, for it is this knowledge that 'robs the child of its childhood' (Kitzinger 1990). This implication was perhaps even clearer when the term 'incest' was in common use. The awfulness of sexual defilement – of the corruption of innocence – seems to divert attention from such mundane matters as violence. This may not be appropriate. For what good reason should the sexual abuse of children not be called rape?

There are complex and troubling issues here, and scientific or medical accounts cannot be taken at face value (Curt 1994: 192). What, if anything, is special about sexual knowledge? What do we presuppose when we set up child protection systems: what is being protected? In what ways can we rethink the notion of natural innocence in the child without opening the floodgates of paedophilia? How can we institutionalize respect for childhood? A naturalistic account of children's devel-opment, their needs or their special characteristics, does not seem to provide any solid ground (Stainton Rogers and Stainton Rogers 1992: 80). Appeals to children's needs in the literature of child protection fail to engage with the socially relative status of such criteria. Appeal is often made to the innocence of children and to the notion of childhood having been 'stolen' from victims of abuse. 'Stolen childhood' also plays a role in advertising for Third World famine relief, a context in which it is also highly problematic (Burman 1994b). Like it or not, concern for children has to recognize the complexities in its task. These complexities, both conceptual and moral, are perhaps as great as in any area of human affairs.

If we are concerned about children, how can we articulate that concern? How can we, with honesty, discuss and analyse situations in which children are exploited or abused? These questions might seem to be central to much of what developmen-tal psychologists concern themselves with. It might be thought that the discipline would have examined these questions very thoroughly in its substantial history. But as Rex and Wendy Stainton Rogers argue, developmental psychology's record in illuminating the abuse of children is a poor one; it has contributed to a situation in which we have 'a concern over "sex" obscuring a concern for the child' (Stainton Rogers and Stainton Rogers 1992: 181). What *Stories of Childhood* sets out to do is to work towards a recasting of our ways of thinking about childhood, with these practical matters of concern very much in mind.

This practical orientation is important to emphasize, because it is on practical grounds – in terms of consequences for children – that the simplicities of available approaches are criticized. The Stainton Rogers are driven to complex theories because of the complexity of real life. The authors' criticisms of conventional psychology centre on its demand for the one true and simple answer to the question of the nature of childhood. The alternative advocated in *Stories of Childhood* is the recognition of complexity: complexity of experience, of culture, of economic conditions. We have to accept, the authors urge, that any account of childhood (for whatever purpose) is but one story chosen from many possible alternatives. Their own name for the position that recognizes this is 'critical polytextualism': the critical recognition of the multiplicity of possible stories that might always be told. Previous and current approaches to child protection, for example, exhibit none of the self-doubt that is central to the Stainton Rogers' own attitude. Yet these available approaches, focusing on children's innocence of sexuality for example, are riddled with inconsistencies and disturbing consequences (ibid.: 70).

The theoretical ground which *Stories of Childhood* comes to occupy is extensively informed by post-structuralism. It treats the scientific claims of developmental psychology with little respect. It approaches developmental psychology, like Henriques *et al.* (1984) and Burman (1994a), as a set of disciplines and discourses which have emerged in history for particular reasons, serving particular ends. *Stories of Childhood* locates the emergence of the human sciences within 'modernism' – a period characterized both by the humanism of the Enlightenment and the effects of the industrialization of Europe. Within the human sciences, it is noted,

> the pursuit of uncovering the mysteries of human development became a central feature of that humanistic project, drawing in particular on the pivotal discipline of psychology, the claimed intercept of the knowledging of the biological and the social.
>
> (Stainton Rogers and Stainton Rogers 1992: 7)

The term 'knowledging' here is shorthand for the production of knowledge (or 'knowledges') through social practice, as examined by Foucault and others.

Their analysis of developmentalism as a modernist project aligns the Stainton Rogers with those critics of modernism who have discerned a successor world-view, 'postmodernism' (Gergen 1992; Kvale 1992; Shotter 1992). From a philosophical point of view, the analysis of postmodernism is accompanied by a thorough-going relativism. The philosopher Richard Rorty (1989) has examined this position, and attempted to salvage a kind of moral integrity from this relativism without making the pretence of absolute foundations for moral judgements. He advocates a 'liberal irony' as a personal and intellectual stance, and the Stainton Rogers endorse this (Stainton Rogers and Stainton Rogers 1992: 188). Rorty insists that we must see other beings as 'one of us', and the Stainton Rogers argue that children must be one kind of 'other being' to whom this attitude must be extended. Critical polytextualism is an 'ironic transdiscipline' which explores, among other things, what such an attitude to children and childhood would involve (Curt 1994). What distinguishes this approach from that of Walkerdine, for example, is its acceptance of relativism and its consequences. This willingness of the Stainton Rogers to reject any kind of realism brings their approach closer to literary styles of analysis such as deconstruction.

Derrida and deconstruction: textual visions

> If everything scientists say about babies is a social construction, how can it be any truer to say that infancy is hell than to call it bliss?
>
> (Bradley 1989: 180)

Deconstruction as a technique of analysis is associated with the writings of the philosopher Jacques Derrida, once a student of Foucault. It can be discerned in Bradley's *Visions of Infancy* which, like *Stories of Childhood*, is concerned with the multiplicity of interpretation. Bradley's book can be read as an illustration of some of the possibilities afforded by Derrida's work.

Derrida's significance for a critical psychology of development emerges from both the philosophical and the literary contexts (Morss 1992b). In common with Foucault, Derrida has exposed the reliance of Western scholarship on some basic commitments. These, according to Derrida, include a commitment to the notion of origin – to explanation in terms of postulated beginnings. Social science, for example, has sought to trace the origins of human civilization in prehistory (Derrida 1976: 121); psychology has sought to trace its origins in the growing individual. Western philosophy, Derrida claims, has treated such postulated origins as 'the truth' – as a situation in which some transcendental reality made contact with mundane life. In an extreme form, this moment might be treated as a moment of 'inspiration', for example in a Biblical context. Derrida's questioning of the explanatory role of origins undermines any conventional explanation in history, evolution or development (Morss 1992b).

In the writings of philosophers and social scientists, Derrida links this notion of the origin with what he calls a 'metaphysics of presence'. 'Presence' is exemplified by the kind of solidity in the here-and-now presupposed in empiricist philosophy. Empiricism, with its focus on immediate sensory experience as the basis for knowledge, has dominated Western accounts of human infancy since the seventeenth century (Morss 1990: 74). Derrida, further, connects the metaphysics of presence with what he discerns as a philosophical devaluation of writing in favour of speech. Speech, says Derrida, has been taken philosophically to relate closely to truth or spirit – as the voice of God perhaps – whereas writing has been taken as a secondary and corrupt human attempt to transcribe that speech. Speech seen in this way is taken as manifesting the immediate presence of spirit. The human invention of writing would thus be seen as a fall from grace. As Sampson notes, the orthodox elevation of speech over writing also privileges the 'ontological status that empiricism grants to whatever has here-and-now, observable, qualities' (Sampson 1988: 9).

Derrida shows that the orthodox evaluation of speech and writing can be overturned, and that what has been said of the one can equally be said of the other. The aim here is not to recuperate writing or to denigrate speech, but rather to demonstrate some of the tensions within the orthodox formulation. The supremacy of speech in that orthodox formulation is not a natural state; it is only maintained by the forced suppression of writing. There is a kind of violence going on, involving forces within the formulation that can be released. With close attention the orthodox hierarchy springs apart – it 'deconstructs itself'. By extension, any hierarchy may be encouraged to do the same. Any dichotomy (true–false, absent–present, appearance–reality) can be identified as a hierarchy in that one pole will be valued over the other. Derrida's method therefore threatens the stability of any argument based on such dichotomies. Given the importance of the dichotomy true–false in Western writing – that is, the importance of Aristotelian logic – the threat is a real one.

The term 'deconstruction' is met fairly often in critical writings in psychology (for example, Burman 1994a; Parker and Shotter 1990) but is used in a variety of ways. Derrida has refused to endorse any narrow definition of the term, and it would be foolish to attempt any legislation over its 'proper' use. But it should be pointed out that there have been numerous methods of criticism before Derrida, and that applying the word deconstruction to them all is unhelpful. Thus, analysing some statement for its ideological assumptions is not necessarily deconstruction, if it is assumed that some definitive answer can be obtained in a particular case. It is more helpful to use the term 'critique' for such an approach. Critique may be guided by Marxism, by feminism or by various other master narratives. Most importantly perhaps, Derrida's deconstruction can never be thought of as being 'done'. Deconstruction has a present tense but not a past tense. To say that some author has 'deconstructed' some statement or value-system is to suggest that something stable has been achieved. But this is to deny the possibility of further deconstruction – indeed it is to suggest that the 'truth' has now been revealed. With respect to Derrida's own work, it would be misleading to state that 'Derrida has deconstructed speech versus writing'. Like sex and housework, as has been said before, deconstruction never stays done.

The sense of deconstruction that I am employing here is perhaps best illustrated in Bradley. In his *Visions of Infancy* (1989) Bradley emphasizes that scientific descriptions of babies, of their competencies and their development, are exercises in interpretation. Any one interpretation obscures all the others. Interpretations are never arbitrary; 'scientific questions about babies always emerge from particular circumstances for particular reasons' (ibid.: 180). Further, psychologists' theories of infant development reflect their presuppositions on human nature in general. What scientists have done, Bradley shows, is to see babies in such a way that the baby exemplifies an origin state in accordance with their chosen developmental theory. Whatever overall theory of development a scientist may adhere to, infancy will fit into it in terms of a starting-point; if the scientist looks for that particular starting-point, it will be found. Infancy, for Bradley, is defined as a scientific project in terms of a search for the origins of adult human nature, for 'babies provide scientists with what is almost a *carte blanche* to speechify about the fundamentals of psychological change' (ibid.: 175).

Deconstruction lurks beneath the surface of Bradley's writings. The reader might at first take Bradley to mean that infancy, specifically, is open to endless interpretation but that childhood and adulthood are not. To make that judgement would be to take at face value the dichotomy between infancy and later life, a dichotomy endorsed (to the detriment of infancy) throughout the history of developmental psychology. For example, infants are said to be governed by biology, children and adults by culture. Deconstructively, Bradley hints that scientific descriptions of children and of adults too must be subject to the same qualifications and conditions as are descriptions of infancy. Adulthood for example cannot be treated as some stable, abstract end-point, any more than infancy can be treated as an abstract starting-point for some naturally regulated 'development'.

Bradley has also discussed how orthodox theories of infant development present a happy, confident baby in a supportive and benign environment. Noting that none of these conditions can be taken for granted, Bradley has shifted the focus of the study of infancy on to the negative side, giving attention to hate and anger and to infancy as 'hell' (Bradley 1991). In many ways this is a deconstructive move, because it makes us rethink the dichotomies of love and hate, paradise and hell and so on, as they relate to our treatment of infants. Bradley is able to point to earlier theorists (especially the psychoanalyst Melanie Klein), who already investigated negativity in infancy. But the deconstructive style allows a more incisive critique of our ways of dealing with infancy, because it does more than explore some neglected area. Bradley's point is that hatefulness and anxiety in infancy are not just further aspects of infancy that need study, as if to complement or balance the more usual treatment. Rather, the usual accentuation of the positive has eliminated the negative – it has led to the denial of negativity. In doing so, it has involved 'interpretive violence' (Bradley 1989: 176). If negativity is observed or reported then it must have come from 'outside' the baby, that is, from the mother. Insisting on dealing with the negative does not just correct an imbalance, it threatens to overturn the overall dichotomy of positive versus negative in that context.

These claims of Bradley therefore involve the continual exposure of conflicting possibilities. Every interpretation involves the suppression of all others. The notion of development cannot survive such treatment unscathed. As Bradley notes, developmental psychology is 'a legitimate target for deconstruction . . . [it] sees "development" as something "in nature" that is prior to the experiments that investigate it and the texts which discuss it' (Bradley in preparation: 183). Developmental explanations involve claims about objective regularities, natural, universal or essential kinds of change. They often appeal to evolutionary biology. But human science, including biology, involves interpretation. Bradley emphasizes the necessity for 'developmental psychology' to move beyond a model of itself as a natural science, towards

> a self-conscious discipline advocating the grounds for change . . . a discipline intended to better the understanding, position and prospects of the most disadvantaged in human affairs – including, when babies are being discussed, the lot of those who look after them.
>
> (Bradley 1989: 10)

Bradley, like Urwin (1986), focuses on the concrete conditions of mothering within which infancy takes place. More generally, he describes the ways that theoretical formulations of infant development systematically blame and devalue women as mothers. As others have shown, the psychiatric literature overwhelmingly blames mothers for pathological conditions in their children. Mothers are set up for blame in a number of theoretical formulations: they are expected to provide a hyper-sensitive interactive partner for the young baby, a partner who is at the same time natural, educationally constructive (but non-directive), and who must at all costs enjoy what she is doing. Mothers must fall in love with their babies as well as serving them. All these points illustrate how theories of infant development assume some quite specific caretaking conditions, but treat them as natural – and hence treat the development itself as natural. As Walkerdine (1991: 142) notes, 'facilitating and nurturant Others (teachers, mothers) are necessary to the facilitation of a "natural" sequence of development in "the child". These contradictions are lived out by girls in pedagogic practices'. In Bradley's words, orthodox accounts insist that the understanding of others is 'naturally endowed . . . rather than having to be repeatedly struggled for' (Bradley 1989: 10). Bradley favours a deconstructive approach, so long as it is taken seriously:

> Let us then have a 'deconstruction' of the place of development in psychology, one that would show, by the deconstruction of certain key texts, *how* mental growth has a 'fictive character' and constantly eludes our grasp. But, for many deconstructive psychologists, this is neither the means nor the end they seek. They have no stomach to dwell amongst the system of uncertainties to which deconstruction would reduce psychology. They have no desire to do what Derrida and de Man have done: painstakingly to apply the techniques of deconstruction to the texts of developmental psychology, and then, inevitably, to confront the problems of ethics and aesthetics which such work would raise.
> (Bradley in preparation: 183–4)

Bradley's focus of concern has been human infancy. Moving to the other end of the life-course, psychologists' treatment of ageing is similarly naturalistic. As Dannefer points out, 'prolonged activity in late life was once claimed as a failure to achieve successfully the life stage of disengagement' (Dannefer 1989). For Dannefer, developmentalism should be thought of as a 'closed text': a narrative that is not open to revision or reinterpretation. Using the textual terms employed by Roland Barthes, Dannefer describes developmentalism as 'readerly' – it describes processes in which 'there is nothing for the human actor to do but oblige, consume, acquiesce, whether with resignation or enjoyment' (ibid.: 15). The alternative is not to bring back the humanist subject, able to make free and rational decisions, but to bring in the subject as part of the same social world as the texts it encounters. Subjectivity will have to be seen not as unfolding but as 'infolding' (Curt 1994: 50). The post-structuralist project, broadly defined, has destroyed the notion of development. Paradoxically, writing about development now becomes more urgent – for 'writing about development' now becomes writing *against* development. The authors whose work has been discussed in this chapter are taking this task seriously.

PROGRESS SO FAR

Growing critical involves the scrutiny of arguments – of their form as well as of their content. Rational argument turns out to be a game of mastery, to involve violence and mutual recognition. As Sherlock Holmes says to Watson: 'I shall keep piling fact upon fact on you, until your reason breaks down under them and acknowledges me to be right'. Knowledge turns out to have intrinsic connections with power and personal relationships.

Knowledge and power are bodily functions, things that we do with parts of ourselves and of others. Statements about development involve these matters. They concern bodies, including children's bodies; they produce knowledge about those bodies; they exert control over, and perhaps manifest desire for, those bodies. Of course, statements about development – what we might now start calling develop-mental discourses – seem more directly concerned with 'children's minds' than with their bodies: with thinking, understanding and so on. Minds seem to be abstract, universal entities, whereas bodies are particular. Any statement about general, regular ways in which children's minds develop is challenged by the post-structuralist attitude. Further, developmental statements about minds often turn out to relate to physical regulation or surveillance.

Post-structuralist work brings together an interest in the history of social practices (such as teaching methods, parenting methods) with an interest in their immediate consequences. Unlike Freud and Marx – as they are usually read at least – the history is not understood as a genetic, developmental explanation for the current state of affairs. Nor, however, are current situations treated as entirely negotiable. To state that all knowledge is relative, then, is by no means to say that 'anything goes'. The socially constituted nature of the lives we lead does not diminish their reality. Our lives could not possibly be more real than they are. Our shifting, interlocking involvement with each other, with each other's bodies and bodies of knowledge, is what makes concrete social reality. Bodies of knowledge and knowledge of bodies shift and reform across time and across space. Everything is relative, but life goes on. The houses and offices we live our lives in are set on shifting fragments of the earth's crust, and are spinning around with the earth, which is spinning around the sun in a universe which is either expanding or contracting – yet our lives remain troublesome, obstinate, concrete and they still cost money. As Bradley insists, the practical aspects of the lives of babies, children and adults must never be lost sight of in discussions about 'development'. It is 'poverty and disease which dominate the lives of millions of children and their minders' (Bradley 1989: 9). The question of whether infancy is to be Heaven or Hell is at the same time a question that calls for deconstruction and a question that calls for action.

Out of my window, down on the campus, a woman student waves her arms in greeting. I think it might be to me although that's unlikely because I'm six floors up. But she's greeting another woman student walking towards her. They meet, hug, and talk for a few moments. They, also, are involved in bodies of knowledge: their waving to each other is a public conversation involving recognition and definition of the other. Hugging is knowledge too – it's something we do as a way of knowing our own bodies, and as a display. Men are beginning to be able to hug women, and women men. Men don't hug men very often, not in New Zealand anyway, except when dressed in shorts and on a muddy field. Rugby also is a body of knowledge. A man walks by pushing a baby in a pram, replacing the two woman students: yet another set of discourses, an intersection of social practices of work, care, and sex. My desires, whatever they are, and my development, whatever that is, come from all this – and from nowhere else.

Chapter 8

Writing against development

Rather than living with the existential dizziness of the fact that our lives are headed essentially nowhere but simply keep on, now this way, now that, perhaps we delude ourselves into supposing that there is indeed some rhyme and reason to what's been happening.

(Freeman 1993: 9)

In this final chapter I present a summary of my argument and some speculative remarks relating to life after development. I am strongly influenced here, both as to style and as to substance, by three recent books: Bradley's *The New Psychology* (in preparation); Burman's *Deconstructing Developmental Psychology* (1994a); and the collectively written Curt (1994) *Textuality and Tectonics*. In very different ways these books suggest that my project has been legitimate. It *is* possible to talk about childhood, and indeed adulthood, without talking about development. It is, perhaps, important to do so.

In challenging orthodox forms of explanation, these writers also find themselves challenging orthodox ways of writing psychology. For Bradley, this involves a recognition of subjectivity – not in general but in particular. Writing about people's lives, or researching into them, is for Bradley an intensely personal affair. For Burman the issue of style involves a directness of approach to the reader and an engagement with contemporary culture. For the Curt collective (which includes Rex and Wendy Stainton Rogers) it involves challenging, teasing and at times infuriating the reader. Each book raises more questions than it answers. *Growing Critical*, by comparison, may seem a little dogmatic. Here I balance the dogmatism of earlier chapters with some partly-baked explorations of the consequences of seeing development for what it is.

ANTI-DEVELOPMENTAL FORMULATIONS: THE STORY SO FAR

The critical psychology of human development is a series of claims and counter-claims that, between them, fragment the notion of development. My aim in this book has been to identify and to bring together some of the currently available anti-developmental work. Critical psychology allows us to recognize the limits and the failings of developmental argument. It does this by distancing us from it, thus allowing us to scrutinize it, and by opening up alternatives to the developmental account. In Walkerdine's words, 'we might then adopt a double strategy: one which recognizes and examines the effects of normative models, whilst producing the possibility of other accounts and other sites for identification' (1991: 57).

It must not be forgotten that there are discernible anti-developmental tendencies even within the Vygotsky tradition (see Chapter 2). Vygotsky's own writings can be employed in an anti-developmental manner (Newman and Holzman 1993), but by and large, the Soviet work has resulted only in a minor deviation from the European path of functionalism. The Soviet line – supposedly a 'sociohistorical' line – continually reconverges with the 'natural line' of Western psychology of development. Perhaps this is inevitable given the extent of influence on Vygotsky of European and American psychology (Van der Veer and Valsiner 1994: 6). Some aspects of Vygotsky's writings have been taken up by those committed to the social construction of the human mind and therefore of development (Chapter 3). The social constructionist reading of Vygotsky has, by and large, chosen to sideline the issues raised by Marxism. In spite of the attention given to the constructive role of human interaction and negotiation, the social construction of development falls short of a critical analysis of development itself. With Vygotsky, the focus shifts from organism-in-environment to persons-in-interaction. There is a new emphasis on the moral responsibilities of the human agent, as she constructs her own and other people's life-careers. But there is at the same time a disavowal of responsibility for larger social processes. Lives are constructed as dances between trusting and innovative partners, each taking turn to lead or to follow. But while some have the liberty to dance, others must polish the dance-floor and sew on the sequins.

Marxism has generated many different approaches to the human life-span and its possible variations (Chapter 5). Although there are important issues in Marx's own writings which remain to be explored, the most obvious line in Marxism is a developmental one. In recent years, Marxist contributions have been most clearly focused in the writings of Althusser, Sève, and the *Kritische Psychologie* group. There is much to be learned from Althusser, although his account turns out to be a Marxist form of socialization theory. The importance of Sève's contribution is, fortunately, not limited to his more detailed and diagrammatic accounts of alternative economic lifestyles. Rather, Sève has identified some of the key elements in an anti-developmental Marxism. The Western Marxism of Sève has not made much impact on the more classical doctrines endorsed by *Kritische Psychologie* – the developmental attitudes of which are explicitly evolutionist (Tolman 1994).

It was through Western Marxism that Adorno, in particular, established a critical distance both from Soviet Marxism, with its complacent, whiggish belief in its historical validity, and from Western Enlightenment traditions. Refusing both of these progressivist options – refusing to trade black magic for white magic – Adorno insisted on being contrary, opposite, surly. The spirit of Adorno still lingers within 'ideology critique', doing battle there with the sheer niceness of Habermas and with the grand Weberian narrative of 'rationalization'. Adorno's negative dialectics continually undermines the positivist aspirations of ideology critique: its attempt to seek the one true political motivation behind each of psychology's claims.

Ideology critique has suffered various forced marriages with psychoanalysis over the last 60 years. I did not attempt to deal with such Freud–Marx syntheses in Chapter 6. Freud, indeed, has to be seen as a major anti-developmental thinker in his own right. He was also a major developmental thinker. If we are prepared to call Freud a psychologist then his critique of developmental versions of psychology has been the most important to have emerged from within the discipline. The distinction between Freud's developmentalism and his anti-developmentalism has not been sufficiently observed by critical writers in psychology. Lacan is perhaps more thoroughly anti-developmental than Freud: while both Freud and Lacan move in and out of developmentalism, Lacan seems more aware that he is doing so. Or rather, perhaps, Lacan desires us to know that he knows that he is doing so. Be that as it may, the developmental stories that Lacan has conjured up have proved too vivid to be resisted. The quickness of the tongue has deceived the eye. Lacan threatens to be the new Piaget: someone who can incorporate every mid-twentieth-century intellectual style into his own system (from formal mathematics to structuralism) and who sees things happening in children that we would like to be able to see.

Something has to rescue us from this impasse, and it is the common sense of Michel Foucault. What, he asks us, is actually going on? What are people doing to other people when that word development is used? What happens as a result of its invocation? How is developmental knowledge spawned? Foucault urges us to maintain the questionings of the discipline. His example encourages us not to be daunted by the paradoxical nature of an anti-developmental approach to development, for Foucault has himself been described as an 'impossible object: a nonhistorical historian, an anti-humanistic human scientist' whose prose style 'manages to seem imperious and doubt-ridden at the same time' (Macey 1993: 432). In Chapter 7, I coupled Foucault with Derrida. Adherents of Foucault are called difficult, adherents of Derrida are called dangerous. To be anti-developmental may involve both – each supplementary to the other. Difficulty and simplicity, danger and safety, must all be dared in the unpicking of the discourses of development. It is not just children who are said to develop, but also peoples and economies (Rahman 1993: 212; Sachs 1992). 'Development' is always said to an inferior by a superior. 'I am your future' says the superior: 'You have no other' (Morss 1995). Developmental talk is a kind of genetic engineering.

The three books mentioned at the start of this chapter represent three very different styles of contemporary critical psychology of development. They all reject orthodox psychology of development, but disagree dramatically over what directions should now be followed: textual, critical, or subjective. The Curt group (1994) focuses on textuality and on discourse, in line with a post-structuralist analysis of knowledge. For Burman (1994a), it is the detailed claims and practices of developmental psychology that must be scrutinized, with post-structuralist notions informing a process of critique. Post-structuralism and deconstruction are to be moderated by political commitments such as a feminist programme. Bradley's (in preparation) argument is an ethical one that finds insufficient respect for personal subjectivity in all the available approaches, both traditional and critical. Bradley is emphatically anti-developmental in the sense I have defined. For example, he endorses William James' rejection of 'genetic' (that is, developmental) forms of explanation. James, writing in the 1890s, argued that it was a fallacy to seek explanation in origins ('By their fruits ye shall know them, not by their roots' (1982: 20)). Bradley discerns the 'genetic fallacy' still at work even in the writings of critical psychologists such as the Curt group, who describe subjectivity as emerging from social discourse. This explanation of subjectivity is for Bradley an inappropriately developmental one, in that it seeks to explain the human mind by appeal to universal and regular processes of transformation: the social becomes the mental. Social constructionism reinvents evolutionism as it posits 'ordering principles to the temporal course of construction' (Lock 1994: 2). Appealing to the social for a comprehensive explanation of human experience is for Bradley no more satisfactory than appealing to God or to the gene. Bradley thus cuts himself off from the broad tradition of social constructionism as well as from its post-structuralist descendants. He seeks a new method of grasping subjectivity in psychological terms, a method not yet articulated either in traditional or critical psychology: 'a new kind of poetic possibility in the study of mental life, one that does not try to climb above the plurality of subjective realities which constitutes the world in which we all, psychologist or not, necessarily dwell' (Bradley in preparation: 192). Personal responsibility has not disappeared from the world. Bradley has in a sense worked his way through social constructionism, and indeed deconstructionism, and out the other side – where he finds himself waiting.

DEVELOPMENT AS FICTION

Subjectivity, in Bradley's radical sense, has usually been thought of as the province of the novelist rather than of the psychologist. What does the novelist have to tell us about truth and fiction as they relate to the description of people's lives? In his Author's Note at the beginning of *The History Man*, Malcolm Bradbury states that his novel is 'a total invention with delusory approximations to historical reality, just as is history itself.' He continues:

> Not only does the University of Watermouth, which appears here, bear no relation to the real University of Watermouth (which does not exist) or to any other university; the year 1972, which also appears, bears no relation to the real 1972, which was a fiction anyway; and so on. . . . The rest, of course, is true.
>
> (Bradbury 1977: i)

The History Man is about sociology lecturer Howard Kirk, a man whose life and personality are totally controlled by the times – that is, by history – and he knows it. Kirk teaches his students that all they need to know in order to understand themselves and society is 'a little Marx, a little Freud'. Bradbury's Howard Kirk is a creature of his times (nowadays he would say 'a little Foucault, a little Lacan'). His consciousness, his teaching, his political and sexual activities are all determined by external circumstances, including intellectual circumstances. Cleverly, Bradbury the author even describes Howard's driving around town as entirely constrained by traffic signals, lane markings and car-park barriers.

Howard Kirk is a fictional character. Marx, Freud, and Malcolm Bradbury are real people: I have even met one of them. Howard Kirk, the character, was created by Malcolm Bradbury the author, who decided what Howard's life-story was to be. So we would say that Bradbury, Marx and Freud 'developed' as people, but Kirk didn't. Kirk was made. So what is the point of Bradbury's reference to 'the real 1972, which was a fiction anyway'? Bradbury is challenging our assumptions about the boundaries between fact and fiction. In effect, he is challenging our assumptions about human development also. Human development, as studied scientifically, is about general, natural changes that take place in the lives of real people. There would seem to be no place for a fictional character in such a scientific enterprise (although 'Kirk' and 'enterprise' do somehow seem to go together). What Bradbury is suggesting, however, is that development is quite the opposite of what science thinks. The notion of development may be based on the kind of coherence that can only happen in books. It may presuppose the kind of ordered regularity, and the making of sense, which can only happen if the plot has been deliberately made up (see Freeman 1993).

Text-books of human development should perhaps be thought of as novels – the hero grows up, acquires knowledge, and is eventually launched into a social world as an adult. The Preface of F. Philip Rice's *Human Development: A Life-span Approach* starts thus:

> The story of human development is an exciting portrayal of life in the process of becoming. From conception to death the drama unfolds, revealing an ever more complex being in the making. This story is about you and me as well as others.
>
> (Rice 1992: vii)

The text-book of developmental psychology is the story of 'the' development of 'the' child. The cute illustrations may appear to be of different children at various ages, but somehow the text reduces this diversity down to an idealized developing child. He is probably white, probably middle-class, probably American at least by cultural aspiration – and probably a 'he'. Perhaps he is the author's own child, sometimes appearing in a photograph with the dedication. Developmental psychology is his life-story, from cradle to grave. Somewhere in the middle he might just become President of the United States.

The argument of this book is that there is no such thing as 'development'. If anything, development is a fiction or a set of fictions. Academic writings about development are part of a tradition that includes *The History Man*, *Jane Eyre*, *The Thorn Birds* and *The Bone People*. Development is a story, or rather a set of stories, each told by a different author with different interests. The many different versions of critical psychology, some of which are discussed in this book, all indicate the impossibility of a comprehensive theory of development. The critical traditions are themselves kinds of story, as some of them recognize. But all stories are not equal. Different stories have different consequences for those who live in or by them: choosing, or having a choice made for us, to live by the Holy Bible is quite different from living by Marx's *Capital*.

We must believe that people are real, and that people's lives are real. Changes in people's lives are real; changes in people's lives that may be referred to as examples of development are real. But the unreflective use of that word development is a step away from reality. It gives the false impression that some particular events have been connected up with some general pattern, explained perhaps as a quasi-natural phenomenon. The critically-minded stories of critical psychology – stories that know they are stories – are our protection against development. Stories that know they are stories keep us safe, if anything can, from stories that do not know they are stories. Developmental psychology aspires to the encyclopedic. Is an encyclopedia fact or fiction? A 200-year-old encyclopedia does not read as factual any more. If it is not true now, was it true then – and if it is not true, why should we believe that our modern encyclopedia is true? The main reason encyclopedias are produced, after all, is because they are purchased under pressure by well-meaning, under-educated parents. Is that the sort of atmosphere in which truth is likely to flourish?

Development is part of the built environment – what used to be called 'man-made'. We have to be prepared to boldly go across the line into fiction and back again, for reality and fiction interpenetrate whether we like it or not. *The History Man* is set in 1972 and was published in 1975. Much of it is written in the present tense ('Now it is autumn again'). When televised, in the 1980s, the time it portrays was already seen retrospectively, with some nostalgia. A sub-title at the end of the series told us that Howard Kirk voted Conservative in the 1979 election which brought Margaret Thatcher to power in the UK. Reading the book now, in the AIDS decades, Kirk's promiscuity seems quaint and innocent. We cannot escape from history even when we read a book.

RESEARCH AFTER DEVELOPMENT

Throughout this book I have emphasized the anti-developmental arguments of critical psychology in its many forms. Has this been a purely destructive enterprise, or can some constructive project emerge from the remains of developmental psychology? It seems to me that the concrete things that people do, and that we might formerly have explained by appeal to development, still need to be described and perhaps explained. Concrete human reality, including the actual lives of infants and children, is more insistently in need of consideration once development is swept away: there is more to talk about, and to take action about, not less. Rethinking development involves rethinking education, for example (Newman and Holzman 1993).

The first way to approach this issue is from the point of view of the current research landscape. An analogy, and perhaps something more than an analogy, is with the ethical scrutiny of research in psychology. Increasingly, researchers are being asked to justify their activities in terms of their possible consequences. Both before empirical research begins, and as it goes along, the 'subjects' or informants of research (or their representatives) are asked to give informed consent to their participation. They are, increasingly, being informed of rights to withdraw their participation in research, to check the researcher's written or taped records, and to veto any usages of the information they may supply to which they have objections. This kind of ethical hygiene is replacing the methodological hygiene of controls and the matching of samples that experimental psychologists have always stressed. The application of such ethical scrutiny to research involving children or babies raises questions many of which are yet unanswered, either theoretically or pragmatically.

However unevenly pursued, the ethical demands which are now coming to be recognized would in principle deal with most if not all of the troubling issues in the psychological investigation of 'development'. One question asked of any researcher using a standardized interview or rating scale is whether any undesirable 'reactive' effects are possible. The researcher might be proposing to probe respondents' feelings in a way that pays insufficient attention to the impact of the questioning. The point made by this ethical scrutiny is that the end of information-gathering does not justify the means, if other consequences also follow. More broadly, the kind of reflection that the ethical procedure encourages must inevitably raise questions about the value of a particular research project. It cannot be denied that much research in psychology takes place merely because research publication is the established professional practice of so many individuals. Taken together, the greater degree of reflection and scrutiny that is coming into play in psychological research could in principle solve the problem of what research should be done into 'development'.

If a research programme currently in place can satisfactorily meet the ethical demands and some criterion of value then it is unlikely that all would not be well. Matters of value are of course subject to various interpretations and interests, but it should be stressed that the editors of journals already exercise such judgement in rejecting a submitted article for failing to add significantly to the literature. However 'cleanly' done in methodological terms, that is to say, a piece of research may at present remain unpublished because it is considered of insufficient interest. Worthwhile-ness is not therefore a new criterion, but perhaps its standards need to be reexamined. However high the current rejection rates in the most prestigious journals, perhaps they are not yet high enough.

Any form of research, even including experimental research, can be carried out honestly and with due regard to ethical procedures and can be directed towards worthwhile goals. In light of the discussions in the present book, however, certain kinds of research are indicated more than others. A focus on the social production of 'developmental' change must necessitate a social scrutiny of the ways in which this production takes place. Why are certain kinds of achievement regulated in particular sequences, or attached to particular chronological ages, in particular settings? What diversity is actually present in existing cultural settings, with which to refute the universality of the norm? What interests are served by developmental regulation in particular contexts? What ways do people find of 'saving' the developmental explanation when disruptions appear? Above all, in a sense, why is developmental explanation so tenacious, and so seductive?

A range of enquiry methods would be appropriate to these kinds of question, including some methods usually labelled 'qualitative' and some versions of 'discourse analysis' (Burman and Parker 1993). More orthodox methods, including various interviewing techniques, would certainly have a part to play. There would be a tendency towards description and explication rather than inferential modelling. As suggested by the ethical dimension discussed above, interrelations between investigators and informants would be more recursive and perhaps less unequal in power terms. Lessons and techniques would be learned from the experience of 'action research' (Carr and Kemmis 1986), particularly in educational contexts. On occasion, the investigator would serve at least in part as advocate of the participant person or group. There would thus, unavoidably, be a political dimension to the kinds of research that would be indicated by a 'post-developmental' attitude to the lives of children and adults. Complex issues of talk and action are raised by any consideration of research, but research informed by the critique of development might be somewhat better equipped to deal with such issues.

The difficult one: infancy

Bearing in mind these issues of research, to what extent does the anti-developmental argument apply to infancy? It is not so difficult to displace development from the adulthood area. We need only say that development implies regularity, and that adult humans are diverse and open-ended in their potential. But the younger the person we discuss, the harder it might seem to be to avoid developmental prescriptions. If it is difficult for childhood in general, surely it is impossible for infancy. Infancy, then, must surely be the most severely testing case for any general claims for anti-developmentalism. Can I really be saying that babies do not develop?

To be consistent I do need to say just that. To say that adults do not develop but that babies do would be an unacceptable retreat: effectively, a retreat to the classical, biological position (Morss 1990). The alternatives, which I think of as liberating alternatives, include the kinds of analysis offered by Bradley and by Urwin, among contemporary critical writers. Bradley (1989) focuses our attention on the role of interpretation in the scientific study of infancy. In studying infants, and in formulating general claims about the ways they change across time, scientists impose their own world-views on infants and their social contexts. There is no such thing as 'atheoretical' development. Development must always be described according to some theoretical perspective or perspectives. 'Scientific' approaches to development are clearly flawed then, if they are meant to be objective accounts of natural change. As Cushman (1991) observes in his analysis of Daniel Stern's infancy theory (Stern 1985), descriptions of natural processes of 'unfolding' are inevitably culture-bound.

Urwin's (1984, 1985) writings about infancy are concerned with the emotional lives of babies and the emergence of language. She considers mothering as unavoidably implied in any account of infant development, even if invisibly. Mothering, in turn, is a set of practices and desires that is socially produced. To write about a baby's 'development' while neglecting mothering is to suppress, and effectively oppress, mothers. Technological accounts of infant competence have the same effect; instrumental rationality in the baby rises above the everyday and the particular. From this viewpoint the developing infant is 'an active processor, a problem solver: hands moving to rattle, feet kicking mobile hanging over crib, grasping, lifting, pushing, coordinating acts, tinkering with action patterns, always experimenting, always learning how to work' (Harris 1987: 41). Parental care is redefined as resourcing. Bradley (1989) argues against such a cold, managerial account of infancy. He urges that a proper psychology of infancy should be about 'advocacy', and that it must be about particular babies rather than some abstract 'baby'. Personal experience cannot and should not be avoided:

> The reality of babyhood cannot be available to anyone who has not shared the brief peaks and long lows of responsibility for the management of feeding and anxiety-provoking illness, bathtime and sleepless nights, screams and smiles, milk-scented excreta and scramble-brained craziness over a period of weeks and months of a baby's life, or long enough, in any case, to entwine that baby's existence with that of the psychologist who claims to be investigating it.
>
> (Bradley in preparation: 208)

The word 'development' directs us away from such issues of particularity and personal experience, and if only for this reason it should be avoided.

In the context of school-age children, I would be confident that development explanations are of little help in weighing educational alternatives or parenting decisions. Consider the statement that a particular 6-year-old child is 'too young' to understand something. The statement may be little more than acceptable short-hand: this child does not yet (seem to) understand X; older children (around here) seem to; it is to be expected that (for whatever reason) this child will come to understand X at some time in the future. This descriptive usage becomes vicious if applied generally, to yield an explanatory statement that '6-year-olds cannot understand X'. In a teaching setting, even the particular usage may be little more than a way of avoiding the scrutiny of teaching.

If this analysis is valid for a school-age child, it is difficult to see why it should not be applied to the infant. For the infant, I would suggest that developmental statements will always hinder rather than help. How solid are the supposedly regular changes in infancy which we would normally consider illustrations of develop-ment? Within the mainstream of developmental psychology, the 'facts' about development are subject to constant revision. No consensus seems imminent on what forms of knowledge or processing capacity, if any, should be thought of as inborn (Karmiloff-Smith and Clark 1993). Babies are challenging beings, and it is their right to challenge theory as well as their parents. What I am claiming is that babies do not develop, they demand (Morss 1995).

Babies are hard work. That work may or may not be 'rewarding' or rewarded, and if unrewarded may well be invisible. One consequence of that work is what we call development. If the work is done by someone other than oneself, it may appear that the results of work are natural changes – the sort of natural changes we call development. A father might perhaps underestimate the work of a mother in this way. In the context of the school-aged child, both parents and teachers might 'forget' each others' work in a similar manner. Developmental explanation facilitates this forgetting; it explains *away*. Development could thus be defined as 'someone else's work'. By and large the someone else is female and in a bizarre, alienating twist she may come to perceive even the results of her *own* work as merely natural. The ultimate accolade for a young mother would then be for an expert voice to confirm that her baby is 'developing normally'. Developmental explanation has immense status in the context of infancy: it seems unassailable, to the extent that alternatives seem incoherent. Yet this hegemony must be challenged. If the anti-developmental project has any validity, it must sooner or later launch an attack on the citadel itself.

CODA: TIME, TENSE, TEXT

There are some kinds of statement that, it seems, must be made in the present tense (this is one). However tentatively expressed, and however qualified, some truth claims are expected of the scientific author and these are particularly marked by tense. General claims or statements ('Children are like this'; 'Adults are like that' – the stuff of developmental psychology) must be expressed in some limitless present, for either past or future tense would destroy their value. To say 'is' is to make a universalist claim. 'Is' is the language of philosophy (British philosophy at any rate). Philosophy would not still engage in debate with Descartes if he had written 'I thought, therefore I was'.

The literature on 'the history of childhood' is subversive for this very reason, for it says again and again that children 'were' like this, adults 'were' like that, at some time in the past. Troubling comparisons are elicited: if they were like 'that' then, but are like 'this' now, then what status does our analysis of 'this' have? If adolescence 'did not exist' at such-and-such a time and now it does, what challenges does that present to a conventional view of the naturalness of adolescence? Science fiction – particularly the pessimistic or 'dystopian' science fiction following George Orwell, Aldous Huxley and so on – is subversive for similar reasons. Cross-cultural comparisons are potentially troubling in an analogous way. The eruption of difference is challenging to any analytic system.

The issue of tense seems important. It has been suggested by de Castro (1992) that adults exert a domination over the present. Adults, she indicates, are people who *are*. Children *will be* in the future, but they are denied full participation in the present. Certainly, young children have classically been considered as perceptually and cognitively limited *to* the present, but their experience has been defined at the same time as erroneous – egocentric, and limited only to appearances. It is because of their status as 'becomings' rather than beings that so much stress is laid on the long-term effects of children's experience (sometimes at the expense of a recognition of immediate effects). Contrariwise, the elderly are those-who-have-been: their existence is only in the past tense. Adulthood thus defines itself in a territorial way – it commands the present, and hence legitimizes the denial of rights to non-adults.

The present tense would represent a claim for the singularity of truth: this is the way it is. This is a denial of textuality, of richness in discourse – now, as well as then. It is a denial of the children in adults, and of the adults in children. It is to deny that people of any age can display terminal serenity or terminal despair. The notion of development does not ignore the past, but it does violence to it. The past is that which is made good by developmental change. In dialectical terms, contradictions become lifted up and recuperated as the tide of history advances. Thinking against development requires some sobering recognitions. Childhood cannot be our icon for this constant upliftingness of the past, for this always-becomingness. All may not be made good. Human life is too important to be left to developmental explanation.

I have three children. Between seeing them this morning and seeing them tonight (now, that's written by a man), their lives, their life-stories, could be snuffed out. A drunk behind a wheel is all it takes. Development is no protection against that: no protection, and no solace.

Endpiece

My daughter's friend saw it first: the skull of a horse, clean and white, protruding slightly from the earth. They, and the boys, insisted I dig it up to take home. It was lying side on, teeth and jaws clearly visible. We scraped away the soil and levered at the bone with sticks. This is what palaeontologists do. You could see that it was in perfect condition – a scientific specimen. It didn't want to be shifted though, until we scraped away beneath the jaw and were able to grip it. It came away from the earth, and underneath was livid green flesh.

Development – as studied by psychologists – is clean, polished, measurable, the perfect scientific phenomenon. It is the anatomy of human growth. But don't look underneath it.

References

Althusser, L. (1969) *For Marx*, Harmondsworth: Penguin.
Appignanesi, L. and Forrester, J. (1992) *Freud's Women*, New York: Basic Books.
Benjamin, J. (1987) 'The decline of the Oedipus complex', in J. Broughton (ed.) *Critical Theories of Psychological Development*, New York: Plenum.
—— (1988) *The Bonds of Love*, New York: Pantheon.
Berger, P. and Luckmann, T. (1967) *The Social Construction of Reality*, Harmondsworth: Penguin.
Bidell, T. (1988) 'Vygotsky, Piaget and the dialectic of development', *Human Development* 31: 329–48.
Boothby, R. (1991) *Death and Desire*, London: Routledge.
Bradbury, M. (1977) *The History Man*, London: Arrow Books.
Bradley, B. S. (1989) *Visions of Infancy: A Critical Introduction to Child Psychology*, Cambridge: Polity Press.
—— (1991) 'Infancy as paradise', *Human Development* 34: 35–54.
—— (1993) 'A serpent's guide to children's "theories of mind"', *Theory and Psychology* 3: 497–521.
—— (in preparation) *The New Psychology: Poetics for a New Vision of Mental Life*.
Braun, K-H. (1991) 'Play and ontogenesis', in C. Tolman and W. Maiers (eds) *Critical Psychology*, Cambridge: Cambridge University Press.
Bronfenbrenner, U. (1979) *The Ecology of Human Development*, Cambridge MA: Harvard University Press.
Broughton, J. (1986) 'The psychology, history, and ideology of the self', in K. Larsen (ed.) *Dialectics and Ideology in Psychology*, Norwood NJ: Ablex.
—— (ed.) (1987) *Critical Theories of Psychological Development*, New York: Plenum.
Bruner, J. (1983) *Child's Talk*, New York: W. W. Norton.
—— (1985) 'Vygotsky: historical and conceptual perspective', in J. Wertsch (ed.) *Culture, Communication and Cognition: Vygotskian Perspectives*, Cambridge: Cambridge University Press.
—— (1990) *Acts of Meaning*, Cambridge MA: Harvard University Press.
Buck-Morss, S. (1977) *The Origin of Negative Dialectics: Theodor W. Adorno, Walter Benjamin, and the Frankfurt Institute*, Hassocks: The Harvester Press.
—— (1987) 'Piaget, Adorno, and dialectical operations', in J. Broughton (ed.) *Critical Theories of Psychological Development*, New York: Plenum.
Burkitt, I. (1991) *Social Selves: Theories of the Social Formation of Personality*, London: Sage.
Burman, E. (1994a) *Deconstructing Developmental Psychology*, London: Routledge.
—— (1994b) 'Innocents abroad: Western fantasies of childhood and the iconography of emergencies', *Disasters: The Journal of Disaster Studies and Management* 18: 238–53.

Burman, E. and Parker, I. (eds) (1993) *Discourse Analytic Research*, London: Routledge.

Carr, W. and Kemmis, S. (1986) *Becoming Critical: Education, Knowledge and Action Research*, London: Falmer.

Castro, L. R. de (1992) 'Temporality and human development', unpublished MS, Catholic University of Rio de Janeiro.

Chodorow, N. (1978) *The Reproduction of Mothering*, Berkeley: University of California Press.

Cole, M. (1985) 'The zone of proximal development: where culture and cognition create each other', in J. Wertsch (ed.) *Culture, Communication and Cognition: Vygotskian Perspectives*, Cambridge: Cambridge University Press.

—— (1988) 'Cross-cultural research in the sociohistorical tradition', *Human Development* 31: 137–57.

—— (1991) 'Conclusion', in L. Resnick, J. Levine, and S. Teasley (eds) *Perspectives on Socially Shared Cognition*, Washington DC: American Psychological Association.

Curt, B. (1994) *Textuality and Tectonics: Troubling Social and Psychological Science*, Buckingham: Open University Press.

Cushman, P. (1991) 'Ideology obscured: political uses of the self in Daniel Stern's infant', *American Psychologist* 46: 206–19.

Dannefer, D. (1984) 'Adult development and social theory: paradigmatic reappraisal', *American Sociological Review* 49: 100–16.

—— (1989) 'Human action and its place in theories of aging', *Journal of Aging Studies* 3: 1—20.

Derrida, J. (1976) *Of Grammatology*, Baltimore, Md: Johns Hopkins University Press.

Döbert, R., Habermas, J., and Nunner-Winkler, G. (1987) 'The development of the self', in J. Broughton (ea.) *Critical Theories of Psychological Development*, New York: Plenum Press.

Donaldson, M. (1978) *Children's Minds*, Glasgow: Fontana/Collins.

—— (1992) *Human Minds*, London: Penguin.

Elbers, E. (1987) 'Critical Psychology and the development of motivation as historical process', in J. Broughton (ed.) *Critical Theories of Psychological Development*, New York: Plenum Press.

Eribon, D. (1991) *Michel Foucault*, London: Faber & Faber.

Forrester, J. (1990) *The Seductions of Psychoanalysis: Freud, Lacan and Derrida*, Cambridge: Cambridge University Press.

Foucault, M. (1972) *The Archaeology of Knowledge*, London: Tavistock.

—— (1977) *Language, Counter-memory, Practice*, Ithaca NY: Cornell University Press.

—— (1981) *The History of Sexuality: Vol 1, An Introduction*, Harmondsworth: Pelican.

Freeman, M. (1985) 'Ricoeur on interpretation', *Human Development* 28: 295–312.

—— (1993) *Rewriting the Self: History, Memory, Narrative*, London: Routledge.

Freud, S. (1922) *Beyond the Pleasure Principle*, London: The Psycho-Analytical Press.

—— (1961) *Civilization and its Discontents*, New York: Norton.

—— (1974) *The Ego and the Id*, London: The Hogarth Press.

—— (1975) *New Introductory Lectures on Psychoanalysis*, Harmondsworth: Penguin.

—— (1979) *Three Essays on the Theory of Sexuality*, Harmondsworth: Penguin.

Frosh, S. (1987) *The Politics of Psychoanalysis*, London: Macmillan.

Geertz, C. (1983) *Local Knowledge*, New York: Basic Books.

Geras, N. (1983) *Marx and Human Nature*, London: Verso.

Gergen, K. (1985) 'The social constructionist movement in modern psychology', *American Psychologist* 40: 266–75.

—— (1991) *The Saturated Self: Dilemmas of Identity in Contemporary Life*, New York: Basic Books.

—— (1992) 'Toward a postmodern psychology', in S. Kvale (ed.) *Psychology and Post-modernism*, London: Sage.

Gergen, K. and Davis, K. (eds) (1985) *The Social Construction of the Person*, New York: Springer Verlag.

Gergen, K., Gloger-Tippelt, G. and Berkowitz, P. (1990) 'The cultural construction of the developing child', in G. Semin and K. Gergen (eds) *Everyday Understanding: Social and Scientific Implications*, London: Sage.

Gergen, M. and Gergen, K. (1993) 'Autobiographies and the shaping of gendered lives', in N. Coupland and J. Nussbaum (eds) *Discourse and Lifespan Identity*, London: Sage.

Grosz, E. (1994) *Volatile Bodies: Toward a Corporeal Feminism*, St Leonards NSW: Allen & Unwin.

Habermas, J. (1979) *Communication and the Evolution of Society*, Boston: Beacon Press.

—— (1987) *The Theory of Communicative Action: Vol 2, Lifeworld and System*, Boston: Beacon Press.

Harré, R. (1974) 'The conditions for a social psychology of childhood', in M.P.M. Richards (ed.) *The Integration of a Child into a Social World*, Cambridge: Cambridge University Press.

—— (1983) *Personal Being: A Theory for Individual Psychology*, Oxford: Blackwell.

—— (1986) 'The step to social constructionism', in M. Richards and P. Light (eds) *Children of Social Worlds*, Cambridge: Polity Press.

Harré, R. and Secord, P. (1972) *The Explanation of Social Behaviour*, Oxford: Basil Blackwell.

Harris, A. (1987) 'The rationalization of infancy', in J. Broughton (ed.) *Critical Theories of Psychological Development*, New York: Plenum Press.

Henriques, J., Hollway, W., Urwin, C., Venn, C. and Walkerdine, V. (1984) *Changing the Subject: Psychology, Social Regulation and Subjectivity*, London: Methuen.

Hermans, H., Kempen, H. and van Loon, R. (1992) 'The dialogical self: beyond individualism and rationalism', *American Psychologist* 47: 23–33.

Higgins, E. T. and Parsons, J. E. (1983) 'Stages as subcultures', in E. T. Higgins, D. Ruble and W. Hartup (eds) *Social Cognition and Social Development*, Cambridge: Cambridge University Press.

Hollway, W. (1984) 'Gender difference and the production of subjectivity', in J. Henriques, W. Hollway, C. Urwin, C. Venn and V. Walkerdine (eds) *Changing the Subject: Psychology, Social Regulation and Subjectivity*, London: Methuen.

—— (1989) *Subjectivity and Method in Psychology*, London: Sage.

Holzkamp, K. (1991) 'Societal and individual life processes', in C. Tolman and W. Maiers (eds) *Critical Psychology*, Cambridge: Cambridge University Press.

Holzkamp-Osterkamp, U. (1991) 'Personality: self-actualization in social vacuums?', in C. Tolman and W. Maiers (eds) *Critical Psychology*, Cambridge: Cambridge University Press.

Howard, G. (1991) 'Culture tales: a narrative approach to thinking, cross-cultural psychology, and psychotherapy', *American Psychologist* 46: 187–97.

Ingleby, D. (1987) 'Psychoanalysis and ideology', in J. Broughton (ed.) *Critical Theories of Psychological Development*, New York: Plenum Press.

James, W. (1982) *Varieties of Religious Experience*, Harmondsworth: Penguin.

Jay, M. (1973) *The Dialectical Imagination*, London: Heinemann.

—— (1984) *Marxism and Totality*, Cambridge: Polity Press.

Karmiloff-Smith, A. (1992) *Beyond Modularity: A Developmental Perspective on Cognitive Science*, Cambridge, MA: MIT Press.

Karmiloff-Smith, A. and Clark, A. (1993) 'What's special about the development of the human mind/brain?', *Mind and Language* 8: 569–81.

Kessen, W. (1979) 'The American child and other cultural inventions', *American Psychologist* 34: 815–20.

—— (1990) *The Rise and Fall of Development*, Worcester MA: Clark University Press.

Kitzinger, J. (1990) 'Who are you kidding? Children, power, and the struggle against sexual abuse' in A. James and A. Prout (eds) *Constructing and Reconstructing Childhood*, London: Falmer.

Kohlberg, L., Levine, C. and Hewer, A. (1983) *Moral Stages: A Current Formulation and a Response to Critics*, Basel: Karger.

Kohli, M. and Meyer, J. (eds) (1986) 'Social structure and social construction of life stages', *Human Development* 29: 145–80.

Kozulin, A. (1990) *Vygotsky's Psychology: A Biography of Ideas*, Cambridge MA: Harvard University Press.

Kritzman, L. (ed.) (1988) *Michel Foucault, Politics, Philosophy, Culture*, New York: Routledge.

Kvale, S. (ed.) (1992) *Psychology and Postmodernism*, London: Sage.

Laboratory of Comparative Human Cognition (1983) 'Culture and cognitive development', in P. Mussen (ed.) *Handbook of Child Psychology Vol 1*, New York: Wiley.

Lacan, J. (1977) *Ecrits*, London: Tavistock.

—— (1988a) *The Seminar of Jacques Lacan, Book I*, Cambridge: Cambridge University Press.

—— (1988b) *The Seminar of Jacques Lacan, Book II*, Cambridge: Cambridge University Press.

Laplanche, J. and Pontalis, J-B. (1973) *The Language of Psycho-analysis*, London: Hogarth Press.

Leach, E. (1974) *Lévi-Strauss*, Glasgow: Fontana/Collins.

Lichtman, R. (1987) 'The illusion of maturation in an age of decline', in J. Broughton (ed.) *Critical Theories of Psychological Development*, New York: Plenum.

Light, P. (1986) 'Context, conservation and conversation', in M. Richards and P. Light (eds) *Children of Social Worlds*, Cambridge: Polity Press.

Lock, A. (1994) 'Against cognitivism: the discursive construction of "mental mechanisms"'. Paper presented to Conference on the Discursive Construction of Knowledge, Adelaide, February.

Macey, D. (1988) *Lacan in Contexts*, London: Verso.

—— (1993) *The Lives of Michel Foucault*, London: Hutchinson.

Mair, M. (1988) 'Psychology as storytelling', *International Journal of Personal Construct Psychology* 1 : 125–38.

Marx, K. (1969) Preface to 'A contribution to the critique of political economy', in L. Feuer (ed.) *Marx and Engels: Basic Writings on Politics and Philosophy*, Glasgow: Collins.

McAdams, D. (1993) *The Stories We Live By: Personal Myths and the Making of the Self*, New York: Morrow.

Morss, J. R. (1990) *The Biologising of Childhood: Developmental Psychology and the Darwinian Myth*, Hove: Lawrence Erlbaum Associates.

—— (1991) 'Beyond Marx and Spencer: myths of progress and myths of origin in developmental psychology', unpublished MS, University of Otago.

—— (1992a) 'Against ontogeny', in P. Griffiths (ed.) *Trees of Life: Essays in Philosophy of Biology*, Dordrecht: Kluwer.

—— (1992b) 'Making waves: deconstruction and developmental psychology', *Theory and Psychology* 2: 445–65.

—— (1993) 'Spirited away: a consideration of the anti-developmental *Zeitgeist*', *Practice: The Magazine of Psychology and Political Economy* 9: 22–8.

—— (1995) 'The development complex', *Psychoculture* 1: 16–17.

Newman, F. and Holzman, L. (1993) *Lev Vygotsky, Revolutionary Scientist*, London: Routledge.

Parker, I. (1989) *The Crisis in Modern Social Psychology – and How to End it*, London: Routledge.

—— (1992) *Discourse Dynamics*, London: Routledge.

Parker, I. and Shotter, J. (eds) (1990) *Deconstructing Social Psychology*, London: Sage.

Pollock, L. (1983) *Forgotten Children*, Cambridge: Cambridge University Press.

Pusey, M. (1987) 'Jürgen Habermas: reason and the evolution of culture', in D. Austin-Broos (ed.) *Creating Culture*, Sydney: Allen & Unwin.

Rahman, A. (1993) *People's Self-development*, London: Zed Press.

Ratner, C. (1991) *Vygotsky's Sociohistorical Psychology and its Contemporary Applications*, New York: Plenum.

Rice, F. P. (1992) *Human Development: A Life-span Approach*, New York: Macmillan.

Richards, M. P. M. (ed.) (1974) *The Integration of a Child into a Social World*, Cambridge: Cambridge University Press.

Richer, P. (1990) 'Psychological interpretation: a deconstructionist view', *The Humanistic Psychologist* 18: 55–63.

Rogoff, B. (1990) *Apprenticeship in Thinking: Cognitive Development in Social Context*, Oxford: Oxford University Press.

Rorty, R. (1989) *Contingency, Irony, and Solidarity*, Cambridge: Cambridge University Press.

Rose, G. (1978) *The Melancholy Science: An Introduction to the Thought of Theodor W. Adorno*, London: Macmillan.

Rose, N. (1985) *The Psychological Complex: Psychology, Politics and Society in England 1869–1939*, London: Routledge.

—— (1990) *Governing the Soul: The Shaping of the Private Self*, London: Routledge.

Sachs, W. (ed.) (1992) *The Development Dictionary*, London: Zed Press.

Sampson, E. (1988) 'The debate on individualism: indigenous psychologies of the individual and their role in personal and societal functioning', *American Psychologist* 43: 15–22.

—— (1990) 'Social psychology and social control', in I. Parker and J. Shotter (eds) *Deconstructing Social Psychology*, London: Sage.

Sartre, J-P. (1963) *The Problem of Method*, London: Methuen.

Semin, G. and Gergen, K. (eds) (1990) *Everyday Understanding: Social and Scientific Implications*, London: Sage.

Sève, L. (1978) *Man in Marxist Theory and the Psychology of Personality*, Hassocks: Harvester.

Shames, C. (1981) 'The scientific humanism of Lucien Sève', *Science and Society* XLV: 1–23.

Shotter, J. (1974) 'The development of personal powers', in M.P.M. Richards (ed.) *The Integration of a Child into a Social World*, Cambridge: Cambridge University Press.

—— (1984) *Social Accountability and Selfhood*, Oxford: Blackwell.

—— (1990) 'Social individuality versus possessive individualism: the sounds of silence', in I. Parker and J. Shotter (eds) *Deconstructing Social Psychology*, London: Sage.

—— (1992) '"Getting in touch": the metamethodology of a postmodern science of mental life', in S. Kvale (ed.) *Psychology and postmodernism*, London: Sage.

—— (1993a) 'Harré, Vygotsky, Bakhtin, Vico, Wittgenstein: academic discourses and conversational realities', *Journal for the Theory of Social Behaviour* 23: 459–82.

—— (1993b) *Cultural Politics of Everyday Life*, Buckingham: Open University Press.

—— (1993c) *Conversational Realities*, London: Sage.

Shweder, R. (1984) 'Anthropology's romantic rebellion against the enlightenment', in R. Shweder and R. LeVine (eds) *Culture Theory: Essays on Mind, Self, and Emotion*, Cambridge: Cambridge University Press.

—— (1990) 'Cultural psychology – what is it?', in J. Stigler, R. Shweder and G. Herdt (eds) *Cultural Psychology: Essays on Comparative Human Development*, Cambridge: Cambridge University Press.

Singer, E. (1992) *Child-care and the Psychology of Development*, London: Routledge.

Smart, B. (1985) *Michel Foucault*, London: Routledge.

Stainton Rogers, R. and Stainton Rogers, W. (1992) *Stories of Childhood: Shifting Agendas of Child Concern*, Hassocks: Harvester.

Stern, D. (1985) *The Interpersonal World of the Infant*, New York: Basic Books.

Sulloway, F. (1979) *Freud, Biologist of the Mind*, New York: Basic Books.

Tolman C. (1994) *Psychology, Society and Subjectivity: An Introduction to German Critical Psychology*, London: Routledge.

Tolman, C. and Maiers, W. (eds) (1991) *Critical Psychology*, Cambridge: Cambridge University Press.

Urwin, C. (1984) 'Power relations and the emergence of language', in J. Henriques, W. Hollway, C. Urwin, C. Venn and V. Walkerdine (eds) *Changing the Subject: Psychology, Social Regulation and Subjectivity*, London: Methuen.

—— (1985) 'Constructing motherhood: the persuasion of normal development', in C. Steedman, C. Urwin and V. Walkerdine (eds) *Language, Gender and Childhood*, London: Routledge.

—— (1986) 'Developmental psychology and psychoanalysis: splitting the difference' in M. Richards and P. Light (eds) *Children of Social Worlds*, Cambridge: Polity Press.

Van der Veer, R. and Valsiner, J. (1991) *Understanding Vygotsky: A Quest for Synthesis*, Oxford: Blackwell.

—— (1994) *The Vygotsky Reader*, Oxford: Blackwell.

Vygotsky, L. S. (1962) *Thought and Language*, Cambridge MA: MIT Press.

—— (1978) *Mind in Society*, Cambridge MA: Harvard University Press.

—— (1986) *Thought and Language*, trans A. Kozulin, Cambridge MA: MIT Press.

Walkerdine, V. (1984) 'Developmental psychology and the child-centred pedagogy', in J. Henriques, W. Hollway, C. Urwin, C. Venn and V. Walkerdine (eds) *Changing the Subject: Psychology, Social Regulation and Subjectivity*, London: Methuen.

—— (1985) 'Science and the female mind', *PsychCritique* 1: 1–20.

—— (1987) 'No laughing matter: girls' comics and the preparation for adolescent sexuality', in J. Broughton (ed.) *Critical Theories of Psychological Development*, New York: Plenum Press.

—— (1988) *The Mastery of Reason*, London: Routledge.

—— (1989) *Counting Girls Out*, London: Virago.

—— (1991) *Schoolgirl Fictions*, London: Verso.

—— (1993) 'Beyond developmentalism?' *Theory and Psychology* 3: 451–69.

Walkerdine, V. and Lucey, H. (1989) *Democracy in the Kitchen*, London: Virago.

Wertsch, J. (1985a) *Vygotsky and the Social Formation of Mind*, Cambridge MA: Harvard University Press.

—— (ed.) (1985b) *Culture, Communication and Cognition: Vygotskian Perspectives*, Cambridge: Cambridge University Press.

—— (1991a) 'A sociocultural approach to socially shared cognition', in L. Resnick, J. Levine and S. Teasley (eds) *Perspectives on Socially Shared Cognition*, Washington DC: American Psychological Association.

—— (1991b) *Voices of the Mind*, Cambridge MA: Harvard University Press.

Wozniak, R. (1975) 'A dialectical paradigm for psychological research', *Human Development* 18: 18–34.

—— (1993) 'Co-constructive metatheory for psychology: implications for an analysis of families as specific social contexts for development', in R. Wozniak and K. Fischer (eds) *Development in Context: Acting and Thinking in Specific Environments*, Hillsdale NJ: Lawrence Erlbaum.

Zinchenko, V. (1985) 'Vygotsky's ideas about units for the analysis of mind', in J. Wertsch (ed.) *Culture, Communication and Cognition: Vygotskian perspectives*, Cambridge: Cambridge University Press.

Name index

Subject index